Using FrontPage 97

Using FrontPage 97

Eric Maloney

and

Joshua C. Nossiter

Using FrontPage 97

Copyright© 1997 by Que® Corporation

All rights reserved. Printed in the United States of America. No part of this book may be used or reproduced in any form or by any means, or stored in a database or retrieval system, without prior written permission of the publisher except in the case of brief quotations embodied in critical articles and reviews. Making copies of any part of this book for any purpose other than your own personal use is a violation of United States copyright laws. For information, address Que Corporation, 201 W. 103rd St. Indianapolis, IN 46290. You may reach Que's direct sales line by calling 1-800-428-5331.

Library of Congress Catalog No.: 96-72206

ISBN: 0-7897-1134-6

This book is sold *as is*, without warranty of any kind, either express or implied, respecting the contents of this book, including but not limited to implied warranties for the book's quality, performance, merchantability, or fitness for any particular purpose. Neither Que Corporation nor its dealers or distributors shall be liable to the purchaser or any other person or entity with respect to any liability, loss, or damage caused or alleged to have been caused directly or indirectly by this book.

99 98 97   6 5 4 3 2 1

Interpretation of the printing code: the rightmost double-digit number is the year of the book's printing; the rightmost single-digit number, the number of the book's printing. For example, a printing code of 97-1 shows that the first printing of the book occurred in 1997.

All terms mentioned in this book that are known to be trademarks or service marks have been appropriately capitalized. Que cannot attest to the accuracy of this information. Use of a term in this book should not be regarded as affecting the validity of any trademark or service mark.

Screen reproductions in this book were created using Collage Plus from Inner Media, Inc., Hollis, NH.

Composed in *ITC Century, ITC Highlander, MCPdigital, Palantino,* and *Symbol* by Que Corporation.

Credits

President
Roland Elgey

Publishing Director
Lynn E. Zingraf

Editorial Services Director
Elizabeth Keaffaber

Managing Editor
Michael Cunningham

Acquisitions Editor
Martha O'Sullivan

Product Development Specialist
Melanie Palaisa

Production Editor
Mark Enochs

Technical Editor
Kyle Bryant

Technical Specialist
Nadeem Muhammed

Editorial Assistant
Virgina Stoller

Director of Marketing
Lynn E. Zingraf

Book Designer
Ruth Harvey

Cover Designer
Dan Armstrong

Production Team
Julie Geeting
Kay Hoskin
Laura Knox
Kaylene Riemen

Indexer
Chris Barrick

For all contributors to the wit and wisdom on the Web.

About the Authors

Eric Maloney earned his M.S. in journalism from the University of Oregon in 1978. He entered computer magazine publishing two years later as a copy editor for *Kilobaud Microcomputing*. Since then, he has been the editor of three magazines and is now co-editorial director of *DOS World* and *Practical Windows*. He and Josh also are co-authors of the Que books *Using Word for Windows 95* and *Using Microsoft Word 97*. Eric lives in New Hampshire with his son, Miles, and a hamster named Cheerio.

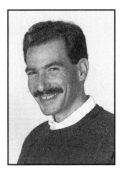

Josh Nossiter received a B.A. in English from Dartmouth College and an MBA in Finance from Columbia University. He's worked in broadcasting in California and in public finance on Wall Street, and is the author of books on WordPerfect, Excel, and (with co-author Eric Maloney) Microsoft Word. Josh is also a novelist. He wrote his first book with a typewriter, and has used just about every generation of word processing software since. He lives in San Francisco with his two children, where he's at work on new novels and computer books.

Acknowledgments

The author's collaboration on this book is the tip of a collective iceberg. Herewith a salute to the talented crew whose unrelenting labors put *Using FrontPage 97* in your hands:

Martha O'Sullivan, Acquisitions Editor, got us afloat, and kept us on course through a sea of treacherous deadlines. No crew ever had a stricter, or kinder, captain.

Melanie Palaisa, Product Development Specialist, turned a tangle of files and figures into a book that's shipshape.

Mark Enochs, Production Editor, poured editorial oil over any choppy prose.

Kyle Bryant, Technical Editor, made many useful suggestions.

We'd like to hear from you!

As part of our continuing effort to produce books of the highest possible quality, Que would like to hear your comments. To stay competitive, we *really* want you, as a computer book reader and user, to let us know what you like or dislike most about this book or other Que products.

You can mail comments, ideas, or suggestions for improving future editions to the address below, or send us a fax at (317) 581-4663. For the online inclined, Macmillan Computer Publishing has a forum on CompuServe (type **GO QUEBOOKS** at any prompt) through which our staff and authors are available for questions and comments. The address of our Internet site is **http://www.mcp.com** (World Wide Web).

In addition to exploring our forum, please feel free to contact me personally to discuss your opinions of this book: on CompuServe, I'm at **73353,2061** and I'm **mpalaisa@que.mcp.com** on the Internet.

Thanks in advance—your comments will help us to continue publishing the best books available on computer topics in today's market.

Melanie Palaisa
Product Development Specialist
Que Corporation
201 W. 103rd Street
Indianapolis, Indiana 46290
USA

Although we cannot provide general technical support, we're happy to help you resolve problems you encounter related to our books, disks, or other products. If you need such assistance, please contact our Tech Support department at 800-545-5914 ext. 3833.

To order other Que or Macmillan Computer Publishing books or products, please call our Customer Service department at 800-835-3202 ext. 666.

Contents at a Glance

Introduction 1

I Everything I Need to Know to Get Started 9

1 Read All About It: FrontPage Essentials 11
2 Start Your Web Adventure with FP Explorer 29
3 Home, Sweet Home Page: Inside the Editor 51
4 Help Is on the Way 61

II Putting Your Pages Together 77

5 Text Typing Tips, Tricks, and Traps 79
6 Editing Tools You'll Learn to Love 89
7 Form and Function: Formatting Text 109

III Interior Decorating 125

8 Color Me Fun! 127
9 Picture This! Adding Graphics to Your Web 149
10 The Miracle of Tables 167

IV Building Your Web Site 193

11 The Best-Laid Schemes: Web Planning and Design 195
12 Webward Ho! Adding Pages to Your Web 207
13 Lights, Action, Click! Hotspots, Video, and Sound 241

V Beyond the Basic Web Page 255

14 It's Good Form: Letting Your Readers Write Back 257
15 WebBots and Other Web Bells and Whistles 287
16 Inducting Your Page into the Hall of Frames 301
17 Templates: Professional Pages, Painlessly 325

18 Let's Talk! The Fine Art of Web Conversation   337

Publishing and Maintaining Your Web   361
19 This Web Is Suitable for Publication   363
20 Maintaining Your Web   381

Index   399

Table of Contents

Introduction

The FrontPage Editor 1

FrontPage Explorer 2

Where we come in 2
- How may FrontPage help? 3
- Something old, something new 4
- The BonusPack 4

What's inside 5
- Part I: Everything I Need to Know to Get Started 5
- Part II: Putting Your Pages Together 5
- Part III: Interior Decorating 5
- Part IV: Building Your Web Site 6
- Part V: Beyond the Basic Web Page 6
- Part VI: Publishing and Maintaining Your Web 6

Nuggets of information 7

Part I: Everything I Need to Know to Get Started

1 Read All About It: FrontPage Essentials 11

What's FrontPage, and what does it do? 12
- The sum of FrontPage's parts 13
- How do networks work (and where does FrontPage come in)? 14
- No HTML spoken here 14

Spinning a web: a hands-on tour 15
- Lay your web foundations in the FrontPage Explorer 16

Add content in the FrontPage Editor   19

Page filled? Add another!   22

Bind your pages with hyperlinks   22

Get the big picture with Link View   25

I need to open (and close) my web   26

How do I turn off the Microsoft Personal Web Server?   27

How do I get rid of this web?   27

How do I publish my web?   28

2 Start Your Web Adventure with FP Explorer   29

Exploring Explorer   31

Tempting Templates   31

FrontPage's FrontDoor   32

The Explorer screen   34

What's what in FrontPage Explorer   37

The menu bar   38

The toolbar   38

Inside the toolbar   40

The status bar   41

View Points   41

Hyperlink View   41

Folder View   45

I'm staring at my new web. Now what?   47

Closing your web   48

Reopening your web with the Getting Started Dialog box   48

I don't have a Getting Started dialog box. Now what?   49

Choosing a web from the Getting Started dialog box   50

Whacking unwanted webs   50

3 Home, Sweet Home Page: Inside the FrontPage Editor   51

The Editor's role in FrontPage   52

Rather like a word processor, but different   54

Tailor the Editing window to suit   55
    Floating toolbars   56
    Don't overlook the Status bar   57

Moving around the page by keyboard and mouse   57
    For faster navigating, use the keyboard   58
    Getting the most (and the least) out of the Editor window   59

4 Help Is on the Way!   61

Context-sensitive help: Shoot first and ask questions later   62
    An object lesson   63
    Help on menu commands   64
    Help on keyboard combinations   64

Searching for help   65
    Contents   65
    1… 2… 3… Help!   66
    Index   67
    Find   67

Inside the Help windows   69
    The FrontPage Help screen: A closer look   70
    Topic screens   71
    Instruction screens   73

Microsoft on the Web—in the land of plenty   74

Part II: Putting Your Pages Together

5 Text Typing Tips, Tricks, and Traps   79

Typing Text: the basics   80
    This is just like my word processor!   80
    This isn't exactly like a word processor after all   82
    I don't want these lines to reach the right margin   83
    No double-spacing? What about columns?   84
    I have a ¥ for special characters and symbols   85
    Bookmarks, the navigational express   86

6 Editing Tools You'll Learn to Love   89

Make your selection   90
    Block parties   92
    Selecting words   92
    Selecting lines of text   93
    Selecting paragraphs   94
    Across wide expanses   94

Deleting, copying, and moving text   95
    Clear the decks!   95
    Moving text with the mouse   96
    Copy that!   98
    Deleting and replacing text in one fell swoop   99

Easy Undoes it   99
    Undoing Undo   99

Spelling bound   100
    What would you like to look up?   100
    Using the Spelling dialog box   100

How to check several pages at once   101
    The Check Spelling dialog box   102

Descrying equivalent expressions with the thesaurus   103
    Inside the Thesaurus dialog box   103

How to change the same word throughout a page   104
    Replacing text in multiple pages   105
    Warning! Replace can be harmful to your health!   107
    Capital ideas   107
    I can delete it for you wholesale   107

Finding a string   108
    I changed my mind—I want to replace the string   108

7 Form and Function: Formatting Text   109

Text in every shape and size, but not for every browser   110
    How do I change fonts?   111
    I need bigger (or smaller) text   115

Use heading styles for text in proportion   116

For text that moves, try a marquee   117

Text formatting at the click of a button   118

Boldface, italics, and underlining spell emphasis   118

Left, right, and center: text alignment made easy   119

Those aren't dents... they're indents   120

Speeding bullets, listing numbers   121

How do I change these bullets?   122

Numbered lists that never lose count   123

Part III: Interior Decorating

8 Color Me Fun!   127

Background colors   129

Pick a color, (almost) any color   130

Up close and personalized—how to make your own colors   131

Basic colors   132

Beyond the basics   133

Add texture with background images   136

The color of text   139

Paging all colors   139

A little daub will do you   140

Default is yours   141

The thin blue (or red, or green) horizontal line   142

I'd like that mauve, please   143

How to create your reference page   144

9 Picture This! Adding Graphics to Your Web   149

Image formats you need to know about   150

Fast art is close to hand   151

I want to import JPEG and GIF files into my web   152

I want to use images that aren't in GIF or JPEG format   155

Fit the image to the page   156
    Moving and resizing your images   156
    I want to wrap text around this image   158
    How can I blend my image into a colored background?   160
    Horizontal lines: add the simplest graphic of all   161

Edit images to suit with the Image Composer   162
    How do I change the colors in this image?   162
    There's a library of ready-to-use images in the Image Composer   164

10 The Miracle of Tables   167

Turning a table with your mouse   169
    Using the Insert Table dialog box   171
    Tables of content   175

Natural selections   176
    Pick a cell, any cell   177
    Selecting just the cell text—what's the difference?   178

Custom alterations   179
    Changing your table's properties   180
    Changing your cells' properties   180

Tables, more or less: Adding and deleting cells   184
    Inserting rows and columns   184
    Cell by cell   184
    Wipeout! Deleting rows, columns, and cells   187

Move it on over: moving rows and columns   187
    Moving and copying cells   189

Let's talk about borders   189
    Coloring the borders   190
    Inside borders: setting a different tone   190

Shady deals   191

Part IV: Building Your Web Site

11 The Best-Laid Schemes: Web Planning and Design   195

What makes a good Web site?   196

Draw visitors into your web by avoiding Web woes   198
- This page loads too slooowly   198
- Semi-literacy isn't close enough   199
- An endless loop of links   200
- Too much of one thing or the other   200
- What's this page all about?   201

Planning a structurally sound web   203
- Well-forged links make a stronger web   204
- Put your web to the test   206

12 Webward Ho! Adding Pages to Your Web   207

Paging all webs!   208
- How do I move from page to page?   209
- Save it now!   210
- Closing pages   210
- Reopening pages   211

Linking your pages   211
- Creating the link   212

Build a link, and the page will come   216
- Links for procrastinators   216

The page that came in from the cold   218
- Importing pages into your web   219
- Other import duties   220
- Live from the World Wide Web!   221

Language barriers   221
- Unknown HTML tags—what can I do with them?   222

Linking to non-HTML files   223

Going by the bookmark—linking to the middle of a page   224
    Section by section—creating the bookmark   224
    Linking to the bookmark   225
    Inside moves   226

Links to the World Wide Web   228
    Doing it by hand   228
    Find me a link   229

Open page, insert here   232
    Open page, insert file   233
    ASCII and ye shall receive   233
    Inserting DOC, XLS, and other non-HTML files   234
    Using the Clipboard   239

13 Lights, Action, Click! Hotspots, Video, and Sound   241

I can see my links in pictures   242
    Hotspots turn images into links   243
    I need a rectangular (or polygonal) hotspot   246
    Moving hotspots   247
    How do I edit this hotspot?   247
    I need to get rid of this hotspot   248

Replace that menu with an image map   248
    An image map example   248
    I can't see my hotspots!   250

Action! Adding video and sound to a page   251
    How do I put a sound in my page?   252
    Web video for those who insist on it   253

Part V: Beyond the Basic Web Page

14 It's Good Form: Letting Your Readers Write Back   257

First things first: how do forms work?   258

Form fields: a quick introduction   260
    A few field notes   261
    Text—by the line or by the box?   262

The name game—renaming your field 265
Hey! You can't type that! 265
What type of data do you prefer? 268
May I have the check? 269
Radio buttons 270
Drop down and give me five (or maybe fifty) 272
Push-button technology 275

Add text and stir 276
Simply marvelous, marvelously simple 277

Gathering your nuts 278
Choosing a handler 278
Secret messages 284

15 WebBots and Other Web Bells and Whistles 287

What are WebBots? 288
Make your web user-friendly with a Search Bot 289
Get a web header with the Include Bot 291
Selling ads? Try the Scheduled Bots 294
Insert an instant TOC with the Table of Contents Bot 295
Keep your pages fresh with a timestamp 297

ActiveX controls? Java applets? Plug-ins? Explain, please 297

16 Inducting Your Page into the Hall of Frames 301

How do frames work? 302
Anatomy of a framed page 303
Start from the beginning! 304

A different frame of mind 309
Adding rows and columns 310
Changing attributes of a framed page, right? 312
Alternate currents 314
The end is near! 315

I'd rather do it myself 315

Connecting your frames 316
Opening a frame 317

Another link in the chain 319
Changing default targets 321
Converting your existing web 322

17 Templates: Professional Pages, Painlessly 325

FrontPage's templates may be all I need 326
One ready-to-wear option: the Corporate Presence Web 327

I need a page template, not a whole new web 329
Add a guest book to your web 329
Getting lost visitors? Add a search page 331

I want my own template 333

18 Let's Talk! The Fine Art of Web Conversation 337

Let's talk about discussion groups 339
More wizardry 342
What will my discussion web include? 342
What shall we talk about? 343
Setting up the Submission form 344
For your eyes only 344
The Table of Contents 345
Search 345
Color coordination 345
How shall we frame our discussion? 346
May I see your passport, please? 347
So what's my discussion web look like? 348

Modifying your discussion web pages 353
Change the banner 354
Have pages, will link 354
READ THIS FIRST! 354
Change the banner 354
Showing good forms 355
Changing your search form 355
A web of a different color 356

Moderating your discussion group 356
You don't say... 357
Put a lid on it! 359

Part VI: Publishing and Maintaining Your Web

19 This Web Is Suitable for Publication 363

How do I publish my web? 364
- What should I know about web publishing? 365
- What do network complications mean for my web? 366

Publishing a web: ways and means 367
- Publishing on an ISP 367
- Publishing on an intranet 368

Can I be my own server? 371
- What about FrontPage's own server software? 371

The Microsoft Personal Web Server can serve a client or three… 372
- How do I turn the Microsoft Personal Web Server off? 373
- Who's in, and who's out: setting Permissions for the FrontPage Personal Web Server 375
- Who's in, and who's out, Part II: administering webs with the Microsoft Personal Web Server 377
- I've got server software other than the Personal Web Server 378

20 Maintaining Your Web 381

When links go bad 382
- Verily, verify 383
- If it's broke, fix it 385
- What's this Edit Link button? 386
- Recalculating Links 387

Getting rid of loose changes 388
- Adding pages 388
- Creating folders and moving pages 389
- Deleting pages 391
- How to rename a file 394

The To Do List: keeping track of loose ends   394
    Lest I forget…   395
    Adding other tasks   396
    Automatic list-building   396
    To Doing it   397
    To Done!   397
    History lessons   398

Introduction

> {I}t is evil that men anywhere be forced to depend, for the information on which they must govern their lives, on the caprice of anybody at all. There should be a great, free, living stream of information, and equal access to it for all.—A.J. Liebling, *The Press*

Legendary journalist A.J. Liebling lived in a simpler age. When he penned those words in 1950, his "living stream of information" was inaccessible to all but newspapers and radio newsrooms that had Teletype machines. The public had to wait patiently at the distant end of a fire brigade of reporters and editors, who passed the news along in small, leaky buckets.

Some 30 years after his death in 1963, Liebling got his wish—the World Wide Web. Just about any computer user with server access can form their own tributary to the information stream, which has turned into a raging river wider and deeper than any Liebling could have imagined. And, although Liebling's dream of equal access remains unfulfilled, all you need is a browser and an Internet connection to trawl the river to your heart's content.

The Internet's infrastructure—the computers and cables that hook the whole thing together—has evolved over decades. But the technology that has turned the Internet into a virtual information utility is relatively new. It's called Hypertext Markup Language, and it's the code that site developers use to create the files your browser translates into pages of text and graphics.

"The press is free to those who own one," Liebling also once said. If the World Wide Web gives users ownership of their own presses, then HTML is the tool that makes their published works attractive, accessible, and easy to read.

The FrontPage Editor

You used to have to learn how to write HTML code to be a Web publisher. That is, you had to become a programmer. Software makers quickly recognized that HTML code was not only an impediment to Web development, but unnecessary, as well. Why not let users create and format a web page the same way they would a word processing document, and let the computer translate the page into the proper HTML code?

Thus was born the WYSIWYG web page editor—the leading example of which is FrontPage Editor.

The Editor is one of two programs contained within FrontPage 97 (we'll talk about the other, FrontPage Explorer, in a minute). FrontPage Editor gives you all the tools you need to create attractive and well-organized pages without so much as looking at an HTML tag. Special text formats, tables, color—Editor provides all of the essential ingredients for designing pages.

Building a web page with FrontPage starts with typing and inserting text. But FrontPage also lets you include graphics, audio clips, and other elements, usually with the help of toolbars and menus. You tie your pages together with hyperlinks that you create by pointing and clicking. Extras such as feedback forms and discussion groups are readily available.

FrontPage Explorer

FrontPage 97 also takes care of many web design and management tasks with its other component, FrontPage Explorer. Explorer simplifies much of the technical work involved in creating, developing, and maintaining your web.

For example, Explorer guides you through creating a web with templates and wizards. Once your web is set up, Explorer gives you a graphical view of your web pages and how they're linked together. It handles file management tasks such as importing, deleting, and renaming. And it helps you quickly troubleshoot your web for bad links. Finally, Explorer provides the tools for publishing and then maintaining your site.

Where we come in

Think of FrontPage as a veneer that hides the inner workings of a complex machine. You no longer have to directly manipulate the machine's cogs and valves to work it. But you now have an array of buttons, dials, and switches that you have to push, spin, and pull. Some of these controls are hidden, and sometimes you need to work them in combination to get a result.

FrontPage's Help files are useful in some measure. But Help seems to work best when you need to find out what a specific command does. Most of us work in the other direction; we know what task we want to perform, and we need to know how to do it. That's where this book comes in.

The goal of this book is to make creating a web with FrontPage 97 as simple as possible. We'll show you the steps that go into building a web and describe the easiest way to do each task. Along the way, we'll shed some light on some of FrontPage's more complex features, such as WebBots, frames, forms, and discussion groups.

We won't wear you out trying to explain every obscure command and function. We won't try to describe every option in every menu and dialog box. But we'll help you lay a foundation that will let you build complex web sites with confidence and direction.

How may FrontPage help?

Perhaps you've obtained FrontPage just because you're curious about what goes into building a web. But it's more likely that you have a specific project in mind: A corporate web to promote your business or provide services to your customers, a site devoted to a hobby or avocation, a place to exchange information with professional colleagues, or maybe just a poster of yourself and your family.

FrontPage 97 is flexible enough to address all of these needs. What's important is not so much the purpose of your web but how complex you want it to be. *Using FrontPage 97* is designed to mirror FrontPage's flexibility. If all you want is a simple site with a few linked pages, you'll be up and running before you're halfway through the book. On the other hand, if you've got a big, complex site, we'll teach you about some of FrontPage's more advanced procedures, as well.

FrontPage 97 has a variety of features that let you add depth to your web. We give you step-by-step instructions, in plain English, on how to use these features. By the time you're done, you'll be able to:

- Quickly add custom colors and background images
- Incorporate graphics, video, and sound
- Organize your pages with tables

- Add pages and hyperlinks in a matter of seconds
- Easily create forms that let readers write back
- Use advanced features such as frames and registration forms

Something old, something new

This book also gives you the latest on FrontPage 97's new features and commands. If you've been using an earlier version of FrontPage, you'll want to know about some of these extras:

- The ability to find and replace text in all of your web pages.
- A spell checker that checks the spelling of all web pages at once.
- A folder view in Explorer that helps to make site management more efficient.
- An Import Wizard that simplifies importing other webs into your site.
- A Preview in Browser button that lets you load pages into your browser directly from Editor.
- Improved text import conversion.

The BonusPack

The FrontPage CD-ROM comes with more than just FrontPage. You also get several valuable programs bundled with the BonusPack. These programs are optional, and which ones you choose to install will depend on your needs and what programs you have already installed. This book covers the BonusPack programs as necessary:

The Microsoft Image Composer is a full-fledged graphics editor that lets you create and edit graphics files in a variety of formats. You can use the Composer to develop images for your web site, but you can also use it by itself for other graphics applications.

The Microsoft Personal Web Server is software you install on your hard drive that lets you preview your web on your own computer before you publish it. You don't have to install the server if you're upgrading from a previous version of FrontPage. The older FrontPage Personal Web Server works with

FrontPage 97, although the Microsoft PWS supports some advanced features. You will want to install the Microsoft PWS if you're installing FrontPage for the first time.

The Microsoft Internet Explorer is Microsoft's web browser. You'll want a browser with which to preview the pages you create with FrontPage. If you prefer, you can use another browser such as Netscape's popular Navigator, but FrontPage is designed to work most effectively with Explorer. You also can use Internet Explorer as a standalone web browser.

The Web Publishing Wizard is a tool you'll need if the server on which you plan to publish your web does not have the FrontPage Server Extensions.

What's inside

OK—you know what FrontPage is, and you know why we're here. So let's take a quick look at some of the important topics we'll cover in this book.

Part I: Everything I Need to Know to Get Started

The first four chapters show you how to create a web and start building pages. We'll talk about how to use FrontPage Explorer to set up different kinds of webs using templates and wizards. Then, we'll discuss FrontPage Editor, the program you use to compose, edit, and save your actual web pages. The section finishes with an overview of FrontPage's Help files.

Part II: Putting Your Pages Together

Once you're settled in, you'll want to start refining your web pages in Editor. Chapters 5, "Text Typing Tips, Tricks, and Traps," and 6, "Editing Tools You'll Learn to Love," cover the basics of adding text and using Editor's tools efficiently. Chapter 7, "Form and Function: Formatting Text," fills you in on how to create an attractive web page with fonts, styles, special text effects, and lists.

Part III: Interior Decorating

What's a web without color? You won't have to find out after visiting Chapter 8, "Color Me Fun!," which explains how to add background color, insert background images, and create custom colors. Continuing with the visual theme, Chapter 9, "Picture This! Adding Graphics to Your Web," tells you all about inserting and manipulating graphics. Finally, Chapter 10, "The Miracle of Tables," discusses tables, one of Editor's most valuable tools for organizing information on a web page.

Part IV: Building Your Web Site

After you're done learning about FrontPage's various components, you'll have to start considering how you want to organize your site. Chapter 11, "The Best-Laid Schemes: Web Planning and Design," shows you how to plan your web with flowcharts and Explorer. Then, Chapter 12, "Webward Ho! Adding Pages to Your Web," get into the details of expanding your site: Creating new pages, adding hyperlinks, and using documents created in other programs. We wrap up the section in Chapter 13, "Lights, Action, Click! Hotspots, Video, and Sound," with a discussion of how to turn graphics into hyperlinks.

Part V: Beyond the Basic Web Page

By this time, you'll have your basic web set up and will no doubt want to explore FrontPage's more advanced features. Chapter 14, "It's Good Form: Letting Your Readers Write Back," explains how to gather information from your users with feedback forms, and Chapter 15, "WebBots and Other Web Bells and Whistles," tells you what you need to know about WebBots. Part V also gives you instructions on how to create framed pages, custom templates, and discussion groups.

Part VI: Publishing and Maintaining Your Web

Like a newspaper that hasn't been printed, a web is useless if other people can't access it. Chapter 19, "This Web Is Suitable for Publication," shows you how to publish your web on a server. And once you've got your web up and running, you'll want to know how to maintain it and how to secure your web with passwords and other restrictions. We cover these topics in Chapter 20, "Maintaining Your Web."

Nuggets of information

Throughout this book, you'll find a variety of special devices that we use to give you special information.

TIP **Tips describe shortcuts and secrets that show you the best way to get a job done.**

CAUTION **Cautions warn you about potential problems that might arise from a particular action.**

Q&A ***Do you have a question?***

We try to anticipate and answer questions or problems you might have about Word's features and procedures.

❝ ***Plain English, please!***

Here we translate **computer terms** and **jargon** into English.

In addition, you'll run across text that is in a different typeface:

A `special typeface` indicates what you see on your screen.

Bold is for new terms or text that you type.

When you see an underlined letter in a command, press the Alt key plus that letter to execute the command. For example, press Alt+F to display the File menu.

Sidebars: entertainment and information

Sidebars are detours from the main text. They usually provide background or interesting information that is relevant but not essential reading.

Part I: Everything I Need to Know to Get Started

Chapter 1: **Read All About It: FrontPage Essentials**

Chapter 2: **Start Your Web Adventure with FP Explorer**

Chapter 3: **Home, Sweet Home Page: Inside the FrontEditor**

Chapter 4: **Help Is on the Way!**

1

Read All About It: FrontPage Essentials

● **In this chapter:**

- **Just what is a FrontPage web?**

- **I want to jump right in and put FrontPage through its paces**

- **Explorer? Editor? Explain, please!**

- **Hyperlinks are nothing to get hyper about**

- **What do I do with my finished web?**

Spinning a FrontPage web is like putting up your own billboard or publishing your own newsletter: it's the fast way to add your voice to the information age chorus. . . . . ➤

From the moment the clock radio goes off in the morning to the last item on the late night news before bed, there's no escaping the information age. Travel to the remotest corners of our national parks, and you'll hear solitary hikers marveling at the wonders of nature—over their cellular phones.

You can't avoid the information age, so join it. Become a purveyor, as well as a consumer, of information. Air your views, publish your work, give, in short, as good as you get. All you need is the right tool, and that's where FrontPage comes in.

With FrontPage you can publish anything you like, from the latest company sales report, to your opinion of hikers talking on cellular phones. Your readership might be your corporate division, or the millions surfing the Internet. Whatever the message, or the audience, FrontPage gives you the chance to be heard.

What's FrontPage, and what does it do?

By now we're all familiar with word processors. And we've had a spin or two on the World Wide Web, where we've viewed some of the millions of Web pages on display. Which makes understanding FrontPage pretty straightforward: it's a word processor for Web pages. As with any modern word processor, you can enter text and format it, insert graphics and position them, and preview your work before you publish it.

The finished product is where FrontPage differs from the word processors you've been using. Where word processors are designed to produce a printed document, FrontPage's final product is a **web**. A FrontPage web is a document meant to be viewed on a computer screen. It consists of pages of text and graphics, just like an ordinary document. But where you might bind an ordinary document with staples or a clasp, the binding in a FrontPage web consists of **hyperlinks**. Hyperlinks are those underlined words or phrases—sometimes they're pictures or buttons—that you click to go from one page to another.

Plain English, please!
> **Hyperlinks** are like cross-references. Just as your encyclopedia might tell you to "see pg. 443," hyperlinks tell the computer to turn to another page on the network. The **Internet** is one such network, a global chain of computers connected by telephone lines and computer modems. The **World Wide Web** is the graphical, user-friendly section of the Internet, where you can post and read pages of the type created in FrontPage.

They're not only the binding of a FrontPage web; hyperlinks are what holds the World Wide Web together. Each hyperlink has the address of another Web page embedded in it. When you click the link, you open the page whose address is embedded therein. It's just like turning the page of a bound document, except that when you click a hyperlink, the page you turn to might be stored in a computer on the other side of the world.

The sum of FrontPage's parts

FrontPage differs from a word processor the same way a stereo system differs from a boom box. Instead of a single unit, which is what you're used to in a word processor, FrontPage consists of separate components that work together. Unlike the average component HiFi system, FrontPage handles all the wiring for you; when you install FrontPage and the FrontPage Bonus Pack, the program hooks everything up automatically.

- FrontPage's main components are the Explorer and the Editor. The Explorer is a combination file manager and outliner for webs. The Editor is a word processor for web pages, which you use to create and format text and graphics. The FrontPage Personal Web Server is installed by default if you choose not to install the Microsoft Personal Web Server. It works in the background and allows you to test and preview your webs.

- The FrontPage Bonus Pack is a bundle of extra components. Though Microsoft treats them as non-essentials, you might find at least some of the Bonus Pack components indispensible. The Microsoft Personal Web Server is a more capable replacement for the FrontPage Personal Web Server. The Microsoft Image Composer is a powerful graphics editing program, while the Web Publishing Wizard helps you get your web to its audience. Microsoft's browser, the Internet Explorer, is also included in the Bonus Pack.

Even if you've already got a different graphics editor, browser, and server software package, you may want to install the Bonus Pack components anyway. Since they're designed to work with FrontPage, they might be easier to live with than your existing programs. And if you don't have similar programs already, the Bonus Pack components are a must.

How do networks work (and where does FrontPage come in)?

Whether it's a company network or the global Internet, computer networks are all built along similar lines. Powerful computers called **servers** hold databases of information, anything from government statistics to *Sports Illustrated* to a corporate home page. Your own computer connects to the server via the phone lines. Once connected, your computer is the **client** of the server, free to browse the information it has stored. Servers can "serve" many clients at once, though the more clients that connect to the server, the slower it's apt to respond. That's one reason why browsing the World Wide Web can sometimes require a lot of patience. Servers can also connect to each other; clicking a link while you're hooked up to one server can take you automatically to a different server.

Just as people do, these far-flung client and server computers need rules and a common language in order to coexist and communicate. The rules that govern computers on a network are called **protocols**; like the laws that keep a society in order, protocols ensure that no one computer can interfere unduly with the rest of the computers on the network.

No HTML spoken here

If you write for a Chinese readership, a good translator spares you the need to learn Chinese. In the same way, FrontPage lets you publish on the World Wide Web, or on the company intranet, without learning a word of the network language, HTML.

HTML? Even though you don't have to become fluent in network-ese, some jargon is unavoidable: Hypertext Transfer Protocol, or **HTTP**, is the set of rules that governs both the computers on the World Wide Web, and on your corporate intranet. Their common language is **HTML**, HyperText Markup

Language, a kind of computer Esperanto. All the documents on the Web are written in HTML. So is any document that you create with FrontPage. In fact, FrontPage acts as an automatic translator, converting your work into HTML pages. Those pages can then be displayed in **Web browsers** like Netscape Navigator or the Microsoft Internet Explorer.

 Plain English, please!

> An **intranet** is a local computer network run by a company information department. Intranets look, and act, like the World Wide Web because they also use HTTP and HTML.

Spinning a web: a hands-on tour

FrontPage does a good job of shielding us from the myriad complexities (and numbing jargon) of computer networks. Putting a web together is a straightforward three-step job:

1 Like an architect drafting the plans for a house, you set up the framework of your web in the FrontPage Explorer.

2 Next, you tackle the interior of the web, entering and formatting text and graphics in the FrontPage Editor. As you complete each page, you link it to the rest of the web with hyperlinks.

3 The last step is publishing your web on the network, which you can do right from FrontPage.

 Plain English, please!

> You get used to it fast, but FrontPage's own jargon can be a little confusing at first. What FrontPage calls a **web** is what you're probably accustomed to thinking of as a web site: one or more related web pages that are linked together. The **FrontPage Explorer** is the component of the program that lets you outline and control the structure of your web, and it's got nothing to do with the Microsoft Internet Explorer (a Web browser) or the Windows Explorer (the file manager that comes with Windows 95).

Lay your web foundations in the FrontPage Explorer

The best way to learn how to spin a FrontPage web is to plunge in and spin one. And the easiest way to do that is to begin with a FrontPage Explorer **template**. Like a stencil, templates provide a ready-made framework for a web, which we'll fill in with pages of text and graphics. To create the skeleton of a FrontPage web:

1 Click Start, Programs, Microsoft FrontPage if you don't already have FrontPage running. You're greeted with the Getting Started with Microsoft FrontPage dialog box shown in Figure 1.1.

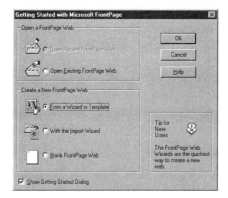

Fig. 1.1
Deselect the Show Getting Started Dialog checkbox if you don't care about seeing this dialog box again.

2 Under the Create a New FrontPage Web options, choose From a Wizard or Template, and click OK in the Getting Started with Microsoft FrontPage dialog box. If the Getting Started with Microsoft FrontPage dialog box doesn't appear when you run the program, just click the New FrontPage Web button on the FrontPage Explorer toolbar.

3 The New FrontPage Web dialog box appears, with a list of templates and wizards. Wizards are more elaborate templates with built-in instructions. Select a template or wizard, and you'll get an idea of what it's about in the Description box. We'll choose the Normal Web template, which gives us the framework for a blank web, as shown in Figure 1.2.

Fig. 1.2
Choosing a template or wizard is the easiest way to tackle a new web.

4. With the Normal Web template selected, click OK in the New FrontPage Web dialog box. The Normal Web Template dialog box pops up (see Figure 1.3). Unless you have a good reason not to, accept the default Web Server or File Location. As shown in Figure 1.3, type a name in the Name of New FrontPage Web text box. Name your web whatever you like, but keep it to one word: spaces are not permitted. The Connect Using SSL (Secure Socket Layer) option has to do with Web site security, and can be skipped for now.

Fig. 1.3
FrontPage checks your Windows 95 network settings to determine the default web location, so you might see something different for your own default.

5. Click OK in the Normal Web Template dialog box. FrontPage goes to work creating your new Web. Depending on your installation, the Name and Password Required dialog box might block your way. If it does, then enter your name and password exactly as you typed them when you first installed FrontPage, and click OK. If you don't type your name and password with the exact spelling and capitalization you used during FrontPage installation, the dialog box keeps reappearing until you get it right.

Q&A I can't remember my password!

FrontPage is very security-minded. Although you might not have realized it at the time, entering your name and password while you were installing FrontPage was a crucial step. If you can't remember your password, you can't create a new web. The only remedy is to uninstall, and then reinstall, FrontPage. And when you reinstall the program, make sure to write down your password!

6 The FrontPage Explorer displays a folder view of the newly created web. So far, the web consists of a single blank HTML document and a couple of empty folders, all created by the Normal Web template (see Figure 1.4).

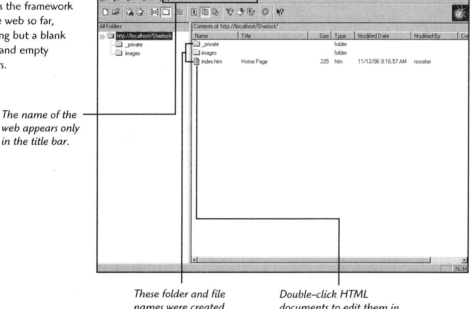

Fig. 1.4
Here's the framework of the web so far, nothing but a blank page and empty folders.

The name of the web appears only in the title bar.

These folder and file names were created by the program.

Double-click HTML documents to edit them in the FrontPage Editor.

Although our web has no content yet, we've got a basic structure in place. Like the blueprint for a house that's yet to be built, it's a start.

Add content in the FrontPage Editor

We've seen that FrontPage is a single program with several components, like a stereo system with separate speakers, amplifier, and so on. The FrontPage Explorer, like an amplifier, controls the system. The FrontPage Editor is the system's tape deck, where you create and edit your web's content. Text, graphics, and links are all created in the FrontPage Editor.

Once your web framework is set up in the FrontPage Explorer, switch to the FrontPage Editor to fill in the blank page:

1. Double-click the blank HTML document listed in the FrontPage Explorer (that's Home Page in Figure 1.4). The Editor window appears with our HTML document, Home Page, loaded.

2. If you're familiar with Microsoft Word, you'll feel right at home in the FrontPage Editor. Even if you're not a Word user, the basic idea is straightforward: type text and format it with the buttons on the Formatting toolbar. To add a title to your home page, for example, type the text for the title. With the flashing cursor in or adjacent to the text, click the Change Style drop-down arrow and select Heading 1. That creates a boldface title in a larger font size, as shown in Figure 1.5.

Fig. 1.5
Like a word processor, the FrontPage Editor formats text with a click of the mouse.

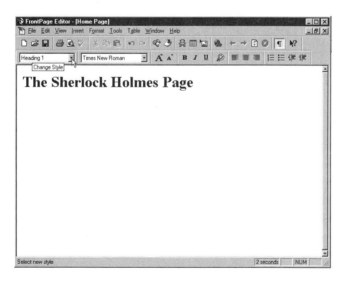

3 Type additional text below your title if you want it. For larger body text, select your text and click the Increase Text Size button. You get a larger font size each time you click the button.

4 Bulleted lists are a common feature of web pages, mostly because they call attention to important information in a space-saving way. To add a bulleted list to your home page, click the Bulleted List button on the FrontPage Editor Formatting toolbar and type the first item. Press Enter, and another bullet is inserted automatically. Type the next item and press Enter at the end of the line. After you type the last bulleted item, press Enter twice to stop inserting bullets.

5 Graphic lines are often used to dress-up web pages. To add a horizontal line to your home page, click Insert, Horizontal Line. A line appears at the insertion point; to move the line, click it, then drag it to a new position.

TIP **To format your horizontal line, right-click the line and choose** Horizontal Line Properties on the context menu. Make your changes in the Horizontal Line Properties dialog box, and click OK.

6 Now that you've put some work into your page, you'll want to save it. Click the Save button on the Editor toolbar. In the Save As dialog box that appears, type a name for your page in the Page Title text box. The Page Title you add here will be seen in browser title bars whenever your page is visited by a passing Web surfer. The Page Title is also used by search services like Yahoo to index and display your page. You don't need to type anything in the File path within your FrontPage Web text box—it fills in with the generic INDEX.HTM for home pages, and a truncated version of your page title for other pages, automatically (see Figure 1.7). By default, the page is saved to the current web. Click OK in the Save As dialog box when you've given your page a title.

7 To get an idea of how your work is going to look to others, click the Preview in Browser button on the Editor toolbar. That loads your Web browser and displays your page (see Figure 1.6). If the Windows Connect To dialog box appears, just click Cancel to avoid connecting to the Internet.

http://www.quecorp.com

Fig. 1.6
Previewing your pages in the Web browser gives you a notion of how Web surfers will see your work.

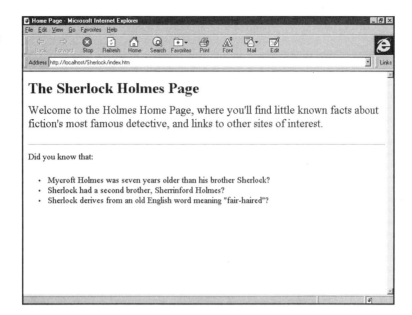

 What you see in FrontPage's Preview in Browser feature won't be exactly what others will see. How your page displays for others will depend, among other things, on what browser they're using.

 Got more than one browser installed? Many of us use both Netscape Navigator as well as the Internet Explorer, for example. You can see how your webs will look in all your different browsers. Click File, Preview in Browser. In the Preview in Browser dialog box that appears, choose a Browser and a Window Size and click Preview.

8. Flip back to the FrontPage Editor to make further changes if you wish. To preview them, leave your browser loaded, return to the browser, and click the Reload or Refresh button on the browser's toolbar (it'll vary depending on the browser you use).

There are plenty of other formatting and editing tricks up the FrontPage Editor's sleeve. See Chapter 3, "Home, Sweet Home Page: Inside the Editor," and Chapters 5 through 10 for details. To add graphics to your pages, see Chapter 9, "Picture This! Adding Graphics to Your Web." And if you have material in word processor files that you want to add to your web page, copy and paste it right into the editor (see Chapter 12, "Webward Ho! Adding Pages to Your Web").

Page filled? Add another!

When your web page holds a screen full of information, consider adding another page instead of extending the page too far out of sight below the bottom of the screen. That'll save your readers some scrolling, for which they'll be grateful. And since we're going to link the two pages together with a handy hyperlink, the new page will be easily accessible from our first web page.

To add a new page to your web-in-progress, click the New button on the FrontPage Editor toolbar. If you're using the Normal Web template, a new window appears, uninspiringly named Untitled Normal Page. Fill in the new page with whatever content you like. Click the Save button on the Editor toolbar to save your work, and the Save As dialog box pops up (see Figure 1.7).

Fig. 1.7
FrontPage web pages have both titles and paths; all you need to do here is give your page a title.

Type a title for the new page in the Page Title text box in the Save As dialog box and click OK. The File path within your FrontPage web text box changes automatically to reflect your new title, so we don't need to type anything there. The file path is part of the web framework we originally set up in the FrontPage Explorer, and needs no further alteration from us.

Bind your pages with hyperlinks

When you print out a report from an ordinary word processor, you reach for a paper clip to bind it together. Once your FrontPage web holds two or more pages, you clip them together with a hyperlink. More than just an electronic paper clip, hyperlinks also act as automatic cross-references, sending readers from page to page within your web, and to other web sites on the network.

To link pages within a web:

1 Press Ctrl+F6 to return to our original home page (or click Window, 1 Home Page if you're keyboard-averse).

Chapter 1 *Read All About It: FrontPage Essentials* **23**

2. Position the insertion point wherever you want the link to appear on the page, then click the Create or Edit Hyperlink button on the Editor toolbar. The Create Hyperlink dialog box pops up, with the Open Pages tab selected. Choose the page you want to link to from the list of Open Pages (see Figure 1.8).

Fig. 1.8
All the open web pages are listed in the dialog box, which makes linking them a simple point and click job.

Select the page you want to link to, and it appears as the destination for the link here.

3. Click OK in the Create Hyperlink dialog box, and the title of the second web page we created appears as an underlined link on the home page. Clicking the link in the Editor doesn't take you to the linked page; instead, right-click the link and choose Follow Hyperlink, as shown in Figure 1.9.

Fig. 1.9
Following links in the FrontPage Editor is a right-click and a context menu choice.

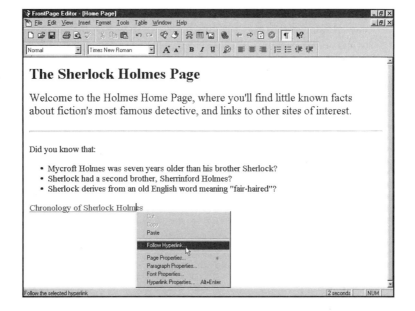

TIP **To see the links as they'll appear to Web surfers, complete** with the familiar pointing-hand that appears when you point at the link, click the Preview in Browser button on the Editor toolbar.

4 Our home page is linked to the second web page we created; now we want a link on the second page that takes us back to the home page. On the second web page, click the Create or Edit Hyperlink button. Double-click Home Page on the list of Open Pages in the Create Hyperlink dialog box, and the link appears at the insertion point.

5 Our pages are linked, but you might want to add a link to another site on the World Wide Web. Select the text you want to use for a link, then click the Create or Edit Hyperlink button. Choose the World Wide Web tab in the Create Hyperlink dialog box.

6 Type the address of the World Wide Web page that you want to link to in the URL text box, as shown in Figure 1.10.

 Plain English, please!

URL, or Uniform Resource Locator, is the Internet jargon for an address. Each page on the World Wide Web, or in your company intranet, has a unique URL. Uniform Resource Locators on the Web have some things in common. Most share the http://www. prefix, and though the other elements of the URL vary, they give you clues as to what a Web site might be about. The bit that follows the www. in the prefix is called the **domain name**. In the URL http://www.mcp.com, mcp.com is the domain name. The domain name is the giveaway: the .com in mcp.com stands for commercial organization (that happens to be Macmillan Computer Publishing's Web site). If the domain name has an .edu suffix, it's an academic institution like a college. Nonprofits like National Public Radio have a .org suffix, and government sites have domain names that end in .gov.

 7 Click OK in the Create Hyperlink dialog box to insert the link at the insertion point. Don't forget to save your changes with a click of the Save button on the Editor toolbar.

Fig. 1.10
Linking to sites on the World Wide Web is no harder than linking pages within your own FrontPage web.

Text selected before you create a hyperlink becomes the text of the hyperlink.

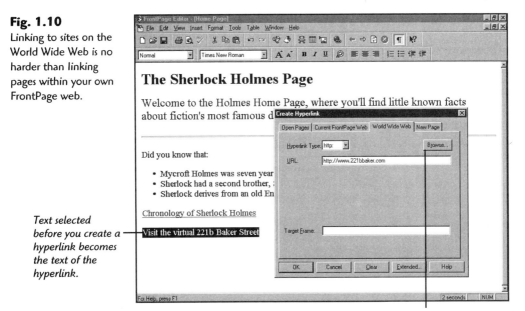

If you don't know the URL of the Web page you want, click Browse to hook up to the World Wide Web and search for it.

Get the big picture with Link View

 Once your web is set up with a couple of saved and linked pages, the FrontPage Explorer shows you how the web hangs together. Click the Show FrontPage Explorer button on the Editor toolbar. That sends you back to where you started in the FrontPage Explorer.

 Now click the Hyperlink View button on the Explorer toolbar. You get a schematic view of your web, with all the links from page to page indicated by arrows, as shown in Figure 1.11.

Fig. 1.11
Hyperlink View shows you how your web is hooked up.

Click any page in the web to view the links it contains.

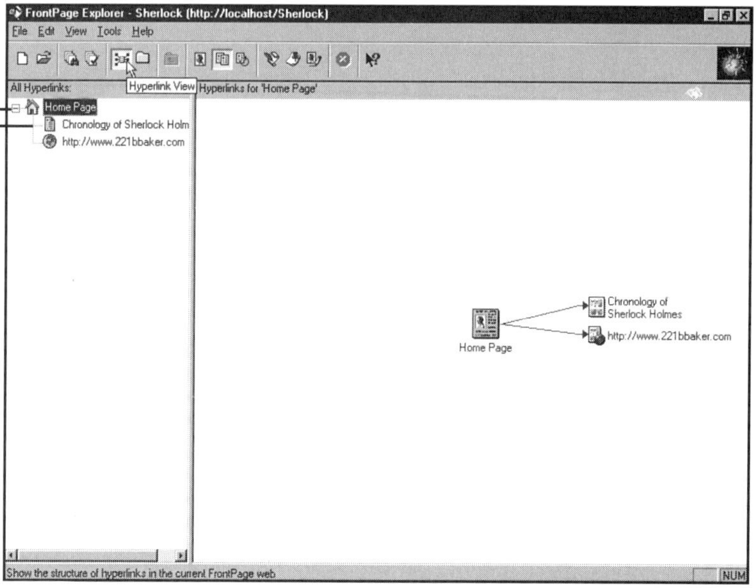

I need to open (and close) my web

Finished working on your web for the day? Make sure you've saved the individual web pages you were working on in the FrontPage Editor. The web itself, whose framework we set up in the FrontPage Explorer, is saved automatically.

To close your web and shut down FrontPage, close each component of the program—just click the Close buttons in the Explorer, Editor, FrontPage Personal Web Server, and the browser (if it's still running). Can't I just turn the whole thing off with one command, you ask? Sorry. You can't.

TIP If you've got several open pages in the Editor, choose File, Save All before clicking the Editor Close button. That'll at least spare you from having to respond to multiple FrontPage Editor Save changes to... message boxes.

When you're ready to go back to work on the web, just click OK in the Getting Started with FrontPage dialog box that appears when you run the program. If you don't see the Getting Started dialog box, click File in the FrontPage Explorer and select your web title from the File menu.

Q&A *I tried to open my web and got "xyz is not a valid host name" error!*

Click the Open FrontPage Web button in the FrontPage Explorer. In the Open FrontPage Web dialog box that appears, make sure that the correct Web Server or File Location is displayed; if it's not, click the Web Server or File Location drop-down arrow and select the correct choice. Now click List Webs. Double-click your web title, and the web should open.

How do I turn off the Microsoft Personal Web Server?

The Microsoft Personal Web Server runs automatically when you start Windows, and it stays in the background whether you're using FrontPage or not. Just ignore it. But if you must shut down the Microsoft Personal Web Server (to free up system memory, for example), double-click the Personal Web Server icon on the Windows taskbar. You'll see it next to the clock at the right end of the taskbar. Choose the Startup tab of the Personal Web Server Properties dialog box that appears, and click Stop. Click OK to finish the job.

To run the Microsoft Personal Web Server again, click Start, Settings, Control Panel. Double-click the Personal Web Server icon in the Control Panel window, and choose Startup, Start, OK in the Personal Web Server Properties dialog box.

How do I get rid of this web?

Trying to delete an experimental web that you've been using to learn on? Open the web, then click File, Delete FrontPage Web in the FrontPage Explorer. Deleting is permanent—your web doesn't go into the Windows 95 Recycle bin, and there's no Undo command for web deletions.

You'll be warned about this by FrontPage. If you're sure, click Yes in the Confirm Delete dialog box that appears.

How do I publish my web?

There's a lot more to learn about FrontPage links, webs, and pages, which we'll tackle in succeeding chapters. Now that you've got a grip on how the program works, the details that follow will make a lot more sense.

When you're finished tinkering with your web, you'll want to get your work published on the network. Members of online services, like America Online and CompuServe, can publish their finished webs through their online services. Some Internet Service Providers offer similar publication facilities. Those on company intranets will have their own guidelines for posting their webs to the network. See Chapter 19, "This Web Is Suitable for Publication," for a complete discussion of publishing a FrontPage web.

Start Your Web Adventure with FP Explorer

● **In this chapter:**

- How to start a web with templates and wizards

- I command thee! How to be the boss of the buttons

- Get the big picture with Hyperlink view

- Folder view: More info on what's in your web

- How do I close, open, and delete a web?

Every journey begins with a first step, and Explorer has all the maps, tools, and supplies you need . . . . ▶

Chapter 1 was quite the whirlwind tour, wasn't it? We feel a bit as if we just gave a rollerblade tour of the entire Smithsonian in 15 minutes. Don't worry if you feel a bit overwhelmed; you can't learn FrontPage in one chapter. But you should have a general sense of how you go about creating a web and its pages. Now it's time to start looking at the details of each step, starting with FrontPage's web-making machine, Explorer.

Creating a web site is like building a house. Before you break out the hammer and nails, you need to know where the walls go. Explorer is FrontPage's drafting table, giving you the tools to create a blueprint for your web site.

And what if you've never built a house before? Don't you need a professional architect to ensure that you don't accidentally put the mud room in the attic and the tub in the garage?

Not with Explorer's collection of wizards and templates. Just pick the design (ranch or colonial?), and Explorer presents you with a complete floor plan. If you happen to require a Jacuzzi in the kitchen, you can later modify the plan to suit your needs.

Of course, once you've become an experienced web designer, you might want to bring your own drafting tools to the job. That's ok, too; Explorer will let you build a web from the ground up.

> *Plain English, please!*
>
> Web this, web that. Before you get started, make sure you understand these web-related terms:
>
> A **web page** is a single document comprising text, graphics, and hyperlinks to other web pages. It includes special codes that let other users view the page with a browser. If you use a word processor, you might think of a page as a single document.
>
> A **web** (or **web site**) is a collection of web pages connected by hyperlinks, as well as the support files that provide such features as graphics, audio, and video. A web, which might comprise a single page or thousands of pages, can reside on your hard drive, the Internet, or your company's intranet. A web on the Internet or an intranet is a **published** web.
>
> The **Web,** capital W, refers to the **World Wide Web**, which, non-technically speaking, is the collection of all the web sites published on the Internet.

Exploring Explorer

Start FrontPage Explorer as you would any other program, by choosing it from Windows' Start, Programs menu or the appropriate folder. FrontPage loads Explorer and then presents you with the Getting Started dialog box, shown in the following graphics page.

The two choices beneath the Open a FrontPage Web heading won't come into play until you've actually created a web. And how do you do that? With one of the options beneath the Create a New FrontPage Web heading.

Tempting Templates

FrontPage can't help you choose the content of your web, but it does give you a variety of pre-formatted webs in which to put it. These prefab webs—called templates and wizards—are designed to save you the work of building a web from the ground up. You select the one that most closely matches the web you want to create, and then modify the content and appearance with FrontPage Editor.

In many programs, such as Microsoft's Word or Excel, you don't use templates and wizards until you learn the software. Templates and wizards play a much more important role in FrontPage. They're the quickest and easiest way to start a web, and they're also the best way to learn how to use FrontPage.

To look at the templates and wizards available to you, choose the From a Wizard or Template radio button in the Getting Started dialog box and click OK. FrontPage displays the New FrontPage Web dialog box in Figure 2.1.

Fig. 2.1
The FrontPage dialog box is like a karaoke machine; you pick the tune and add your own lyrics.

FrontPage's FrontDoor

The Getting Started dialog box lets you open an existing web or start a new one from a wizard or template.

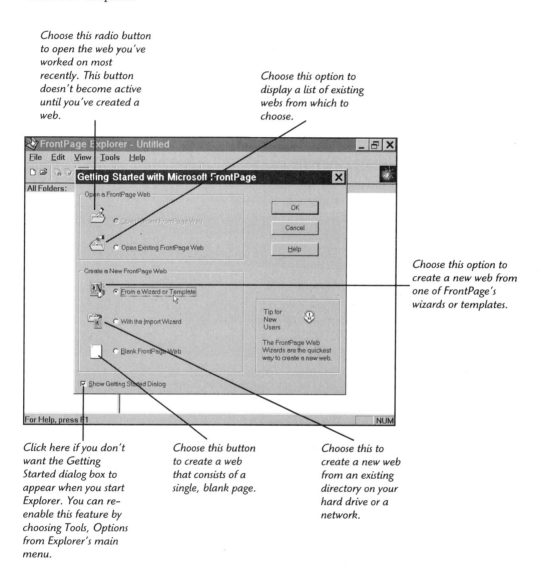

Choose this radio button to open the web you've worked on most recently. This button doesn't become active until you've created a web.

Choose this option to display a list of existing webs from which to choose.

Choose this option to create a new web from one of FrontPage's wizards or templates.

Click here if you don't want the Getting Started dialog box to appear when you start Explorer. You can re-enable this feature by choosing Tools, Options from Explorer's main menu.

Choose this button to create a web that consists of a single, blank page.

Choose this to create a new web from an existing directory on your hard drive or a network.

Click any template or wizard once to get a description at the bottom of the dialog box. Click twice to load the template or wizard.

66 Plain English, please!

A **template** is a preformatted web site in which you fill in blanks, replace dummy text, and add design elements. A template does not cast your web site in stone; you can add or delete web pages as needed. A **wizard** in essence lets you make your own template; you answer a series of questions about what you want the template to include. 99

TIP Once you're inside Explorer, you can create a new web at any time by clicking the New FrontPage Web button on the toolbar or choosing File, New, FrontPage Web from the menu bar. Explorer displays the New FrontPage Web dialog box shown in Figure 2.1.

An example of a template

The best way to see how templates and wizards work is to try one out. We'll start with the Personal Web, which is one of the more useful and adaptable of the templates.

You load the template from the New FrontPage Web dialog box (see Figure 2.1). In the Template or Wizard list, double-click the Personal Web template. FrontPage displays the Personal Web Template dialog box, shown in Figure 2.2.

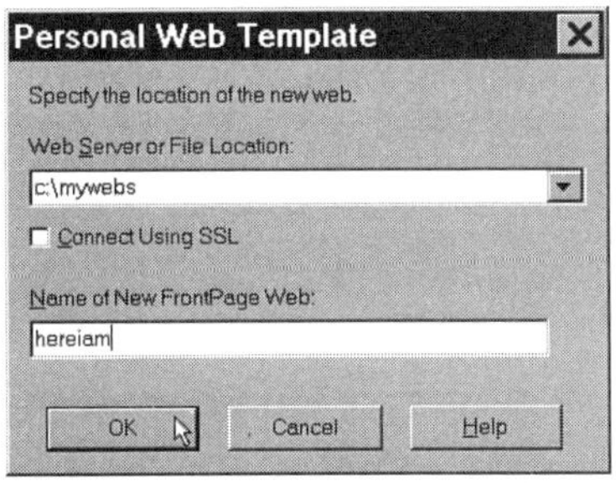

Fig. 2.2
Use the Template dialog box to name your web.

This dialog box can be confusing, and to understand it fully you need to know something about servers and directory structures. Since our goal here is to get a web up and running, we'll forego some of the technical details.

If you have access to a web server, you'll see the name of the server in the Web Server or File Location dialog box, as in Figure 2.2. (FrontPage automatically detects this server during setup.)

And what if no server is available? Not to worry—FrontPage lets you create a web on your hard drive, in the default folder C:\FrontPage Web\Content\. Type the name of your web in the Name of New FrontPage Web text box.

Different servers have different rules governing the length of your filename and what characters you can use. If you don't know what those rules are, you can't go wrong with an eight-letter name containing no spaces.

Click OK. FrontPage displays a message at the bottom of the screen telling you that it's creating your web and then opens the web in Explorer.

TIP **Are several people using your computer for their own web** projects? Things can get confusing if you're all using the same default folder, C:\FrontPage Web\Content\. Consider giving each user a different folder in which to place his or her webs. In the Web Template dialog box, simply enter the new folder's path name under Web Server or File Location. For example, if you're going to put your webs in the folder called mywebs, enter C:\mywebs. FrontPage creates the folder if it doesn't already exist.

Q&A *If I create my web on my hard drive, will I be able to publish it?*

Yes. We'll cover that topic fully in Chapter 19, "This Web Is Suitable for Publication."

The Explorer screen

Let's assume for a moment that we've created a web called **hereiam** with the Personal Web template. Depending on how Explorer has been configured, the web can appear in one of two views—Hyperlink (see Figure 2.3) or Folder (see Figure 2.4). You can switch between the two views by clicking the Hyperlink View or Folder View buttons on the toolbar. Don't worry for now about trying to interpret the content of these views; we'll get to that in a moment.

FrontPage's Templates and Wizards

FrontPage's templates and wizards run the gamut from single, empty web pages to complex webs with multiple pages and special features. Most require some knowledge of FrontPage before they can be modified, but you should feel free to try them on for size; you can't do any damage to FrontPage, and you can always delete the webs you create when you're done playing with them. Here's a rundown of what you'll find and what each template might be good for:

Normal Web. The Mondrian painting of FrontPage templates—a single, empty page. Use this template when you're creating a web from the ground up.

Corporate Presence Wizard. Use this to build a site for your company, large or small. The wizard lets you decide among a variety of features you want the site to include. It's particularly good at helping you build a site for promoting products and services. Another strength: the wizard steps you through creating a customized feedback form. The wizard even gives you some control over graphics and colors. This is a powerful wizard that requires some knowledge of FrontPage and web design.

Customer Support Web. Provides a basic structure for such customer support services as downloads, a feedback form, discussion groups, and FAQs (frequently asked questions). Aimed at software companies (it includes a bug report form), but can easily be adapted for other types of businesses.

Discussion Web Wizard. Lets you create a discussion forum, in which visitors can post and read messages on a topic of your choice. The wizard makes it easy to choose, for instance, if your forum will be public or private and how messages will appear. New users should read Chapter 18, "Let's Talk!: The Fine Art of Web Conversation," before they tackle this one.

Empty Web. This template creates the folders for a web but without any web pages. You do all the work in Editor.

Import Web Wizard. Lets you create a web from existing documents. You can, for example, import a web and create a new web that includes only selected pages from the original.

Learning FrontPage. For use with the Learning FrontPage tutorial in the Getting Started with FrontPage manual, which comes packaged with the FrontPage software.

Personal Web. A no-frills web for publishing information about yourself. As is, this web is geared toward the workplace, with such headings as Employee Information and Current Projects. However, you can easily change these headings so that they're suitable for a web introducing your family or promoting a home business. The comments and suggestions form is particularly handy.

Project Web. Helps you design a web site for a project's participants. It sets you up with a member listing, a schedule, monthly status reports, and discussion groups.

Fig. 2.3
Hyperlink view gives you a picture of your web and its hyperlinks.

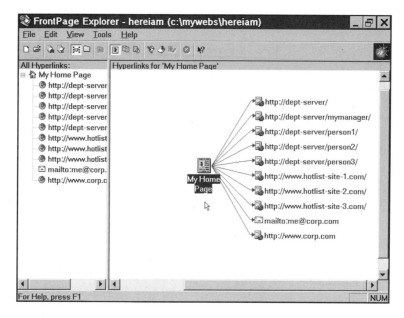

Fig. 2.4
Folder view shows you the folders and files that make up your web.

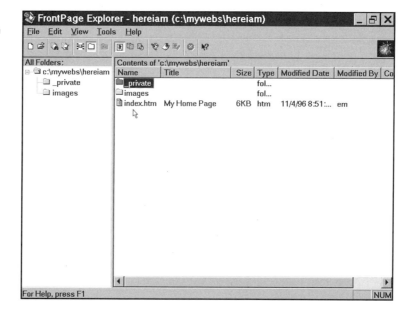

First, let's take a look at the various components of the Explorer screen as seen on the "What's what in FrontPage Explorer" graphics page. Then, we'll examine the more important Explorer components in detail.

What's what in FrontPage Explorer

Explorer's menu bar and toolbar give you access to your commands; the window (in this case, in Hyperlink view) gives you information about your web's pages and hyperlinks.

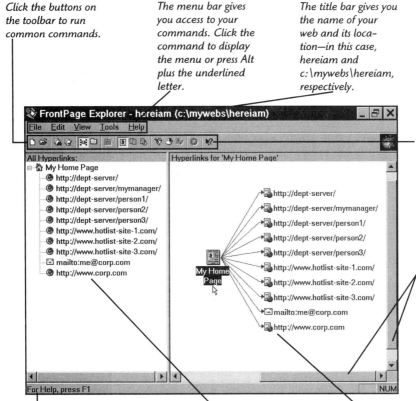

Click the buttons on the toolbar to run common commands.

The menu bar gives you access to your commands. Click the command to display the menu or press Alt plus the underlined letter.

The title bar gives you the name of your web and its location—in this case, hereiam and c:\mywebs\hereiam, respectively.

Use the Help button for quick help on any part of the screen; click it once, drag the question mark to the element on which you want help, and click again.

The scroll bars let you use your mouse to scroll the Explorer windows so that you can display hidden elements.

The status bar gives you descriptions of menu commands and buttons; touch a command or button with your mouse to display the description.

In Hyperlink view, this panel displays a list of your web's hyperlinked pages. Click a page name to display the hyperlinks to and from that page in the Hyperlinks For panel.

In Hyperlink view, this panel graphically displays the hyperlinks to and from the page you've selected in the All Hyperlinks panel.

The menu bar

If you've used other Windows programs for more than five seconds, the menu bar you see in Explorer will look familiar. It behaves just like any other menu bar you've used; you display a menu by clicking once on the option or by pressing the Alt key plus the underlined letter (for example, press Alt+F for the File menu).

Plain English, please!

Alt in the Alt+F combination above represents the Alternate key on your keyboard. You'll also find references in this book to Ctrl, which stands for the Control key. You use Alt and Ctrl in combination with other keys to run commands or perform other tasks. For example, Alt+E displays the Edit menu, or Ctrl+N starts a new FrontPage web.

When you use the Alt key, you can press and release it and then press the second key, or you can press the two keys together. But you must hold down the Ctrl key while you press the second key.

You run a menu command by sliding the arrow down the menu to the command and clicking your mouse button once. If you're using the keyboard, press the underlined letter (for example, press O to run the Open command in the File menu).

Run commands fast with quick menus

You occasionally can save time by using one of FrontPage's quick menus. Just right-click an object in the Explorer window and choose from the menu that pops up.

The quick menu changes depending on what view you're in and what you're clicking. It provides a short list of the main menu commands that you'll probably use the most. Figure 2.5 displays the quick menu you get if you right-click a file name in the Contents panel when you're in Folder view.

The toolbar

The toolbar, just below the menu bar, lets you execute common commands without going through the menu bar. For example, to create a new web, click the New FrontPage Web button instead of choosing File, New, FrontPage Web from the menu bar.

Fig. 2.5
An alternative to the menu bar: right-click an object and choose from the quick menu.

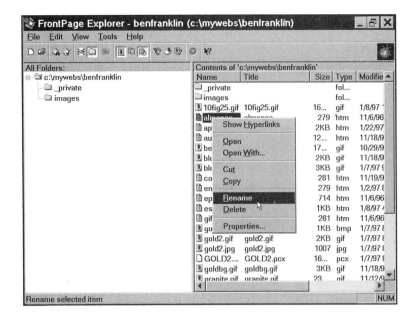

The graphics on the buttons don't always tell you what the buttons do, but you can get a short description or any button by touching it with your mouse pointer. For example, if you touch the button under the View menu item that looks a bit like a spider, a little box called a **ScreenTip** tells you that it's the Hyperlink View button. Meanwhile, in the Status bar at the bottom of the screen, you'll see a fuller description: "Show the structure of hyperlinks in the current FrontPage web."

The following page, "Inside the toolbar," describes what the toolbar buttons do.

Get fast answers with context-sensitive help

As you poke around the Explorer screen, you might find the Help button on the far right end of the toolbar to be particularly useful. The button is a sort of Help Lite, giving you concise, specific information about any item in the Explorer window. It's no replacement for the beefier help functions that we'll discuss in Chapter 4, "Help Is on the Way!" but it's a good tool for learning Explorer.

Inside the toolbar

Toolbar

New FrontPage Web
Starts a new web

Open FrontPage Web
Opens an existing web

Cross File Find
Finds words in FrontPage web pages

Cross File Spelling
Runs spell checker on all web pages

Hyperlink view
Shows structure of hyperlinks in web

Folder view
Shows list of current folder and files in web

Up one level
Move up one folder level in Folder View

Hyperlinks to Images
Shows or hides hyperlinks to graphics images

Repeated hyperlinks
Shows or hides repeated hyperlinks

Hyperlinks Inside Page
Shows or hides hyperlinks inside pages

Show FrontPage Editor
Loads FrontPage Editor or shows editor if loaded

Show To Do List
Shows list of tasks to perform

Show Image Editor
Loads image editor or shows editor if loaded. Active only if image editor installed.

Stop
Stops operation in progress. Button is red during an operation but is otherwise gray.

Help
Context-sensitive help. Click this button, point to item on the screen, and click again.

http://www.quecorp.com

When you click the Help button, a question mark attaches itself to your mouse pointer. Move the pointer to the part of the screen on which you want help (you don't need to hold down the mouse button). Click the mouse button again, and FrontPage displays a screen of information from its Help files.

You can even use the Help button on menu commands. Click the button, open the menu, point to the command, and click the button again.

Press the Esc key to cancel Help.

The status bar

The status bar has two functions. First, it gives more detailed information about any command you've highlighted in a menu. For example, if you click File and touch Import, the status bar displays the message, "Import existing files into the FrontPage web."

Second, the status bar tells you when an operation is in progress. For example, if you choose Tools, Recalculate Hyperlinks, the status bar displays the message, Update hyperlinks, and text indices.

View Points

We've spent most of this chapter dancing around the edges of the Explorer screen. It's time to get to the meat and potatoes—the Explorer window.

As we saw earlier, Explorer offers two ways of viewing your web: Hyperlink View and Folder View. Each provides different information, and each plays an important role in helping you conceive and develop your web.

Hyperlink View

The Hyperlink View lets you look at a picture of the links that make up your web. Click the Hyperlink View button on the toolbar or choose View, Hyperlink View from the menu bar. The left panel, All Hyperlinks, provides a list of hyperlinks; the right panel, Hyperlinks for..., graphically displays the hyperlinks to and from the hyperlink selected in the left panel.

TIP **You navigate the Explorer panels much as you do in Windows Explorer.** Use your arrow keys to move up and down the All Hyperlinks panel. A plus sign next to a page indicates that the page has its own hyperlinks. Click the plus sign or double-click the page name to expand the list. The plus sign changes to a minus sign. Click the minus sign or double-click the page name to collapse the list. Use the tab key to move between the left and right panels.

In Figure 2.6, for example, Home Page has been selected in the left panel. The right panel, Hyperlinks for... provides the following information:

Fig. 2.6
The web site called Benfranklin has a home page with one incoming hyperlink, listed on the left, and nine outgoing hyperlinks, listed on the right.

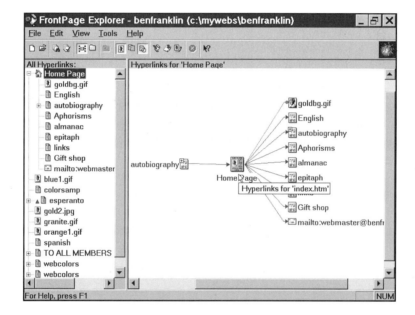

Home Page has nine outgoing hyperlinks, listed to the right of Home Page. For example, the Home Page has a hyperlink called Autobiography that, when clicked, takes you to a page containing Ben Franklin's autobiography.

Seven of the nine links go to other pages, one (goldbg.gif) goes to a graphic, and one (mailto) goes to an e-mail address.

Home Page has one incoming link, from Autobiography. This indicates that the Autobiography page has a link that takes the visitor back to the Home Page.

Notice that each type of hyperlink is represented by a different type of icon. For example, the graphic features a little picture while the e-mail address displays an envelope. Titles don't always tell you what kind of hyperlinks you've got, and the icons can serve as important visual aids.

TIP **The titles of the pages that are linked are not necessarily the file** names of those pages. For example, in Figure 2.6, the Autobiography link points to a page whose title is Autobiography but whose file name is autobio.htm. You can view the file names while in Hyperlink view by touching the title in the right panel; FrontPage displays a ScreenTip that includes the file name. In Figure 2.6, for example, the ScreenTip reveals that the page titled Home Page is saved as the file Index.htm.

Q&A *The line that runs from Home Page to English.htm is broken. How come?*

A broken line means a broken hyperlink, which can indicate, among other things, that the link in Home Page points to a page that hasn't been created yet, has been renamed, or has been deleted. Fixing broken links is something you don't want to try until you get your feet wet creating webs, but you can do it by choosing Tools, Verify Hyperlinks from the menu bar. You'll learn more about fixing broken hyperlinks in Chapter 20, "Maintaining Your Web."

Expanding your view

You'll notice that some icons in the right panel have plus signs indicating that they're pages that include links of their own. You can expand your right panel view to include these links by clicking the plus sign. Figure 2.7 shows the results of expanding the Autobiography link.

Q&A *How do you change the panel's width to accommodate a larger web, such as in Figure 2.7?*

Touch the border between the two panes with your pointer until the pointer changes into two vertical bars flanked by arrows. Click the mouse button and drag the border to its new position.

Fig. 2.7
You can expand any hyperlink in the Hyperlinks For... panel by clicking the plus sign in its icon.

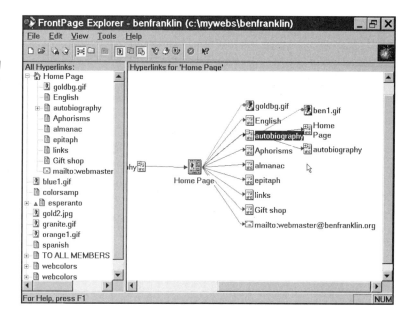

I'd like to look at a different page, please

You can view the hyperlinks for any page by clicking the page title in the All Hyperlinks panel. For example, clicking Autobiography displays the Hyperlinks for "Autobiography" panel in Figure 2.8.

Fig. 2.8
Clicking Autobiography in the All Hyperlinks panel displays the hyperlinks to and from the Autobiography page.

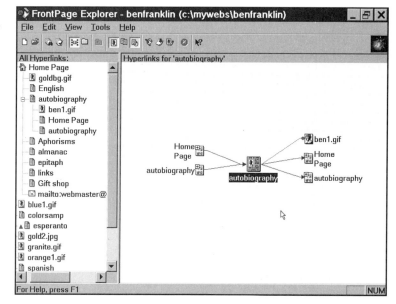

http://www.quecorp.com

Q&A *The Autobiography page in Figure 2.8 has a hyperlink to itself! How is this possible?*

A hyperlink in a web page can take you to another part of the same page that has been tagged with what is called a **bookmark**. In this case, the Autobiography page includes a link at the bottom of the page that takes you back to the top of the page. If you touched the Autobiography link at the bottom of the right column in Figure 2.8, the ScreenTip would read, "Bookmark in: autobio.htm." We'll discuss bookmarks in depth in Chapter 12, "Webward Ho! Adding Pages to Your Web."

Narrow views

The screen shots in this chapter that show the Benfranklin web site display all hyperlinks. But there are times when you'll want to narrow the links you display. For example, a web site might include dozens—perhaps hundreds—of graphics that do nothing but clutter the Hyperlinks For... panel when you want to look only at your web pages. The View menu has several options that will help to simplify your Explorer window, or you can click the corresponding button on the toolbar:

- To hide links to graphics, turn off the View, Hyperlinks to Images option.

- If a page has numerous links to another page, each link will show up in the Hyperlinks For... panel. Turn off View, Repeated Hyperlinks to represent all these links with a single title.

- Turn off Hyperlinks Inside Page to hide links that a page might have to itself, such as with bookmarks.

On the View menu, a check mark precedes the option when it's on; turn an option on or off by clicking it. On the toolbar, the option is on when the button appears to be in 3-D and off when the button is flat gray; turn the option on and off by clicking the button.

Folder View

Hyperlink View is best for tracing the hyperlinks in your web, but the time might come when you need to manage the actual files that your web comprises. Enter Folder View.

Think of Folder View as Explorer's version of Windows Explorer. The left panel, All Folders, shows the folders on your drive that contain your web's files. The right panel, Contents Of..., shows the files, as well as any folders nested in the selected folder.

Choose Folder View by clicking the Folder View button on the toolbar or choosing View, Folder View from the main menu. Explorer automatically shows you the folders and files in the main, or top, folder. In Figure 2.9, for example, the top folder is c:\mywebs\benfranklin. It contains the folders _private and images, as well as the files shown in the right panel. You can view the contents of another folder by clicking it in the left panel or double-clicking it in the right panel.

Fig. 2.9
The Folder View displays the names of the files that make up your web, as well as other useful information.

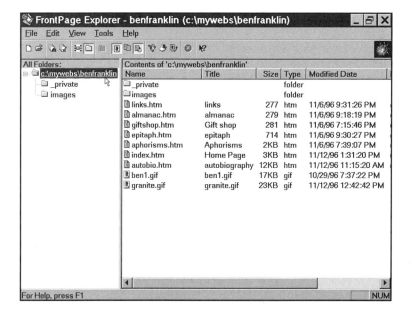

Folder View yields a great deal of information that might not be useful to newcomers but is invaluable to more experienced users. Here's a quick rundown of what you'll learn from the Contents Of... panel:

- In the Name column are the names of the files that make up your web site.

- The Title column lists the titles you've given your pages as you've created them.

- The Size column lists the size of each file, in bytes or kilobytes. File sizes won't be a concern when you start a web, but they can become a factor as your web grows if your server limits how large your web site can be.

- The Type column tells you what types of files are in the folder, if it's a file type that Windows recognizes. Otherwise, the Type column repeats the extension of the file.
- The Modified Date column indicates the last time the file was changed.
- The Modified By column shows you who made the last change. This information can be useful when several people have author access to the same web.

TIP **You can sort your Contents Of… list by any column by clicking the** column head. For example, click Size to sort the files by file size in ascending order; click Modified Date to sort by date modified, most recent files first.

Q&A *How do I change the widths of my columns in the Contents Of… panel?*

You can change column widths in one of two ways. To change the width to automatically fit the longest entry in the column, touch the column title's right border with your mouse pointer; when it changes to a double-headed arrow, double-click. To change the column to a width of your own choosing, touch the column title's right border; when you see the double-headed arrow, click the mouse button and drag the border to the position you want.

I'm staring at my new web. Now what?

Of course, a new web isn't going to do you much good just sitting there empty. So your next step will probably be to open your Home Page in FrontPage Editor and start adding text, hyperlinks, graphics, and other elements. Just double-click the Home Page icon in Hyperlink View or Index.htm in Folder View. If Editor isn't open, FrontPage opens it for you and loads the page, ready for editing. You can load any other HTML page the same way.

Chapter 1, "Read All About It: FrontPage Essentials" includes a crash course in how to proceed once you've got the web page open in Editor. For details on Editor, hold on; we'll get to them in Chapter 3, "Home, Sweet Home Page: Inside the Editor."

Closing your web

You close a web by choosing File, Close FrontPage Web from the main menu. This closes the web but keeps Explorer open.

There's a catch to closing a web if you've still got pages open in Editor—you can't save those open pages once your web is closed. So make sure you save and close all pages in Editor before closing the web in Explorer.

If you accidentally closed the web, don't panic; you can reopen the web without losing your work in Editor. When you try to close the pages in Editor, FrontPage automatically switches you to Explorer (opening Explorer if it isn't open already) and displays the Open FrontPage Web dialog box for you. Reopen the web, return to Editor, close the pages, and close the web again.

If you configured the Getting Started dialog box to display itself each time you run Explorer, it will also appear when you close a web.

TIP If you're going to open another web or create a new one, you don't need to close the current web first; FrontPage closes it for you.

Reopening your web with the Getting Started Dialog box

Remember the Getting Started dialog box we discussed at the beginning of the chapter? Refer to the graphics page on **p. 32** if you need to refresh your memory.

That dialog box included a grayed out button at the top called Open Recent FrontPage Web. Once you've created a web, the button changes to list the web you've worked on most recently, whether the dialog box appears just after you close your web or the next time you run Explorer. In Figure 2.10, for example, the button reads Open "benfranklin." To open the web, simply choose the OK button.

Fig. 2.10
Once you've created a web, its name appears as part of the first choice in the Getting Started dialog box; in this case, Open "benfranklin."

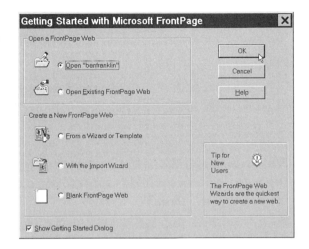

I don't have a Getting Started dialog box. Now what?

If Explorer isn't set up to display the Getting Started dialog box, click the Open FrontPage Web button on the toolbar or choose File, Open FrontPage Web from the main menu. Explorer displays the Open FrontPage Web dialog box in Figure 2.11. Follow these steps:

Fig. 2.11
To open an existing web from a server or file location, choose the List Web button and double-click the name of the web you want to open.

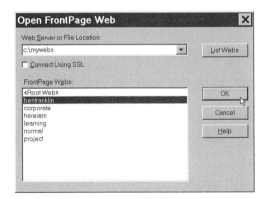

1 If the correct web server or file location is listed in the Web Server or File Location text box, choose the List Webs button.

2. If you've got more than one web server or file location in which you're creating webs, click the right arrow next to the Web Server or File Location text box and choose the appropriate server or location.

3. When you're done with either of the previous steps, you'll see a list of the existing webs. Either click the name of the web you want and click the OK button or double-click the name.

Q&A *The FrontPage Webs list box in the Open FrontPage Web dialog box includes something called <Root Web>. What's that?*

The Root Web is simply a web that FrontPage sets up by default when you install the program. You don't need to work with the Root Web until you start dabbling with permissions settings. See Chapter 19, "This Web Is Suitable for Publication," for more information.

Choosing a web from the Getting Started dialog box

How do you open an existing web, other than the most recent one, from the Getting Started dialog box? Easy—just choose Open Existing FrontPage Web. FrontPage displays the Open FrontPage Web dialog box. Follow the three steps described above.

Whacking unwanted webs

Maybe you've created a web with a template and found it didn't meet your needs. Or you've got a web hanging around that you don't need any more. In either case, you can delete the entire web in one stroke of the mouse. Open the web that you want to delete, then choose File, Delete FrontPage Web from the main menu.

CAUTION **When you delete a web, it's gone for good; you can't get it back.** Neither can you restore deleted web files from Windows' Recycle Bin. Make sure you rescue any individual files that you might need later. Do not delete a web using Windows Explorer or File Manager. While you will successfully delete this web, the name of the web will continue to be listed in the Open FrontPage web dialog box.

Home, Sweet Home Page: Inside the FrontPage Editor

● **In this chapter:**

- What does the Editor do?
- I could have sworn this was a word processor
- Can I get a little more room to work?
- How do I get around in here?

Get acquainted with the FrontPage Editor, the word processor for webs. . . . . >

The editors' lot is not always a happy one. Writers hog all the credit for good writing, but when does anybody ever say of bad writing, "That could have used a good writer?" Instead, it's always, "This sure needed a good editor." Back when politicians were capable of wit, Adlai Stevenson, Governor of Illinois and Presidential candidate, defined the editorial role for all time: "An editor is one who separates the wheat from the chaff and prints the chaff."

Editors grow accustomed to such abuse, and carry on regardless, in true workhorse fashion. The FrontPage Editor is a case in point. Compared to a word processor, its functions are constrained by the limitations of HTML. You might, therefore, be tempted to curse its occasional clumsiness. But the Editor is the FrontPage workhorse, the component of the program in which you'll do most of your work. Get to know its quirks, and you'll find the Editor an indispensable web-building partner. Furthermore, if a web ends up with more chaff than wheat, the FrontPage Editor is blameless. Separating one from the other is entirely in your hands.

The Editor's role in FrontPage

Although it's a distinct component of the program, you probably won't use the FrontPage Editor as an independent component. Because of the way FrontPage requires you to lay out a web in the Explorer, even blank Editor pages begin life as part of a web that's already assembled. FrontPage users begin in the Explorer, either by opening or creating a web. Only after that vital first step does the Editor come on the scene to refine or add pages to a web.

TIP **Which isn't to say that you can't use the Editor as a standalone** program. If you create a new page in the Editor without opening a web in the Explorer, that's exactly what you'd be doing.

http://www.quecorp.com

Chapter 3 *Home, Sweet Home Page: Inside the FrontPage Editor* **53**

To run the FrontPage Editor:

1. Click File in the FrontPage Explorer and select an existing web from the File drop-down menu. Or click File, New, FrontPage Web to create a new web (see Chapter 2, "Start Your Web Adventure with FP Explorer," for details on opening and creating webs in the FrontPage Explorer).

2. With your web opened in the Explorer, click the Folder View button on the Explorer toolbar. That gives you a handy list of the web's files and folders, as seen in Figure 3.1.

Fig. 3.1
Even if your pages are blank, they still show up in the Explorer's Folder View.

Items of the HTM (Hypertext Markup) type are pages ready to be edited in the FrontPage Editor.

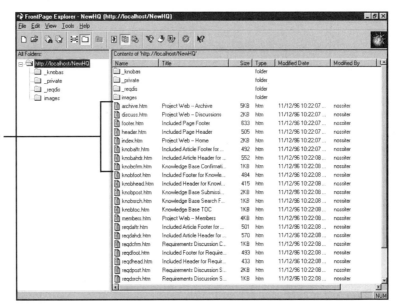

3. Double-click any file of the HTM type on the Explorer's list. The Editor opens with the selected file loaded in the editing window, ready for alterations major and minor. Figure 3.2 shows the FrontPage Editor's main features.

Fig. 3.2
It looks like a word processor, it acts like a word processor, but the Editor isn't exactly like the word processors you're used to.

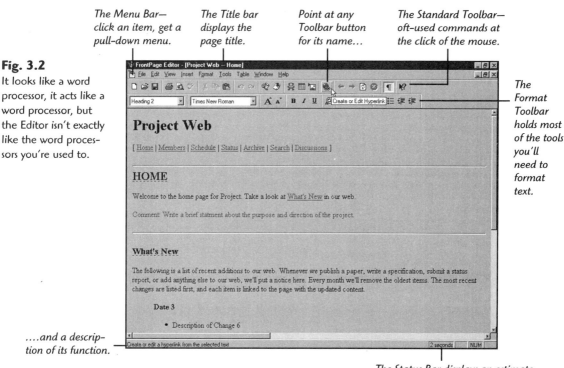

The Menu Bar—click an item, get a pull-down menu.

The Title bar displays the page title.

Point at any Toolbar button for its name...

The Standard Toolbar—oft-used commands at the click of the mouse.

The Format Toolbar holds most of the tools you'll need to format text.

....and a description of its function.

The Status Bar displays an estimate of how long the current page will take to load in a browser.

Rather like a word processor, but different

The FrontPage Editor is a cousin of your word processor, a close relation but not immediate family. When you start typing in the editing window, you'll quickly discover a few unique Editor traits:

- The Tab key doesn't work. There are no tab stops in the Editor, so if you want to indent paragraphs, click the Increase Indent button on the Format Toolbar.

- There are no page numbers. Since webs are designed to be viewed, not printed, readers scroll down a single long page instead of turning multiple shorter pages. If you type a screen full of text, you can add another page and link it with a hyperlink (see Chapter 1, "Read All About It: FrontPage Essentials"). But that added page is a separate HTML document, not another page of the same document.

http://www.quecorp.com

- The Enter key inserts a blank line whenever you press it to end a paragraph. Poets and others who need to snap off a line of text before it hits the right margin can click Insert, Break, Normal Line Break, OK to break a line without inserting a blank.

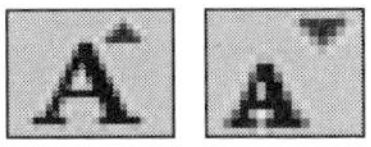

- There's no font size button. Instead, select text and click the Increase or Decrease Text Size buttons.

Apart from these oddities, there are a few other Editor quirks that we'll look at when we edit and format text in Chapter 5, "Text Typing Tips, Tricks, and Traps." When you consider that the whole idea of the Editor is to produce viewable, rather than printable, pages, these quirks and oddities are really not so quirky and odd. The fair-minded will think of them as differences instead.

Tailor the Editing window to suit

No matter how many toolbars, menu bars, and other gadgets there are in the FrontPage Editor, the area where you do your work is a blank space. That's all to the good, since you need room for your own material. Furthermore, the workspace is adjustable. You can clear some of the gadgets off the screen, or add more. Some gadgets can even be moved around if they get in your way.

Features like the Status bar and the various toolbars can be hidden or displayed from the View menu. Click View, then select or deselect the features of your choice. Activated items have check marks beside them, as seen in Figure 3.3.

Fig. 3.3
Give yourself more room to work, or add more gadgets to the screen, with your choices on the View menu.

TIP **If you do put the Format Toolbar out of sight, you can still access** formatting features from the keyboard. Press Ctrl+B to apply boldface, Ctrl+I for italics, and Ctrl+U for underlining. To indent, press Ctrl+M. Shift+Ctrl+M decreases indenting.

Floating toolbars

The top of the page is what your readers will see first when they visit your web, so you'll likely put a lot of effort into getting it right. To give yourself more room at the top of the window while keeping the toolbar gadgets within easy reach, try dragging the toolbars to the bottom of the window.

Just drag the toolbars out of their "docked" position at the top of the window and move them wherever you like. To dock them again, double-click the toolbar's title bar, as shown in Figure 3.4.

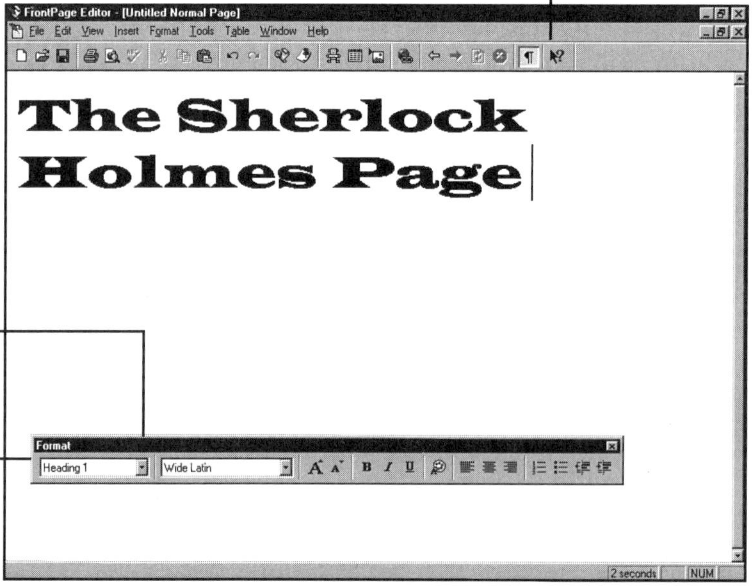

Fig. 3.4
To free up workspace at the crucial top of the page, drag the toolbars down to the bottom of the window.

This toolbar is docked.

Double-click here to dock a floating toolbar.

This toolbar is floating.

TIP **Puzzled about a toolbar button or menu command? Click** the Help button on the Editor Standard Toolbar, and your pointer is joined by a question mark. Now click any button or menu item, and a help explanation pops right up.

Don't overlook the Status bar

It's inconspicuous, but the Status bar at the bottom of the Editor window displays a lot of useful information. It shows the function of any toolbar button you point at and the number of seconds the current page will require to download into a browser. That's crucial information if you want to avoid losing web surfers who might become impatient waiting for a very slow page. The Status bar displays the estimated time the page will require to download at the speed of your current modem. If the download time starts to inch past thirty seconds, consider eliminating a graphic or three from your page.

The Status bar has another trick up its sleeve. Point at any link on your page, and the link's destination is displayed at the left side of the Status bar.

Moving around the page by keyboard and mouse

For all the amazing things they can do, computers are far from perfect at some basic tasks. Displaying text for easy reading, a job at which books and magazines excel, is not the computer's strong suit. Text on a screen is harder to read than text on a page, and no gadget for scrolling from screen to screen will ever duplicate the ease of turning a printed page. When it comes to document navigation, computers have turned the clocks back to the days when books were written on long scrolls instead of bound pages. The ancient Egyptians would have sympathized with a modern Web surfer wearing out a wrist scrolling down a long page. Still, the FrontPage Editor has a few navigational shortcuts that an ancient scroll reader might have envied.

The scroll bar, that familiar Windows gadget, is what you use to get around the page without moving the cursor. Click the scroll bar above or below the scroll box to advance or retreat one screen at a time. Click the Up or Down scroll buttons to move one line at a time, and drag the scroll box up or down to move variable distances (see Figure 3.5). As you fill up your page, the scroll box shrinks, indicating how far you'll have to drag it to reach the bottom of the page.

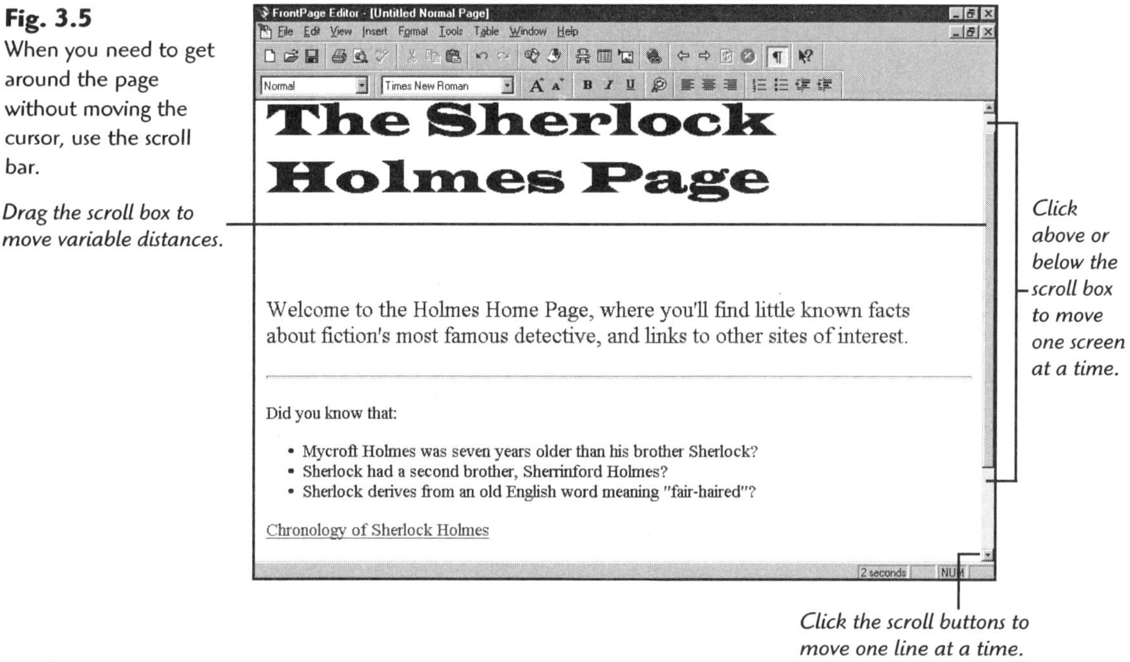

Fig. 3.5
When you need to get around the page without moving the cursor, use the scroll bar.

Drag the scroll box to move variable distances.

Click above or below the scroll box to move one screen at a time.

Click the scroll buttons to move one line at a time.

For faster navigating, use the keyboard

The scroll bar is fine for reading, but if you're still batting out your text, you won't want to lift your hands from the keyboard to get around. Table 3.1 below shows you how to navigate the page right from the keyboard.

Table 3.1 Navigate the page with keyboard convenience

To move the cursor...	Press these keys
Up one screen	Page Up
Down one screen	Page Down
To the top of the page	Ctrl+Home
To the bottom of the page	Ctrl+End
To the end of the line	End
To the beginning of the line	Home
Left one word	Ctrl+Left Arrow

http://www.quecorp.com

To move the cursor...	Press these keys
Right one word	Ctrl+Right Arrow
Up one paragraph	Ctrl+Up Arrow
Down one paragraph	Ctrl+Down Arrow

Of course, you can move the cursor anywhere you like with the mouse as well. Just click wherever you want the insertion point to appear.

 Q&A *Where's the horizontal scroll bar?*

The FrontPage Editor horizontal scroll bar only appears if you type past the right margin on any line.

Getting the most (and the least) out of the Editor window

Like all Windows programs, FrontPage comes equipped with two Control bars at the upper right corner of the window. The top Control bar minimizes, maximizes, and closes the program window; the bottom toolbar does the same things for the document window.

By default, the FrontPage Editor loads in a window. To give yourself more room to work, just click the top Maximize button to make the program full screen.

Help Is on the Way!

● **In this chapter:**

- Instant help: just point and click!

- How to find information in FrontPage's Help files

- Getting there from here: how to navigate Help

- In your own words: adding comments to a Help screen

- Hello, Microsoft! Digging for treasure on the World Wide Web

FrontPage helps those who help themselves. Learning how to use its help tools is a key to mastering FrontPage's commands and features..................... ●

Patience is a virtue, except when you've got three projects due tomorrow. Suddenly, that new program you're trying to learn becomes a morass of hidden commands, confusing procedures, and buried secrets. You need help, and you need it *now*.

Don't panic—the cavalry is on the way. FrontPage's help system gives you a variety of tools that can answer pressing questions and step you through unfamiliar tasks.

Of course, it's an immutable law of computing that eventually you'll run into a quandary from which even the help files can't save you. That's where the World Wide Web comes to the rescue. FrontPage lets you directly access Microsoft's online services, where you'll find a wealth of tips, shortcuts, and solutions.

Context-sensitive help: Shoot first and ask questions later

FrontPage offers extensive help files that you can query in a number of ways through the Help command on the menu bar. But what you often need most is immediate help on a specific command or task. Enter **context-sensitive help**. Instead of wading through layers of menus and windows, you get a few paragraphs of information that relate specifically to a toolbar button or menu command.

For example, if you want to insert a table in Editor, you point at the Insert Table button on the toolbar or the Insert command on the Table menu and click. FrontPage displays a window explaining the Insert Table command.

Context-sensitive Help can save you a lot of time. And it'll significantly lower your blood pressure; pointing and clicking is a lot easier than trying to remember the exact term you need to look up in Help's (or the manual's) index.

 TIP **Explorer and Editor share the same help files, so you can get help** on Explorer from inside Editor and vice versa.

An object lesson

Context-sensitive help works with almost any object on the screen. Click once on the question mark at the far right of the toolbar. Point the question mark at the object and click again.

In Figure 4.1, the question mark has been pointed at Explorer's Folder View button. Clicking the button again displays the Help screen shown in Figure 4.2.

Fig. 4.1
Want to know what a toolbar button does? First, click once on the Help button and aim the pointer at the button...

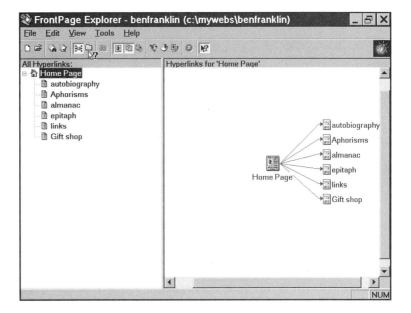

TIP You can "click" the help button from the keyboard by pressing Shift+F1. Thus, you can get context-sensitive help on an object by pointing at the object first, pressing Shift+F1, and clicking the object. Pressing F1 only displays the Help Topics dialog box discussed later.

Q&A *The Help window blocks part of the screen that I want to see. Can I shrink or move it?*

You can do either. To resize the Help window, drag the borders in and out with the mouse pointer. The new size becomes a permanent part of your FrontPage configuration until you resize it again.

You can move the window by clicking its title bar and dragging the window to another part of the screen.

Fig. 4.2
...and then click again. FrontPage displays a window that explains the button's function.

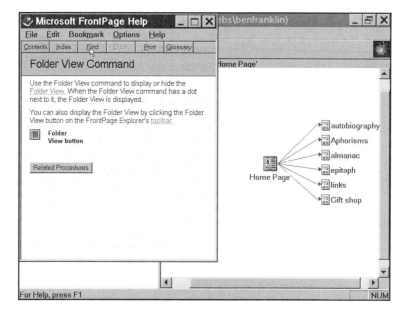

Help on menu commands

The Help button works with menu commands, too. Let's say, for example, that you want help on Explorer's Tools, Spelling command. Click the help button and then choose Tools. Point at the Spelling command and click again.

You also can get help on menu commands with the F1 function key. This method is faster if you're one of those users who likes to use the keyboard as much as possible. For example, here's how you get help on creating hyperlinks in Editor:

1 Choose Edit from the menu bar.

2 Point at Hyperlink with your mouse, or scroll the selection bar to Hyperlink.

3 Press F1.

Help on keyboard combinations

The help button even lets you get help on keyboard combinations. For example, Ctrl+F runs the Find command; to get help on Find, click the Help button and press Ctrl+F.

Searching for help

The Help button is the drive-thru window of FrontPage's help system; it lets you grab a fast bite quickly and easily. But if you want to belly up to a real meal, you'll have to go inside and order from the full menu.

FrontPage offers a smorgasbord of search features that lets you get comprehensive instructions on commands and tasks. Start by choosing Help, Microsoft FrontPage Help from the menu bar or pressing the F1 function key. FrontPage displays the Help Topics dialog box, in which you can choose one of three panels (see Figures 4.3A, 4.3B, and 4.3C on the following graphics page):

- **Contents** gives you a table of contents, much like the one you'd find in a book, that collects topics under category headings. This is a good place to start if you want an idea of what subjects the Help files cover. You'll also find it useful for getting an overview of FrontPage's features.
- **Index** provides an alphabetical list of topics.
- **Find** searches all Help files for any instance of a selected word or partial word.

Contents

Remember when reference books actually were books? So does FrontPage. The Contents panel (refer to Figure 4.3A) uses the traditional tome as its metaphor, organizing the help files' information much like a manual would.

Contents displays a list of general Help subjects, called **books**, each of which is preceded by a closed-book icon. Click twice on a book to drop down the book's table of contents.

The table of contents can include books, topics (which are preceded by question mark icons), or both. Double-click a book to get another table of contents, or double-click a topic to get a Help screen.

For example, in Figure 4.3A, the table of contents for the book titled "Working with Tables" includes one topic and eight other books. One of those books, "Inserting Tables," covers two topics.

1... 2... 3... Help!

FrontPage's Help command presents you with three tools for finding information. These figures show the different ways in which you can find help on inserting tables in Editor.

Fig. 4.3A
The Contents panel includes a book titled "*Working with Tables.*" In that book are several more books, one of which is called *Inserting Tables*, which in turn is divided into two chapters on the subject.

Fig. 4.3B
If you search the index for "insert table," the Insert Table Command entry appears as soon as you type "insert t."

Fig. 4.3C
If you search for the words "insert table" in the Find panel, you'll get a variety of topics that include the words "insert" and "table."

Index

While Contents is fine for browsing, Index is more useful when you need help on a specific task. Let's say you want to learn how to insert a table. The fastest way is to search the Index for the topic "insert table" (refer to Figure 4.3B).

In the Type The First Few Letters… text box, start typing the words **insert table**. As you type the text, FrontPage takes you to the first match in the Click the Index Entry text box. When you type the **t** in **table**, FrontPage jumps to "Insert Table Command." To retrieve the help screen, click "Insert Table Command" twice or choose the Display button.

Find

Find is similar to Index, except that it looks for words and phrases rather than for topics. It identifies all occurrences of the search term in all Help files (refer to Figure 4.3C).

For example, the Click A Topic… text box lists all entries that include the words "insert" and "table."

At first blush, Find might seem like the best way to go if you're not sure of the specific topic you're looking for. But using Find is like trawling a pond—your net will gather some fish, but you'll also dredge some mud and old tires. Sifting through the flotsam can be tedious and frustrating. You'll often have better luck if you use Find only after you've run into a dead end with Index.

 Q&A ***Is it possible to search for entries that include either of several words—for example, "URL" or "hyperlink"?***

Yes. In the Find dialog box, choose Options. In the Find Options dialog box that appears, click the option called At Least One Of The Words You Typed.

When I click the Find tab, I get a Find Setup Wizard dialog that tells me I have to create a database first. Is this normal?

Yes. FrontPage has to create a word list from its Help files before Find is functional. This is a simple, one-time-only procedure. Choose Minimize Database Size, the recommended option. The wizard steps you through the job.

Refining Find

The Find panel offers you several options that will help you conduct your searches more efficiently. Here are some quick tips and shortcuts:

- You can use the list beneath Select Some Matching Words… to eliminate topics you don't want. For example, if you click Table in Figure 4.3C, the list of topics changes to include only those entries that have the word "Table," with a capital T (see Figure 4.4).

- You can choose several matching words by clicking each one while holding down the Ctrl key.

- To start a new search, choose the Clear button. Find will delete the text in the Type the Word(s) You Want to Find text box and place your insertion point in the box.

- Want to re-launch a search for words you've cleared from the text box? Click the arrow to the right of the box. Find displays a drop-down menu of recent searches; click the one you want. You also can select the text box and use your up- and down-arrow keys to scroll through the search history.

Fig. 4.4
Click a matching word to refine your list of topics. You can choose more than one matching word by holding down the Ctrl key as you click each choice.

Inside the Help windows

Learning Help is like finding your way around a new shopping mall. Once inside the building, you still need directories to get to the right shops, as well as walkways and elevators to move from one part of the mall to the other.

FrontPage's Help screens have several features that will make your shopping a little easier. For instance, many Help screens also include links to other Help screens that have related information. You can print a Help screen, copy the information into a document, and even add your own notes (see the following graphics page).

You'll find two types of Help screens as you poke around, and you can identify them by the icon at the far left end of the title bar. Screens with overview information and lists of topics have a book icon, while screens with specific instructions have a question mark icon. To make this discussion easier, we'll call the former **topic screens** and the latter **instruction screens**.

These are the same icons that you see in the Contents panel of the Help Topics dialog box. Notice, however, that the Help screen icons don't always correspond to the ones you see in the Contents panel. If this seems confusing, don't worry about it; what's important is that the two types of Help screens have different arrays of menu items and toolbar buttons.

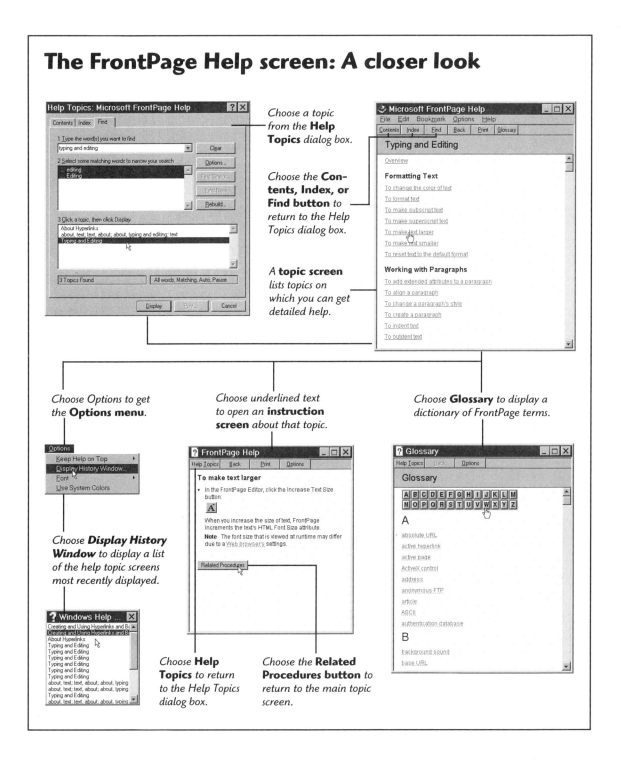

Q&A ***Can I return to my document without closing the Help window?***

Yes. You have three choices: click the Help window's Minimize button, click anywhere in the document window, or press Alt+Tab. The Help window will remain in the background. You can bring it back by pressing Alt+Tab.

Topic screens

Topic screens offer a number of important features that will help you organize, navigate, and use Help. You access these features the same way, whether you're in Explorer or Editor, with the main menu and button bar. We'll start with the commands that are designed to move you from one screen to another in the sometimes labyrinthine help-file maze.

Home, sweet home

No matter where you are in the Help file system, you can always return to the main Help Topics dialog box by clicking the Contents, Index, or Find button on the button bar (see the graphics page).

History lessons

It's sometimes easy to lose track of where you saw something in the Help files. You know you recently ran across a heading that offered help on adding header cells to a table, but where? And how do retrace your footsteps to the proper screen?

Rather than go to Help Topics and start searching all over again, try Help History—a list of all the topic screens you've visited in your current session.

To display the Help History window, choose Options, Display History Window from the menu bar (see the graphics page). You can go to any topic screen listed in the window by clicking it twice.

The Help History window does not include instruction screens.

You can also return to previously viewed help screens with the Back button on the button bar. This button takes you to the last topic screen you looked at, not the previous screen listed in the Help History window.

Bookmarks hold the spot

Do you ever find a help screen that you know you'll want to return to often? You can mark the screen with an electronic bookmark and return to it at any time by choosing it from a list.

You bookmark a screen by choosing Book<u>m</u>ark, <u>D</u>efine from the menu bar. Help opens a Bookmark Define dialog box like the one in Figure 4.5. The name of the screen you're bookmarking is displayed in the <u>B</u>ookmark Name text box, while previously created bookmarks are shown in the list box below. Type a new name for your bookmark if you don't like the default name and click the OK button.

Fig. 4.5
The Bookmark command lets you create a list of shortcuts to important Help screens.

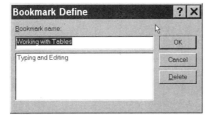

Whenever you want to go to a bookmarked screen, choose Book<u>m</u>ark from the menu bar. Beneath the <u>D</u>efine command, you'll see a numbered list of all your bookmarks. Click the bookmark you want or press the appropriate number.

Printing a Help screen

You can't take your Help screens with you to study in the tub. For this, you'll need paper copies. Click the <u>P</u>rint button to open the Print dialog box, from where you can send the Help screen to your printer.

Comments from the peanut gallery

You can't make your own Help screens from within Help, but you can add comments—**annotations** in Help parlance—to the screens Help provides. The Annotate command is useful if you want to emphasize important information or add a reference to another page that has related material.

Choose <u>E</u>dit, <u>A</u>nnotate from the menu bar. The Annotate dialog box pops up, like the one shown in Figure 4.6. Type your note in the Current <u>A</u>nnotation text box, then click <u>S</u>ave.

Fig. 4.6
Add comments to a Help screen with the Annotate command.

Click the paper clip to see your annotation.

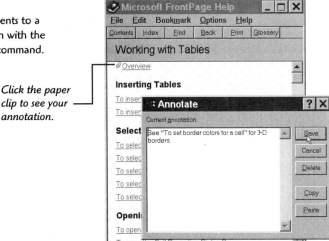

A small paper clip appears at the beginning of the Help screen's text (in Figure 4.6, in front of the word Overview). Click the paper clip to display the Annotate dialog box.

Q&A *My Help screens disappear whenever I switch to Editor or Explorer. Can I keep a screen visible at all times, so I can refer to it while I work?*

Yes. In any Help screen, choose Options and select Keep Help On Top, On Top. This option will let you move between the Help screen and FrontPage by clicking inside one or the other or by pressing Alt+Tab. Choose Not on Top to reverse the process.

Pardon my jargon—the FrontPage Glossary

The Internet has introduced a lot of new terms to the world, and many of them appear in FrontPage's Help files. You can get quick definitions of many terms by clicking the Glossary button on the button bar.

Instruction screens

As you can see, topic screens provide myriad tools and resources for using the help system. What they don't generally offer are step-by-step instructions on how to handle a specific task. These are contained in instruction screens, which you get by clicking a topic in a topic screen. For example, in the previous graphics page, clicking the heading "To Make Text Larger" opens the instruction screen that tells you how to make text larger.

You won't find as many features in an instruction screen as you do in a topic screen, but you can still perform the most important tasks. Here's a summary:

- Choose Help Topics to return to the Help Topics dialog box.
- Choose Back to return to the previous instruction screen.
- Choose Print to open the Print dialog box.
- Choose Options, Annotate to add comments to a help screen. The Annotate command works the same as it does in topic screens.
- Choose Options, Copy or press Ctrl+C to copy a screen.

Microsoft on the Web—in the land of plenty

Most of us have a dictionary on our desks, but few of us own an unabridged dictionary. Chances are that we'll eventually need to find a word that isn't listed, sending us to another resource such as the library or the Internet.

Similarly, the odds are you'll one day run into a problem for which your help files can't provide a solution. Your local library probably won't be of much help, but the Internet will. In fact, nothing gives you more promise for expanding your help resources than the World Wide Web. User groups, vast databases, and collections of tips offer a plethora of information, all available to you from within FrontPage.

The place to start is Microsoft's Web site. Here's where the people in Redmond gather a range of information, from practical to esoteric, in a variety of formats. Included are:

- Answers to frequently asked questions
- Access to technical information in the Microsoft Knowledge Base
- Tips on how get more out of FrontPage

- Newsgroups in which users swap information and get problems solved
- Information on other support services

To access Microsoft's Web site, just choose Help, Microsoft on the Web in Explorer or Editor. FrontPage loads your browser and connects you to the site. Microsoft rearranges its pages occasionally, so you might have to poke around to find all of the available services. Use the Search and Site Map options to help you find the information you need.

Part II: Putting Your Pages Together

Chapter 5: **Text Typing Tips, Tricks, and Traps**

Chapter 6: **Editing Tools You'll Learn to Love**

Chapter 7: **Form and Function: Formatting Text**

Text Typing Tips, Tricks, and Traps

● **In this chapter:**

- Where are my tabs, double-spacing, columns?

- I insist on indented first lines

- This page needs special characters

- FrontPage bookmarks never disappear inside the book

Technology puts all kinds of web publishing glitz at our disposal, but the meat of any web page is still solid text.....

Flashing ads, animations, startling graphics—Web page designers strive for arresting effects. Considering that there are tens of millions of pages on the Web, all trying to get the attention of passing surfers, maybe that's not too surprising.

The motto of the average Web page could have been written by Adlai Stevenson: "Man does not live by words alone, despite the fact that sometimes he has to eat them." Still, for a Web page that readers can really sink their teeth into, you need well-presented text. Catching a Web surfer's eye won't be much use unless you can also hold it.

Entering text in web pages is a straightforward chore with the FrontPage Editor. Like a word processor, the Editor makes typing and editing easy. The real challenge is the same that's faced by any writer: choosing your words. With care, you'll never have to eat them.

Typing Text: the basics

Putting words on a page hasn't changed much since the days of the typewriter. Press a key, get a character. What could be simpler? The FrontPage Editor works on the same principle, so there's nothing mysterious about it. In fact, the only difficulty you might run into with the FrontPage Editor is finding it. When you run FrontPage, the Explorer is what you see first. If you're working on an open web, double-click any of the .HTM documents listed in the Explorer to run the FrontPage Editor.

For a new blank web page, click the View FrontPage Editor button on the Explorer toolbar. With the Editor up and running, click the New button on the Editor Standard toolbar to open a blank web page.

This is just like my word processor!

Start typing in the Editor, and characters appear at the insertion point, also called the cursor, the flashing vertical line that precedes your typed characters. Like a beacon, the cursor lets you know where your next typed character is going to go. Type a full line of text, and the cursor automatically moves to the beginning of the next line. That's the **word wrap** feature word processor users know and love. At the end of a paragraph, press Enter. That inserts a blank line and moves the cursor to the beginning of a new paragraph.

Figure 5.1 shows a paragraph of body text typed in the FrontPage Editor.

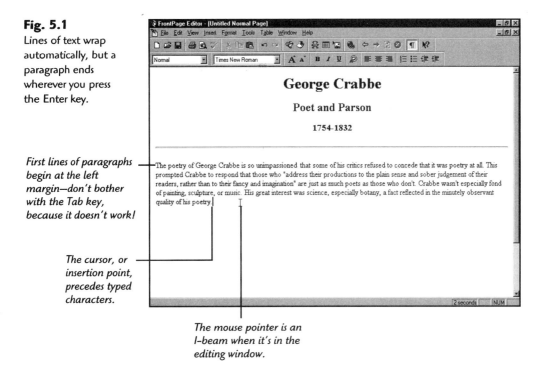

Fig. 5.1
Lines of text wrap automatically, but a paragraph ends wherever you press the Enter key.

First lines of paragraphs begin at the left margin—don't bother with the Tab key, because it doesn't work!

The cursor, or insertion point, precedes typed characters.

The mouse pointer is an I-beam when it's in the editing window.

The familiar mechanics of typing in word processors apply to the FrontPage Editor:

- Keep typing past the right margin. Your text automatically wraps to the next line, so you press Enter only at the end of paragraphs.

- To correct mistakes on-the-fly, use the Backspace and Delete keys (see Chapter 6, "Editing Tools You'll Learn to Love," for more on editing text).

- Click the mouse pointer I-beam or press the arrow keys to move the cursor anywhere in the editing window where you've inserted text or blank lines. Just as in a word processor, you can't advance the cursor further into the editing window than you've already typed.

This isn't exactly like a word processor after all

So far, so good—word processor veterans won't find many surprises when it comes to basic typing in the FrontPage Editor. Still, there are a few things to get used to. Because many Web browsers ignore extra white space on the page, the Editor doesn't let you insert some of the spacing that's traditional on a printed page.

In the Editor's Normal paragraph style, which is what you get by default, the Tab key doesn't work. You also can't insert more than one space at a time with the Spacebar, so there's no way to indent the first line of a paragraph. And if you automatically press the Spacebar twice after a period, as most typists are trained to do, that second space is ignored—only one space at a time with the Editor Spacebar, remember?

66 Plain English, please!

A **style** is a collection of formatting options—fonts and alignments, for example—that are named and saved. The current style appears in the Change Style box on the FrontPage Editor Format toolbar. The Editor gives you the Normal style by default; to change a paragraph to a different style, click the paragraph, then click the Change Style drop-down arrow and choose another style from the list. 99

I can get indented first lines and extra spaces after all?

If you insist on indented first lines for your paragraphs, and on two spaces after periods and colons, you *can* get them. It just requires a little extra effort. To insert more than one space, even at the beginning of lines, press Shift+Ctrl+Spacebar. The Shift+Ctrl+Spacebar combination lets you insert as many blank spaces as you want, although not every browswer will display them.

Fast typists won't want to slow down to press Shift+Ctrl+Spacebar all the time. For the speedy-fingered who need tabs and spaces, a switch to the Formatted style might be the more convenient way to get them.

Click the Change Style drop-down arrow on the Format toolbar and choose the Formatted style. The Formatted style does allow multiple spaces and the use of the Tab key. There are, however, a couple of serious drawbacks to the Formatted style:

- You lose the word wrap feature, so that your typing extends past the right margin.
- The default font for the Formatted style is Courier New, a **monospaced** font (in which all characters are the same width) which imitates the look of old-fashioned typescript. That may not be exactly the effect you want, as shown in Figure 5.2.

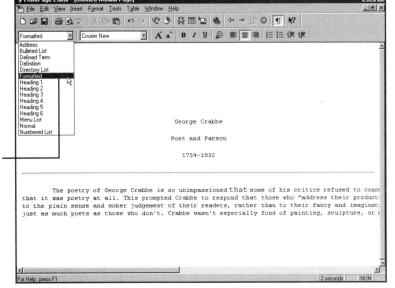

Fig. 5.2
With all that computing power at our disposal, the Formatted style yields pages that look typewritten.

Choose the Formatted style if you must have extra spacing (and if you don't care about word wrap or unattractive fonts!).

See Chapter 7, "Form and Function: Formatting Text," for more on formatting web pages and changing styles.

I don't want these lines to reach the right margin

Anyone who's ever used a typewriter appreciates the way word processors wrap lines of text automatically at the right margin. And if you're writing poetry or song lyrics, with short lines that don't go all the way out to the right margin, word processors make it easy to break a line wherever you wish: you just press Enter after each line.

Poets and song writers typing short lines of text in FrontPage might be disconcerted by the fact that the program adds a blank line at each press of the Enter key. Furthermore, you can't adjust that formatting quirk. Press Enter in the FrontPage Editor, and you get a blank line whether you want it or not.

What to do if you want short lines of text with no blank lines between them? Press Shift+Enter at the end of each line. Shift+Enter inserts a **line break,** a formatting code that snaps off a line of text wherever it's inserted. If the Show/Hide button on the FrontPage Editor toolbar is clicked (it's activated by default), you'll see the line break symbols at the end of each line (see Figure 5.3).

Fig. 5.3
Poets, or even poetry quoters, will find line breaks indispensable.

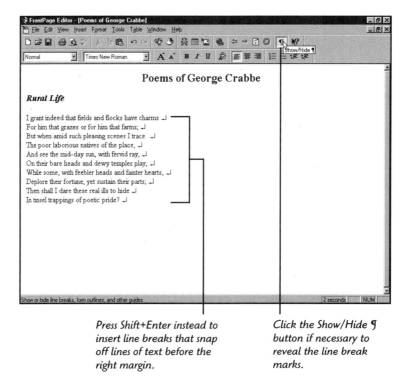

Press Shift+Enter instead to insert line breaks that snap off lines of text before the right margin.

Click the Show/Hide ¶ button if necessary to reveal the line break marks.

No double-spacing? What about columns?

FrontPage's goal is to display pages in a browser. The aim of every right-thinking word-processor is to print pages on paper. That's why the FrontPage Editor doesn't allow certain text maneuvers that look better on paper than on the screen. Double- or triple-spacing, the favorite dodge of any writer trying to fill up pages, isn't available in the Editor. You can insert blank lines by pressing Enter if you need more white space, but that's about it.

Columns, a useful text formatting device for both the printed page and computer screens, aren't supported in the FrontPage Editor. It's easy to get the effect of columns with a table, however. In fact, tables are FrontPage's principal layout tool, and you can read all about them in Chapter 10, "The Miracle of Tables."

I have a ¥ for special characters and symbols

Building a web page denominated in Yen, not Dollars? Maybe you'd like to insert a copyright symbol to protect your work. FrontPage has a built in collection of symbols and special characters for every occasion. To insert trademark, copyright, and other special characters, click Insert, Symbol to pop up the Symbol dialog box.

Click a symbol, and it appears at the bottom of the Symbol dialog box in an easier-to-read format, as shown in Figure 5.4.

Fig. 5.4
Tiny symbols are easier to see if you click them first.

To pop the selected symbol into your page at the insertion point, click Insert.

Q&A *The symbol I need isn't in the FrontPage Symbol dialog box!*

If you can't find what you're looking for in the FrontPage Symbol dialog box, Windows has a built-in assortment of special characters of its own. Click Start, Programs, Accessories, Character Map. In the Character Map dialog box that pops up, double-click any of the symbols on display to copy them to the Windows Clipboard. If you still don't see what you need, click the Font drop-down arrow and select another font. Switch back to the FrontPage Editor and press Ctrl+V to paste the symbol at the insertion point. FrontPage automatically converts the imported symbol to HTML for you, and displays a message saying that it's doing so.

Bookmarks, the navigational express

In a book, the bookmark's job is humble, vital, and self-explanatory. Bookmarks in the FrontPage Editor similarly mark your place, but they might require a little more explanation. FrontPage bookmarks are selected sections of text that you mark with a name so that you can jump right to them whenever you wish. If you've ever done research in a fat reference book and stuck bits of paper between the pages so that you could flip back and forth with ease, you'll appreciate the value of bookmarks. In a long web page, bookmarks can make getting around a lot more efficient.

 Plain English, please!

> Netscape Navigator users are familiar with bookmarks, but of an entirely different kind. Netscape **Bookmarks** are just like the **Favorites** in the Microsoft Internet Explorer. They're World Wide Web pages whose address and titles you've saved for future visits.

To create a bookmark:

1 Select the section of text you want to mark. It can be anything from a single word to several paragraphs. Headings make useful bookmarks, especially if your page has a lot of them. (If you need some tips on selecting text, check out Chapter 6.)

2 With the text selected, choose Edit, Bookmark. That pops up the Bookmark dialog box shown in Figure 5.5.

3 You'll notice that your selected text appears in the Bookmark Name text box. If you want something else for a bookmark name, type it in. Otherwise, just click OK to create the bookmark.

Chapter 5 Text Typing Tips, Tricks, and Traps

Fig. 5.5
Bookmarks are convenient navigational aids in long web pages.

This selected text is the bookmark; by default, it's also the bookmark name.

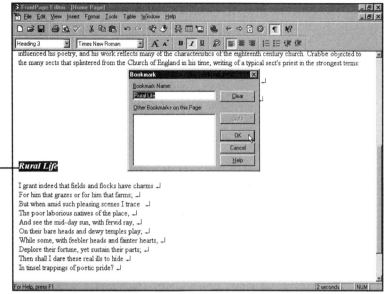

 If the Show/Hide ¶ button on the Editor toolbar is selected, your bookmarked text is displayed with a dashed blue underline. Add other bookmarks to the page as needed.

To visit existing bookmarks, click Edit, Bookmark. In the Bookmark dialog box that appears, double-click a bookmark on the list of Other Bookmarks on this Page. The display scrolls immediately to the selected bookmark.

To get rid of a bookmark, click Edit, Bookmark. In the Bookmark dialog box, select the bookmark you no longer want and click Clear.

 TIP **If you get tired of clicking Edit, Bookmark on the menu bar, try** this alternate route to the bookmark dialog box: right-click any bookmarked text and choose Bookmark Properties on the context menu.

Bookmarks are also invaluable when paired with a hyperlink. Bookmark-hyperlink combinations let readers go directly to a section of a page when they click the hyperlink. You also use them to link sections of other web pages to the current page. See Chapter 12, "Webward Ho! Adding Pages to Your Web," for details on combining bookmarks with hyperlinks.

Editing Tools You'll Learn to Love

● **In this chapter:**

- **Mark my words: how to select text**
- **Deleting text the quick and easy way**
- **On the move with cutting and pasting**
- **May I have the spell check, please?**
- **In other words: the FrontPage thesaurus**
- **How to find and replace text**

Editing a FrontPage document isn't nearly as exciting as, say, an oil change, but you'll save a ton of time if you learn the right way to delete, move, correct, and otherwise rolf your text . . . . ▸

In the heyday of the American diner, the kitchen often was open to public view. While you waited for your root beer float, you could watch the short-order cook simultaneously flip a dozen burgers, mix three shakes, and chop an onion, all the while chewing the fat about Friday night's big game against Crosstown High.

The cook was able to perform his prodigious feats of prestidigitation for two reasons. First, he knew how to use his implements. Second, he followed the same steps over and over until they became as reflexive as putting your foot on the brake when you want to stop your car.

FrontPage Editor lacks the sounds and smells of a sizzling grill, but it functions much the way a kitchen does. Your editing tools are your knives and spatulas; your keyboard provides your ingredients; and your Editor window is the stove on which you cook. When you're done, you have a tasty meal ready to serve up to your customers at the El Webbo Diner.

In this chapter, we're going to concentrate on the knives and spatulas—where they are, what they're good for, and how to use them efficiently. That means learning the best methods for deleting, copying, and moving text. It also means learning how to do each task the right way from the start, so that you don't have to break bad habits later.

Make your selection

Most editing requires that you first select text. Once you learn the quickest way to choose the words, lines, paragraphs, tables, and other elements, changing and formatting your page becomes easy.

Let's look at a simple example. How would you delete the selected paragraph in Figure 6.1? First, you might select the text in one of several ways:

- You could click at the start of the paragraph, hold down the shift key, and press the arrow keys until the paragraph is selected.
- You could click at the start of the paragraph and drag the mouse to the end of the paragraph.

Then, you could go to the Edit menu and choose Clear.

Fig. 6.1
Shift+Click or click and drag to select a paragraph

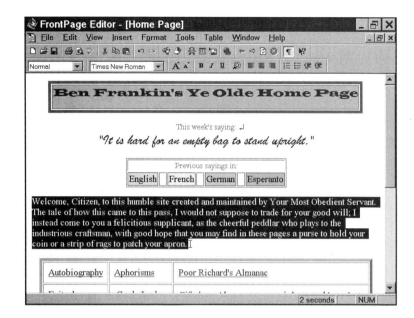

Easy? Yes. Efficient? Not really. Here's a method that's much quicker:

1 Move your mouse pointer to the beginning of the first line until it turns into an arrow.

2 Double-click.

3 Press the Delete key.

FrontPage has similar shortcuts for selecting words, lines, sentences, or entire documents. You can even select from your insertion point to the beginning or end of a document. Learn these shortcuts now, and you can concentrate on the more interesting work of designing and building your web site.

 FrontPage does not include many of the more advanced editing tools provided by most word processors. For example, it doesn't have an equivalent to Word's AutoText, Columns, Change Case, or Hyphenation commands. If you're editing a document that needs a lot of work, you might want to consider fixing it in your word processor first, then bringing the finished text into your web page with the Insert, File command or via the Clipboard. See Chapter 12, "Webward Ho! Adding Pages to Your Web," for more information.

TIP Don't forget that you can instantly change the appearance of an entire paragraph by placing the insertion point in the paragraph and choosing a style from the Style selection box on the Format toolbar. See Chapter 7, "Form and Function: Formatting Text," for a complete discussion.

Block parties

You can select, or **mark**, any block of text in one of three ways. These methods are best for selecting part of a line, paragraph, or page:

- Place your insertion point at the beginning of the block you want to select, put the mouse pointer at the end of the block, hold down the Shift key, and click the mouse button.

- Click at the beginning of the block and, holding down the mouse button, drag the mouse insertion point to the end of the block. Move from left to right to select text character by character; move up or down to select text line by line.

- If you prefer the keyboard, place the insertion point at the beginning of the text. Hold down the Shift key and press the appropriate arrow key. For larger blocks, you can press the Page Up or Page Down key.

Selecting words

These brute-force methods are overkill if you want to select only a word or two. It's quicker to use these techniques:

- To select a word, click twice anywhere in the word.

- If your insertion point happens to be at the beginning of the word, press Ctrl+Shift+right arrow. If it's at the end of the word, press Ctrl+Shift+left arrow.

- To select several words, click twice on the first word and continue to hold down the mouse button after the second click. Drag across the next or previous words.

- You can select several words from the keyboard, too. Put the insertion point at the beginning of the first word and press Ctrl+Shift+right arrow. Repeat the arrow as many times as you need to. You can select

http://www.quecorp.com

previous words using Ctrl+Shift+left arrow; note, however, that you must select each space between words as well as each word.

- If you want to select from the middle of a word, put the insertion point where you want to start the selection. Press Ctrl+Shift+right arrow to select to the end of the word, and Ctrl+Shift+left arrow to the beginning of the word.

Selecting lines of text

A line of text is one that occupies a single line in your document, regardless of punctuation or length. Use these techniques to select lines:

- Move your mouse pointer to the left of the line until it points northeast (see Figure 6.2) and click once.

- At the keyboard, place the insertion point at the beginning of the line, and press Shift+End.

- Select multiple lines with the mouse by clicking the space to the left of the line and dragging the mouse pointer up or down.

- Select multiple lines with the keyboard by pressing Shift+End, then pressing Shift+up arrow or Shift+down arrow.

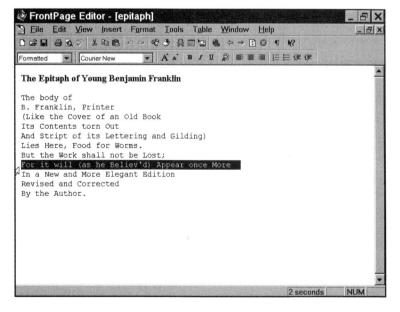

Fig. 6.2
Select a line of text by moving the mouse cursor to the beginning of the line and clicking once.

You also can use Shift+End and Shift+Home to select from your insertion point to the line's end or beginning, respectively.

Selecting paragraphs

One of my old college texts defines a paragraph as an incident or a speech of a character, a segment of thought, or a related group of sentences. FrontPage's definition is a lot less highfalutin—a paragraph is the text between two paragraph marks. Thus, a paragraph can consist of a single word, a line, or a thousand lines.

FrontPage offers three techniques for selecting a paragraph:

- Double-click the space to the left of the paragraph.
- Press the Alt key and click anywhere in the paragraph.
- Put your insertion point at the beginning of the paragraph and press Shift+Ctrl+down arrow.

Across wide expanses

Situations will arise when you'll want to select large expanses of a document. Use these shortcuts:

- Select from the insertion point to the end of your document by pressing Ctrl+Shift+End (see Figure 6.3).
- Select from the insertion point to the beginning of your document by pressing Ctrl+Shift+Home.
- Select the entire document by pressing Ctrl+A.

When you use one of these methods, remember that you'll also mark any tables, links, and graphics that are in the part of the document you're selecting.

 TIP **Cancel your selected text by clicking anywhere in the text or by** pressing an arrow key.

Fig. 6.3
Ctrl+Shift+End selects your text from the insertion point to the end of the page.

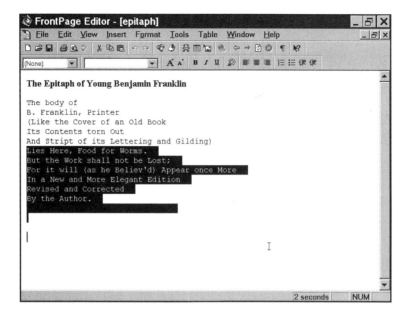

Deleting, copying, and moving text

You select text in FrontPage for a variety of reasons, among which are changing the text's format and turning text into a hyperlink. We cover many of these topics in other chapters (turn to Chapters 7 and 8, "Color Me Fun!," for more information about formatting and Chapter 12 to learn about hyperlinks). For now, we'll focus on the main editing functions: deleting, copying, and moving.

Clear the decks!

In FrontPage, deleting is called **clearing**, and that's the way it appears on the Edit menu. The two are one and the same, but the word "delete" is, well, clearer.

The fastest way to delete selected text is to press the Delete key. If your pinky finger needs some exercise, you can stretch it a little farther and hit the Backspace key.

Don't confuse deleting with cutting. Delete and Backspace keys delete your text for good, whereas cutting places your text on the Clipboard. We'll talk about cutting text in a moment.

TIP **FrontPage offers a time-saving keyboard trick that lets you delete** words without having to select them first. To delete a word you just typed, press Ctrl+Backspace. To delete a word that's in front of your insertion point, press Ctrl+Delete.

Moving text with the mouse

If you're an inveterate furniture-rearranger, the chances are you'll be a compulsive text-mover, too. How do you get a paragraph from the bottom of the page to the top without rewriting it? FrontPage offers a couple of tools that let you move text quickly and easily.

Moving text can be a drag

The first is the drag-and-drop method; you select your text and drag it to its new location.

Point to the highlighted block and hold down the mouse button. A small checkered box attaches itself to the bottom of the pointer (see Figure 6.4).

Fig. 6.4
When you drag and move selected text, a gray insertion point lets you know exactly where FrontPage will place the block.

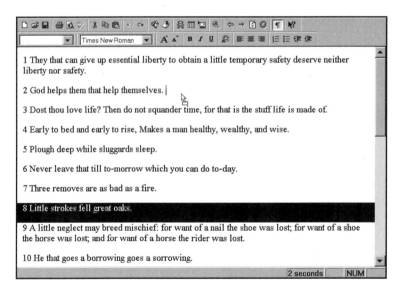

Drag the block to its destination. As you drag it, you'll see a gray insertion point that moves with your pointer. This insertion point marks precisely where FrontPage will insert the block. When the insertion point is where you want to put the text, release the button, and FrontPage drops the block into its new location (at the end of item 2 in Figure 6.5).

Fig. 6.5
The move started in Figure 6.4 is complete.

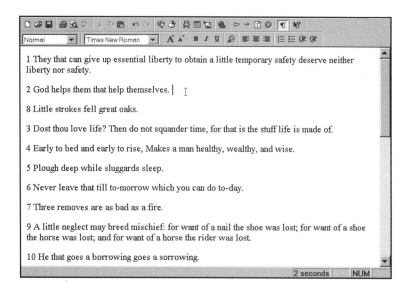

Dragging and dropping text is most effective when you're moving text from one part of the visible window to another. It's less practical if you have to scroll your window to another part of the document. The better alternative in such cases is to use method no. 2: cut and paste.

 TIP If you start dragging your selected text and decide you don't want to move it after all, move the mouse pointer outside the document window. When it turns into a circle with a line through it, release the button. You also can cancel the move by pressing the Esc key.

Cutting and pasting

The other way you can move text is by using FrontPage's cut and paste tools. If you've used cut and paste in other Windows programs, then you already know the procedure:

Select your text and click the Cut button in the toolbar. The text vanishes, deposited in the Windows storage bin known as the **Clipboard**.

 Putting text on the Clipboard is like removing a block from a Lego project and putting it back in the box. The block is out of immediate sight, but it still exists, in storage, until you need it again.

 Next, position the insertion point where you want to move the text and click the Paste button. FrontPage takes the text out of storage and inserts, or **pastes**, it at the position of your insertion point.

TIP **You can paste text from the Clipboard as often as you like. This is** a time-saving trick if you have a line of text that you want to repeat several times.

You can also cut or paste a block by clicking the right mouse button and choosing the Cut or Paste from the shortcut menu.

TIP **To move a block of text with the keyboard, cut it by pressing** Ctrl+X, move the insertion point to the point of insertion, and paste it by pressing Ctrl+V.

Copy that!

The steps you use to copy text are almost identical to those we just described for moving text. You can use either method—drag and drop or the Clipboard.

Ctrling your copy

Remember the steps for moving a block of selected text by dragging it with the mouse, as shown in Figures 6.4 and 6.5? Well, if you want to copy the text instead of move it, just hold down the Ctrl key while you drag. FrontPage lets you know it's copying the block by putting a plus sign in the little box attached to the mouse pointer's tail.

Copying with the Clipboard

Likewise, the steps for copying via the Clipboard are the same as they are for moving via the Clipboard. Instead of clicking the toolbar's Cut button, you click the Copy button. Next, move the insertion point to where you want to copy the block and click the Paste button.

As is the case with cut and paste, you can copy and paste by clicking the right mouse button and using the quick menu.

TIP **To copy a block using the keyboard, press Ctrl+C to copy and** Ctrl+V to paste.

CAUTION **When you cut or copy a block of text to the Clipboard, it replaces** and permanently deletes any text that is already on the Clipboard.

Deleting and replacing text in one fell swoop

You can delete text and replace it with new text in one operation. Select the text you want to replace; then:

- Start typing new text, or
- Paste text from the Clipboard

Easy Undoes it

What if you make a mistake and delete, copy, or move text accidentally? Simple: FrontPage has an Undo command that will reverse the action. Restore the text by clicking the Undo button on the toolbar, pressing Ctrl+Z, or choosing Edit, Undo Clear from the menu bar.

The Undo command works on your most recent action, so you should undo your change immediately. However, all is not lost if, for example, you've already typed new text into the spot once occupied by your deleted text. Simply repeat your Undo until FrontPage undoes the delete.

Depending on what your last edit was, the Undo command on the Edit menu changes to tell you what action you've just taken. For example, if you've just dragged and dropped a block of text, the item on the Edit menu is Undo Drop. If you undo the drop, the item on the Edit menu reverts to the previous action and reads Undo Drag.

CAUTION You can't undo file commands such as Open, Close, and Save.

Undoing Undo

None of us is perfect, and we all occasionally undo an action that we didn't want undone. For example, you might drop a block of text and accidentally Undo the drop. Rather than go through the process of dragging and dropping the text again, use Redo. Either press Ctrl+Y or click the Redo button on the toolbar.

Spelling bound

A misspelled word on a web page sticks out like the proverbial sore thumb. Even readers who themselves are poor spellers will notice. "Gee," they'll wonder, "Why can't this person take the time to look up these words in a dictionary?"

If your desk is like ours, you probably don't even have room for a dictionary. Luckily, FrontPage does. Not only that, but FrontPage will automatically check every word in your web page and help you correct the ones that are wrong.

Actually, FrontPage uses the Office 97 dictionary. So if you have ever spell-checked a document in another Office 97 program, such as Word or Excel, FrontPage's spelling checker will look familiar.

What would you like to look up?

You start your spell check by pressing F7 or clicking the Check Spelling button on the Standard toolbar. You can start anywhere in the page. FrontPage starts at the top of the page and checks everything to the end.

If you want to check just a part of your page, select the text and run the checker. FrontPage spell checks only the text in the defined block.

Using the Spelling dialog box

When you start a spell check, FrontPage finds the first word it doesn't recognize and displays the Spelling dialog box shown in Figure 6.6.

Fig. 6.6
The spelling checker provides a list of alternative words when it finds a word it doesn't recognize.

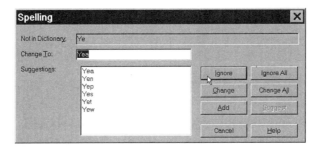

The unrecognized word appears in the Not In Dictionary text box. Possible replacements appear in the Suggestions list box, with the most likely one at the top.

Click the Change button to accept the suggested change. If you want another word on the list, double-click it. To delete the word or replace it with one that is not in the Suggestions box, make the correction in the Not in Dictionary box and click Change.

Click Change All to change all instances of the word in the page or selected block.

Click Add to add the word to your dictionary.

To keep the word as is, click Ignore. The checker will, however, query you again if the word reappears. Click Ignore All if you want the checker to accept the word for the entire page.

CAUTION Remember that when you add a word to your dictionary, the addition applies to spelling checks you might do in other Office 97 programs.

How to check several pages at once

You don't have to check each page of your web individually. You can gang them together and check them all at once, using Explorer's Cross File Spelling command.

First, you need to decide if you want to check selected pages in the web or all pages. To choose selected pages, you must be in Folder View; click the Folder View button on the toolbar or choose View, Folder View from the main menu. Then, holding down the Ctrl key, click each page that you want to check.

Then, whether you're checking all or only selected pages, click the Cross File Spelling button on the toolbar or choose F7. Word opens the Spelling dialog box shown in Figure 6.7. Click the All Pages button if you're checking all pages in your web, or click Selected Pages if you're checking only the pages you selected in the Explorer window.

If you want to run the spelling checker but don't want to correct any misspellings until later, put a check next to Add Pages with Misspellings to the To Do List. When you're ready to make corrections, just display the To Do List and choose the task from there (see Chapter 20, "Maintaining Your Web," for details on the To Do List).

Fig. 6.7
You can spell check all of the pages in your web or select individual pages for checking.

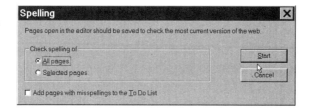

The Check Spelling dialog box

Once you've made all your choices in the Spelling dialog box, click the Start button. FrontPage opens the Check Spelling dialog box and begins checking each page. When done, the Check Spelling dialog box displays a list of pages that contained unrecognized words, as in Figure 6.8. Each page is preceded by a red bullet, indicating that the page has been checked but not corrected.

Fig. 6.8
Explorer produces a list of pages that contain words unrecognized by the spelling checker; you can correct pages immediately or add them to your To Do List for later correction.

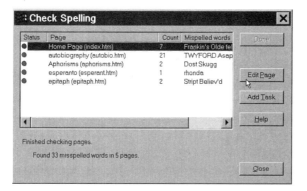

To correct a page on the list, select the page and choose Edit Page or double-click the page. FrontPage opens the page in Editor and displays the Spelling dialog box. Step through your spell check as explained above in the section "Using the Spelling dialog box."

When you're done correcting the page, FrontPage displays a dialog box called Continue With Next Document? Here, you have the option of saving and closing the document; you then can choose to correct the next document listed in Explorer's Check Spelling dialog box (see Figure 6.8) or canceling the cross spell check.

After you've finished correcting the last page listed in the Check Spelling dialog box, FrontPage displays a Finished Checking Documents dialog box. Choose OK to complete the spell check.

Next, switch back to Explorer; you'll see that the bullets in the status column of the Check Spelling dialog box have changed from red to yellow and are followed by the word Edited, indicating that the pages have been checked and corrected. Choose the Close button to finish the job.

> **TIP** **After FrontPage opens the Check Spelling dialog box in Explorer** and spell checks the selected pages, you can add any individual page on the list to the To Do List for later correction. Select the page and choose the Add Task button (refer to Figure 6.8).

Descrying equivalent expressions with the thesaurus

Lost for words? You could sit there staring at a blank screen while you rummage through your brain for that perfect thought. Or you could use FrontPage's thesaurus to help you prime the intellectual pump.

The thesaurus lets you find synonyms for any word. Just put your insertion point on the word and press Shift+F7 or choose Tools, Thesaurus. The Thesaurus dialog box pops up, as shown in Figure 6.9.

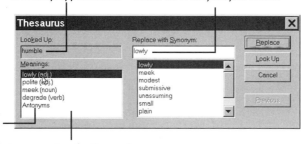

Fig. 6.9
When you're groping desperately for the perfect word, try FrontPage's Thesaurus.

Click Antonyms for a list of opposite meanings.

The word that you want to look up appears here.

The selected meaning appears here with a list of its synonyms below.

Various meanings for the word appear here; click one to select it.

Inside the Thesaurus dialog box

The word for which you want a synonym appears in the Looked Up text box. The Meanings text box displays the different uses of that word. The meaning that is selected in the Meanings text box also appears in the Replace With Synonym text box. Beneath that is a list of synonyms for the meaning.

For example, in Figure 6.9, the word being looked up is "humble." The thesaurus offers synonyms for the adjectives that mean "lowly" and "polite," the noun that means "meek," and the verb that means "degrade."

To replace a word with a synonym, follow these steps:

1 Click the appropriate word in the Meanings list; the word appears in the Replace with Synonym text box, and a list of its synonyms appears below it. If you're looking for an antonym, click Antonyms in the Meanings list.

2 To look up any word in the either list, click it; then click the Look Up button. Continue to click words until the word you want to use is in the Replace with Synonym text box.

3 Click the Replace button to replace the word in Looked Up with the word in Replace With Synonym.

Choosing an option

When you have a word in the Replace with Synonym box that you want to substitute for the original word in your text, select Replace. Your other options are:

- To look up synonyms for a word in the Replace With Synonym list box, double-click the word, or click the word and choose Look Up.

- To look up synonyms for another word in the Meanings list box, click the word.

- To look up a new word, type the word in the Replace With Synonym text box and choose Look Up.

- To retrace your steps, click Previous.

How to change the same word throughout a page

Your company, Acme Tongue Depressors, has just been bought by AAA Mouth Probes. You're assigned the job of replacing all instances of the old name with the new one. Of course, you'd like to do everything possible to avoid missing one or two of the name changes. How can you make sure that you replace every single reference to Acme Tongue Depressors?

The answer is to let the Replace command do the work. Just tell FrontPage to replace every instance of "Acme Tongue Depressors" with "AAA Mouth Probes."

Select Edit, Replace or press Ctrl+H to display the Replace dialog box. Type the text you want to replace in the Find What text box and the replacement text in the Replace With text box (see Figure 6.10).

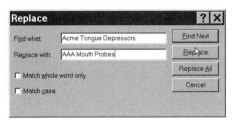

Fig. 6.10
Editor's Replace command lets you replace every instance of a text string with another text string.

Choose Replace to find and replace the first instance of the text. Keep choosing Replace until FrontPage tells you you're done.

The alternative, and sometimes preferable, method is to choose Find Next instead of Replace. FrontPage finds the first occurrence of the string and highlights it. To replace the string, click Replace. To skip the string and go to the next occurrence, click Find Next.

To replace all instances of the text in the document, click Replace All.

 Don't use Replace All unless you're sure of the results. Replacing strings one at a time is slow and sometimes tedious, but it's safer.

 To move the Replace dialog box out of the way so you can see more of your document, click the title bar and drag the box to another part of the screen.

Replacing text in multiple pages

Just as you can spell check many pages in your web from Explorer, so you can search and replace text:

1. Switch to FrontPage Explorer.

2. To choose selected pages, click the Folder View button on the toolbar or choose <u>V</u>iew, <u>F</u>older View from the main menu. Hold down the Ctrl key and click the pages that you want to search.

3. Choose Tools, Replace from the main menu or press Ctrl+H. FrontPage opens the Replace in FrontPage Web dialog box.

4. Enter the string you're searching for in the Fi<u>n</u>d What text box and the replacement string in the Replace With text box.

5. Choose <u>A</u>ll Pages or <u>S</u>elected Pages under the Find heading.

6. Check Match <u>W</u>hole Word Only and Match <u>C</u>ase as appropriate.

7. Choose the OK button.

FrontPage opens the Find Occurrences Of... dialog box and searches the selected pages for the search string. When done, the dialog box displays a list of the pages that contain the string. Select a page and choose Edit Page; FrontPage opens the page in Editor and displays the Replace dialog box. Proceed with your Replace as usual.

When you've finished the page, you'll get the Continue With Next Document? dialog box. Save and close the document and choose the Next Document button to open the Replace dialog box in the next document listed in Explorer's Find Occurrences Of... dialog box. Choose the Cancel button if you want to cancel the search and replace.

When you're done with the last page, FrontPage displays the Finished Checking Documents dialog box. Choose OK to complete the search and replace.

When you return to Explorer, you'll find the status of each page listed in the Find Occurrences Of... dialog box has changed to Edited. Choose the Close button to complete your search and replace.

TIP **Once FrontPage finds the pages that contain the string to be** replaced, you can add any page on the list in the Find Occurrences Of... dialog box to the To Do List. Select the page and choose the Add Task button.

Warning! Replace can be harmful to your health!

Replace is a deceptively powerful command that can do more harm than good if you're not careful. By default, FrontPage searches for *all* instances of a text string, whether it's a whole word or embedded in a larger string.

For example, if you look for the string `car`, FrontPage finds not only all instances of the word `car`, but also the words `uncaring` and `Carolina`. If you use the Replace All option to change all instances of the word `car` to the word `Buick`, you'll also change `uncaring` to `unbuicking` and `Carolina` to `Buickolina`.

To avoid such accidents, check Match Whole Word Only in the Replace dialog box.

Capital ideas

Replace also ignores capitalization unless otherwise instructed. For example, a search for `Jay` will find `Jay Leno` and `I saw a blue jay in my back yard`. If you change `Jay` to `comedian`, you'll end up with `comedian Leno` and `I saw a blue comedian in my back yard`.

To replace only instances of Jay, capital J, check the Match Case option in the Replace dialog box. Note that you'll need to type both the Find What and Replace With strings in the proper case.

I can delete it for you wholesale

Replace is a handy tool for deleting all instances of a word in a document. Leave the Replace With text box blank. Make sure, though, that you've checked Match Whole Word Only and Match Case if necessary, and use the Find Next and Replace buttons to replace each instance of the string individually.

TIP   You can reverse a bungled Replace with Undo.

TIP   **As you search and replace, you might find other changes you want** to make in your document. You don't have to close your Replace dialog box to return to the document; simply click the document window. The

Replace dialog box stays active. Click the dialog box to return to it. You also can move between the document and dialog box by pressing Alt+F6.

Q&A Can I replace fonts and formats?

Sorry, you're out of luck. Unlike many full-fledged word processors, FrontPage Editor does not have this ability; you'll have to change fonts and formats manually.

Finding a string

If you just want to find a string without replacing it, use the Find command on the Edit menu (the keyboard shortcut is Ctrl+F). The Find dialog box includes the same Match Whole Word Only and Match Case options available in the Replace dialog box.

The Find command lets you search forward (the Down button) or backward (the Up button) from the insertion point. However, once it reaches the bottom or top of your document, it does not search the rest of the document. If you want to search the entire document, make sure your insertion point is at the top of the page and the Down button is on.

TIP You can find all pages in your web that contain a string by choosing the Cross File Find button on the toolbar in Explorer (you also can press Ctrl+F or choose Tools, Find from the main menu). Cross file find works almost identically to Explorer's Replace command; see "Replacing Text in Multiple Pages" for details.

I changed my mind—I want to replace the string

Occasionally, you might use Find to locate a string and then decide that you want to replace the string with something else. You can switch from the Find to the Replace dialog box without closing the Find dialog box first and without having to retype the string. Once you've started your search, simply use your mouse to choose Edit, Replace from the Editor's menu bar. FrontPage closes the Find dialog box and opens the Replace dialog box with the string already in the Find What text box.

Form and Function: Formatting Text

● **In this chapter:**

- This page needs a font makeover

- Text that blinks? And what's a marquee?

- How do I align my paragraphs?

- This long quote needs to be indented

- Automatic bullets and numbered lists that do the counting? Now you're talking!

Web pages may not have covers, but they're apt to be judged by their appearance. A little formatting ensures a favorable first impression . . . .

How a thing looks depends on who's looking at it. Jack Kerouac typed the manuscript of *On the Road* on a continuous roll of teletype paper. From the author's point of view, this was a perfectly functional format. His publisher, balking at the job of reading the awkward, paper-towel sized roll, hinted that revisions might be needed. Kerouac grabbed his novel and left, outraged at the suggestion.

However inspired the writing, it's the formatting that readers see first. Of course, an author like Kerouac could depend on a handsome volume from his publisher (eventually), no matter how difficult his manuscript.

FrontPage web spinners are their own publishers, and can't afford to be so cavalier about the way they present their work. The FrontPage Editor is loaded with formatting tricks to help make web page text attractive and readable. The result may not be a Kerouac-style modern classic, but no reader will mistake it for a roll of paper towel.

Text in every shape and size, but not for every browser

Whether we're aware of it or not, the first thing that strikes us about the text we read is probably the font the text is set in. Every font has its own personality, from the understated Times New Roman, to the futuristic Umbra. Matching the right font with your text is like choosing a pleasing wallpaper for a room; it's art, not science, and it's entirely a matter of taste and judgement. Since Windows comes with a slew of fonts, and there are still more fonts that install with Microsoft Office, FrontPage, and the other programs you use, you won't lack for choices.

> ### Plain English, please!
>
> **Fonts** are families of letter styles. Times New Roman is a familiar font; Arial is another common one. Times New Roman is a **serif** font; its characters have little tails, or serifs. Arial is a **sans serif** font—there are no serifs attached to its characters. Fonts are sometimes named for their designers, Goudy for example, or Cooper, whose artistry was devoted to producing readable, attractive type.

Once you settle on a font face, FrontPage provides a battery of special effects for text. Text that blinks, text in color, text that scrolls across the screen in ticker-tape fashion—they're all part of your design arsenal. But before you spend a lot of time perfecting the typography of your web pages, consider this sobering fact: not all browsers will display your work as you've designed it. Like a gallery-goer viewing a Picasso Blue Period painting wearing rose-tinted glasses, certain browsers will simply display web pages in whatever font the reader has chosen.

Figure 7.1 shows a FrontPage document displayed in two different browsers with notably different results.

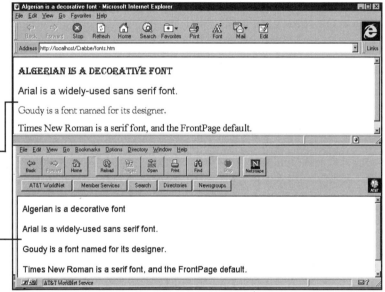

Fig. 7.1
Not all browsers will display your work the way you intended it to be viewed, but that's a problem faced by any artist.

Microsoft Internet Explorer 3.0 displays the fonts as they were intended.

Netscape Navigator 2.1 converts all the text to the same display font.

That some browsers won't display your work in its best light shouldn't discourage you from designing your pages with care. Many surfers will see your pages as you conceived them, and their numbers will grow as more users switch to the latest versions of their favorite browsers.

How do I change fonts?

The FrontPage Editor's Normal style gives you Times New Roman by default, a perfectly serviceable font in common use. If you want a different font, click the Change Font arrow on the Editor Format toolbar and select a font on the drop-down menu. Any text typed from the insertion point on will be in the new font, until you change fonts again.

To change the font of text you've already typed, select the text first, and then make your choice on the Change Font drop-down menu. Only the font of the selected text will change; any other text on the page will be unaffected.

Not sure what a particular font looks like? Click F̲ormat, F̲ont to summon up the Font dialog box. Make a selection on the F̲ont list, and a preview appears in the Font dialog box Sample window, as shown in Figure 7.2.

Fig. 7.2
The Font dialog box lets you preview fonts before you make any changes.

If you've selected text before calling up the Font dialog box, the selected text will change to whatever font you've chosen in the Font dialog box as soon as you click OK. If you haven't selected text before choosing F̲ormat, F̲ont, any font change made in the Font dialog box takes effect from the insertion point on.

TIP **To select a word for a change of font (or for any other reason),** double-click it. To select a line of text, move the pointer over to the left margin at the beginning of the line. When the pointer I-beam changes to an arrow pointing right, click to select the line.

Do too many fonts spoil the page?

Faced with this cornucopia of fonts, you're likely to wonder which ones to use. You can't expect to get the results of a professional typographer without plenty of training and experience, but a few font choice guidelines might help you make up your mind:

- Serif fonts like Times New Roman are most often seen in body text. The serifs guide the eye from one character to the next, which makes for easier reading.

- Sans serif fonts like Arial are often used in headings. Their lack of serifs makes them stand out from body text, which can give pages pleasing contrast and variety.

- You don't want too much variety on the page, however. Too many different fonts can make a page look cluttered and busy.

- Decorative fonts like Algerian get attention, but should be used sparingly. Your goal is a page that's easy to read, and decorative fonts, however attractive, are not necessarily designed for readability.

A little trial and error will take you a long way when mixing and matching fonts. You might also take a look at well-designed Web pages and their use of fonts. One example is shown in Figure 7.3.

Fig. 7.3
A font that looks like it belongs on a fancy invitation makes for an inviting Web page. Try Shelley Volante or Ribbon131 for a similar effect.

Font effects you'll use sparingly

The Font dialog box holds a box of special text effect tricks that may or may not come in handy. Click F*o*rmat, *F*ont, and peruse the Effects options. *U*nderline puts a line under selected or new text if you click the checkbox; Stri*k*ethrough puts a line through new or selected text. Neither effect contributes to readability, and both should be used sparingly, if at all.

The third Font dialog box Effect, Typewriter, makes all the characters in selected or new text the same width, just like old-fashioned typescript. FrontPage suggests using Typewriter for examples of computer code, or to indicate text that readers are to type into a form. And who are we to argue?

Font Special Styles, for the occasional special occasion

HTML is rich in formatting codes for specialized text, and some of those codes and formatting attributes are options on the Special Styles tab of the Font dialog box. They're there mostly to help you edit imported HTML documents, whose formatting codes you can switch on and off with the Font dialog box Special Styles tab options.

Some Special Styles effects can only be seen when you preview the page in your Browser. One such style is Blink, the Special Style option that makes text blink on and off. Difficult to read, and a serious annoyance in the opinion of many, text that flashes on the page may be a passing fad. But if you really want blinking text, select your text, click Format, Font, Special Styles, then click the Blink checkbox and OK. To view your blinking text, click the Preview in Browser button on the Editor toolbar.

Writing up math or chemical formulas? Or maybe you want 1st to look like 1st. If that's the case, one item on the Special Styles tab will come in handy. The Vertical Position option lets you create superscript and subscript characters—letters or numbers above or below the line of the adjacent text. To create superscript or subscript characters:

1 Select the character(s) you want to format as superscript or subscript.

2 Choose Format, Font, Special Styles. Click the Vertical Position drop-down arrow, and select Superscript or Subscript, as shown in Figure 7.4.

3 Click Apply to see the superscript or subscript effect immediately, and click OK in the Font dialog box to finish the job.

Fig. 7.4
Formatting characters as subscript or superscript is easy, provided you know where to look.

A subscript character.

By default, superscript and subscript characters go one point above or below the character that precedes them. Set a different value here for higher or lower characters.

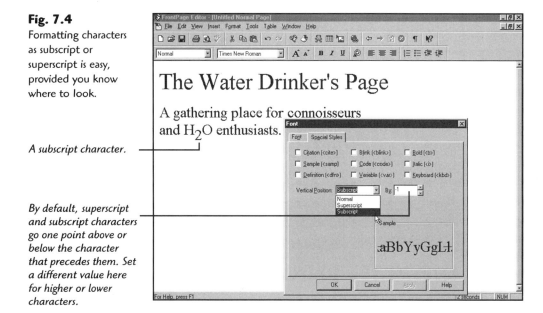

I need bigger (or smaller) text

Bigger isn't necessarily better, but if you're calling attention to a line of text, a bigger font size can certainly help. The FrontPage Editor gives you a choice of seven font sizes, ranging from 8pts to 36pts.

 **Plain English, please!**

Font sizes are measured in **points**, one point being 1/72 of an inch. FrontPage's biggest font size, 36pts, gives you characters half an inch tall.

To make existing text bigger or smaller, select the text and click the Increase Text Size or Decrease Text Size buttons on the Format toolbar. Each click of a button changes the text size to the next higher or lower value. If you click the Increase Text Size or Decrease Text Size buttons without selecting text first, any text that you type will be in the new size.

Use heading styles for text in proportion

Not all browsers will display the different font sizes you select in the FrontPage Editor, and most browsers allow users to adjust the size of the displayed text anyway. If you want to preserve the relative size of different blocks of text on the page, even when your readers monkey around with their browser's text size, consider using the Editor's heading styles.

The six heading styles format text in boldface in different point sizes, ranging from Heading 1, the largest size, to Heading 6, the smallest (see Figure 7.5).

Fig. 7.5
Heading styles keep the relative sizes of your heads in proportion, even when browsers are set to a different display size.

The Change Style box indicates the current style.

Heading styles 1-6.

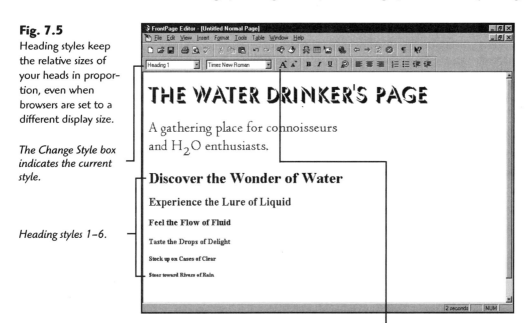

For text larger than Heading 1, select the text and click the Increase Text Size button.

To apply a heading style, click the Change Style drop-down arrow and select one of the headings from the menu. Start typing, and your text is formatted in the selected heading style. When you press Enter to end the paragraph, the style changes automatically back to Normal.

Heading styles also help keep your pages consistent and logical. Assign a different style to headings of differing importance throughout your web, and the result will be crisper pages.

For text that moves, try a marquee

Straight from Times Square to your web page, a marquee is text that rolls across the screen. Once a novelty on the Web, scrolling text now seems to be everywhere. Some marquee text repeats itself in an endless loop, a bit like an old LP with a sticking needle. While it may appear engaging at first reading, many find marquees irritating by the umpteenth repetition. FrontPage has marquee options that allow for a much less annoying effect. Still, if you include a marquee in your web, consider revising the scrolling text at frequent intervals.

To create a marquee, type the text and select it. Click Insert, Marquee for the Marquee Properties dialog box shown in Figure 7.6.

Fig. 7.6
FrontPage lets you create marquees that won't irritate your readers.

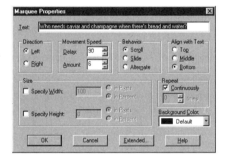

The default values shown in Figure 7.6 will be fine for most purposes, but the one change you'll want to consider making is in the marquee Behavior.

The Scroll option gives you the stuck record effect, with text that loops endlessly across the window. You can fix that by deselecting the Repeat Continuously check box, but the Slide option might be a better choice. Click the Slide checkbox for Marquee text that slides across the window once, then comes to a halt. That gives you the fun of animated text, without the annoying repetition, for which your readers will be grateful.

 Click OK in the Marquee Properties dialog box when you've made your selections. To see the marquee actually working, click the Preview in Browser button on the Editor toolbar. The Editor window displays the marquee with a dashed-line box around it (if you don't see the box, click the Show/Hide ¶ button), but it won't show you the text moving.

To get rid of marquee text, click the dashed-line box to select it and press Delete.

Text formatting at the click of a button

It's the householder's dream—and the interior decorator's nightmare. Room redecorating at the touch of a button doesn't happen outside of science fiction, but in a modest way, FrontPage lets you do something similar with your web pages. The buttons on the Format toolbar give plain pages anything from a formatting tweak to a complete makeover. Best of all, they're easy to use.

Boldface, italics, and underlining spell emphasis

All writers like to think their unadorned words pack all the punch they need, but that doesn't stop publishers from lending a typographical hand—think of book covers. As a web builder, you have to add your own typographical lift. For emphasis and variety on the page, boldface, italics, and underlining are all quick fixes.

To apply boldface, italics, or underlining to existing text, just select the text and click the Bold, Underline, or Italics buttons on the Format toolbar. To apply any (or all) of the three formats to new text, click the buttons and type. Click the buttons again to turn off the formatting for new text. And to remove boldface, italics, or underlining, select the formatted text and click the appropriate button.

Unless it's absolutely needed, avoid underlined text. Underlined words on the Web mean hyperlinks; text that's merely underlined, not linked, will cause confusion.

TIP **Keyboardists can skip the Format toolbar buttons and press Ctrl+B** for boldface, Ctrl+I for italics, and Ctrl+U for underlining. Like the toolbar buttons, the key combinations toggle the formatting on and off. If you're applying the formats to new text, press the key combination, type the text, then press the key combination again to turn off the formatting.

Left, right, and center: text alignment made easy

Text typed in the FrontPage Editor starts at the left margin and proceeds to the right margin, where it wraps to the next line and you start again. Perfectly logical, but not at all inevitable. You can, if you prefer, center your text between the left and right margins, or you can align your text with the right margin. Varying the default left-to-right lines of text with centered and right-aligned paragraphs makes text so formatted stand out. It also adds variety and interest to the page.

To center or align new text with the right margin, click the Center or Align Right buttons on the Format toolbar. The cursor moves to either the center or the right margin of the page; now start typing. Press Enter at the end of the paragraph, and you'll see that the selected alignment applies to the next paragraph as well.

Q&A *I want centered and left- and right-aligned text on the same line! How do I do it?*

Text with different alignments on the same line is one word processing trick that the FrontPage Editor just can't do. You can get the same effect with a table though. See Chapter 10, "The Miracle of Tables," for details.

When you're ready to return to ordinary, left-aligned text, just click the Align Left button on the Format toolbar.

To center or align left or right an existing paragraph, just click the paragraph, then click one of the Format toolbar alignment buttons. Figure 7.7 shows text that's centered and aligned with both the left and right margins.

Fig. 7.7
Formatting paragraphs with different alignments breaks up the page and calls attention to sections of text.

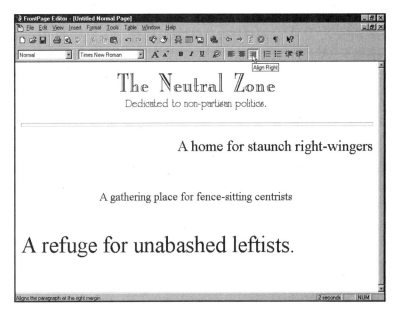

Those aren't dents... they're indents

Indenting a paragraph, like centering it or aligning it with the right margin, is a device to make key text stand out. Indented paragraphs are also used for long quotations. To indent an existing paragraph, click the paragraph, then click the Increase Indent button on the Format toolbar. The first indent level moves both the left and right margins in towards the center of the page; to indent the paragraph further, keep clicking the Increase Indent button. When text is indented from both the left and right margins like this, it's sometimes called a double-indent.

If you've taken your indenting too far, click the Decrease Indent button to move the paragraph margins back towards the page margins.

TIP **If you don't like to reach for the mouse for indenting maneuvers,** press Ctrl+M to increase the indent, and Shift+Ctrl+M to decrease the indent.

http://www.quecorp.com

Speeding bullets, listing numbers

Bulleted lists, in which list items are each preceded by a small typographical symbol called a bullet, are seen everywhere on the Web. They compress a lot of information into a compact space, and they're easy to read at a glance, two useful features of any web page element. Numbered lists are often used to guide readers through a series of steps, or to outline successive points in an argument. Both kinds of lists are easy to add to a FrontPage web page.

To create a quick bulleted list:

1 Click the Bulleted List button on the Editor Format toolbar. That indents the current line and inserts the first bullet.

2 Type your first list item and press Enter. The next bullet is automatically inserted at the beginning of the current line.

3 Continue typing your list items, pressing Enter after each one. At the end of your list, press Enter twice. That stops the automatic insertion of bullets and parks the cursor back at the left margin. Figure 7.8 shows a bulleted list.

Fig. 7.8
Creating a bulleted list is a snap; just don't forget to press Enter twice to stop the speeding bullets.

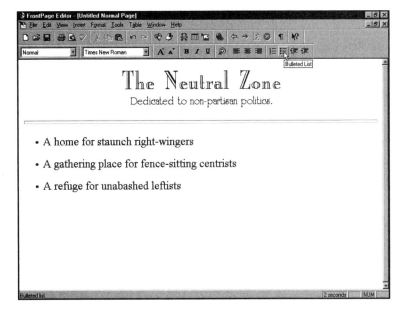

122 Part II *Putting Your Pages Together*

Q&A ***How do I create a bulleted list without blank lines?***

The default bulleted list style seen in Figure 7.8 inserts a blank line each time you press Enter. If you want a bulleted list without blank lines between each item, click the Change Style arrow on the Format toolbar. Choose Menu List on the drop-down menu. That inserts your first bullet. Type the list item, and press Enter. The next bullet is inserted automatically on the next line. Press Enter twice at the end of the list to stop inserting bullets

TIP **If you want to turn a list you've already typed into a bulleted list, just click the paragraph, and then click the Bulleted List button on the Format toolbar.**

How do I change these bullets?

You get solid round bullets with the Bulleted List button on the Format toolbar, but that's not your only option. For a different style of bullet, right-click your bulleted list and choose List Properties on the context menu that pops up. That gets you the Bulleted tab of the List Properties dialog box shown in Figure 7.9.

Fig. 7.9
If you prefer your bullets square or unfilled, here's the place to make the change.

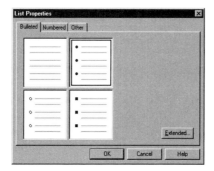

Select the bullet style you want in the List Properties dialog box, and click OK to change your bulleted list.

http://www.quecorp.com

Numbered lists that never lose count

Here's a handy FrontPage Editor tool: automatic numbered lists that keep track of the numbering for you. Just click the Numbered List button on the Format toolbar, type the items, and press Enter after each one. FrontPage numbers each line automatically.

At the end of the list, press Enter twice to stop the automatic line numbering.

To change your numbering style, or to start the list with a number other than one, right-click your list and choose List Properties on the context menu. The List Properties dialog box appears with the Numbered tab selected (see Figure 7.10).

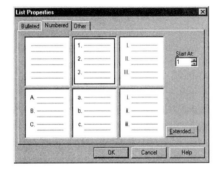

Fig. 7.10
Numbered lists don't have to use numbers. Choose upper- or lowercase letters or Roman numerals if you prefer them.

TIP **For numbered or bulleted lists in the center of the page instead of** at the left margin, put your list inside the cell of a table. See Chapter 10 for details on laying out pages with tables.

Part III: Interior Decorating

Chapter 8: **Color Me Fun!**

Chapter 9: **Picture This! Adding Graphics to Your Web**

Chapter 10: **The Miracle of Tables**

Color Me Fun!

● **In this chapter:**

- **Setting the mood with background colors**
- **Custom colors: pigments of your imagination**
- **How to use background images**
- **Creating text to dye for**
- **How do I add color to horizontal lines?**
- **Decisions, decisions: how to pick the right colors**

Put on your painter's cap and pick up your brush; FrontPage has the colors to add just the right mood to your web . . . . ▶

"**E.C. (Bud) Frye Jr., president of Frye International, which manufactures Larmarle Airtight Calendarware,** said his company has seen an increase in customer orders for blue lids on clear containers in recent months." *HFD—The Weekly Home Furnishings Newspaper, August 31, 1992.*

You probably weren't aware of the revolution in food container colors. That's right—people are just plain sick of seeing all those traditional tans and whites in their freezers.

Why should you care? Because colors are as important to your web as they are to designers of food containers and other product packaging. Colors can re-enforce or overwhelm your message, invite or repel your reader, and ultimately determine if people will forget you or return for another visit. And besides, playing with colors is just plain fun.

Businesses spend millions of dollars annually to find out what colors are best for their products. That's why we see more reds in the laundry detergent aisle than we do in the dairy case, why food manufacturers use a browning ingredient in microwave dishes, and why most computers are off-white. (All this despite the fact that blue is America's most popular color.) It only makes sense that you spend some time thinking about which colors are right for the product you call your web.

Much of your color might come from graphics and other images. But your web includes a variety of elements that you also must consider: background, text, hyperlinks, and, if you use them, horizontal lines. This chapter explains in detail how you change the colors of these elements. Along the way, we'll talk about some of the factors you should consider as you determine your web's color scheme.

Editor uses a variety of dialog boxes to change the color of various elements. For your convenience, here's a table that summarizes where you go to do what:

To change this...	Use this
Background color	Format, Background, Background
Background image	Format, Background, Background Image
Default text color	Format, Background, Text
Selected text color	Text Color button on Standard toolbar
Selected text color to default text color	Format, Font, Color
Default hyperlink	Format, Background, Hyperlink
Default visited hyperlink	Format, Background, Visited Hyperlink
Default active hyperlink	Format, Background, Active Hyperlink
Color of horizontal line	Horizontal Line Properties (right-click menu)

Background colors

Different interiors require different colors. A hospital paints its patients' rooms in soothing pastels; a daycare center uses gay primary colors on its walls. Meanwhile, the local tavern uses woody browns to give customers an appropriate sense of being in a murky sanctuary (and to hide the stains).

Figuratively speaking, your web's interior is the page upon which you place your text and graphics—the **background**.

Depending on the purpose of your web site, adding a background color plays a major role in establishing mood. White and gray, for example, are conservative choices appropriate for businesses and resumes. Fuchsia, on the other hand, is a garish color that draws attention to itself and suggests that the reader can expect informal or unconventional editorial content.

Beyond decoration, background colors also have a practical use: you can use them to distinguish sections of your web, subtly cueing readers where they are in your web's hierarchy. For example, a corporate web might use white for pages that include product information and a pastel blue for pages that provide product support.

Whatever you choose for your background color, your priority is to make sure that your text is readable. Green text against a fuchsia background might look tangy, but most of your readers will be reaching for the Advil.

You can change the color of a single page, or you can set the color for multiple pages with one deft stroke of your brush. Let's look at how you add color to a single page first.

Pick a color, (almost) any color

Choosing a new background color is simple. Open your page in FrontPage Editor and follow these steps:

   1 Choose Format, Background from the menu bar. This opens the Background panel of the Page Properties dialog box (see Figure 8.1).

Fig. 8.1
The Background option in the Page Properties dialog box lets you change the color of your page.

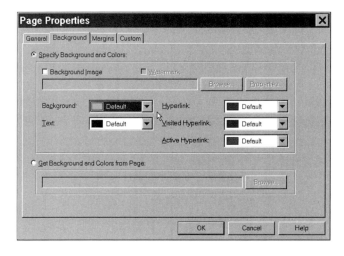

   2 Make sure the Specify Background and Colors option is selected and that the Background Image option is not.

   3 Click the arrow next to the Background selection box. Holding down your mouse button, point to the color you want, and release the button (see Figure 8.2).

Fig. 8.2
Choose from among the standard colors Editor offers on the menu, or choose Custom to create your own colors.

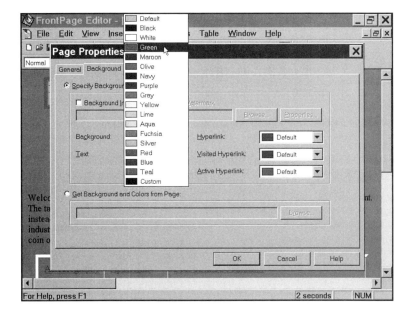

4 Click the OK button.

Q&A *Can I choose a different background color for a portion of the page, such as a single paragraph or heading?*

No. However, you can put that part of the page in a table, and then change the background color of the table. Tables also are invaluable tools for creating horizontal and vertical bands of color, which in turn can help you organize the material you're presenting on a page. We'll look at how to use colors and tables in Chapter 10, "The Miracle of Tables."

Up close and personalized—how to make your own colors

Your local Sherwin-Williams dealer wouldn't stay in business long if he or she sold only 16 colors, especially if the selection included some of the, uh, less-than-appealing choices offered in Editor's Page Properties dialog box. (Fuchsia might be appropriate for a dating service, but Microsoft should have named "olive" "Linda Blair green.")

However, your dealer knows which side of the bread is painted and will mix just about any color you want. So, too, will Editor.

To start mixing, choose F<u>o</u>rmat, Bac<u>k</u>ground from the menu bar; Editor displays the Background panel of the Page Properties dialog box. Click the arrow next to the Background selection box and choose Custom from the menu of colors (it's the last item on the menu). Editor opens the Color dialog box shown in Figure 8.3.

Fig. 8.3
The Color dialog box lets you create just about any color of the rainbow.

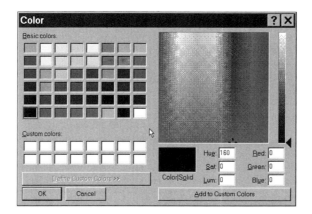

CAUTION Playing with custom colors is lots of fun, but it's important to remember that many users will not see the colors as you intended them to be seen, or may not see any color at all. The reasons are several. First, some people use low-resolution monitors that have a limited color palette. Second, some browsers can't display all colors. In both cases, your custom colors might be replaced by colors that are the closest match or might be eliminated entirely. The bottom line: if you use custom colors, preview the pages in several browsers and at different screen resolutions to make sure that your pages are legible to all users.

Basic colors

The Color dialog box offers several ways in which you can create a custom color. The choices under the <u>B</u>asic Colors heading are a good place to start. Editor displays up to 48 colors, depending on the capabilities of your graphics adapter and display driver.

To use one of the basic colors for your background, click your choice under the Basic Color heading and choose OK. Editor returns you to the Page Properties dialog box. If the color you chose already is on the Bac<u>k</u>ground menu, you'll see it in the selection box. If you chose a new color, the

Ba*c*kground selection box displays Custom, along with a sample of the color. Choose OK again to return to your page and check out your new background color.

Hither and dither

As you experiment with the basic colors, you'll notice a couple of events that might confuse you initially. First, the Color|S*o*lid box to the right of the custom colors sometimes shows *two* colors. Second, when you return to the Page Properties dialog box, you'll see the solid color, not the color you thought you chose, in the Ba*c*kground selection box. For example, if you choose the basic color that looks like pumpkin, Color|S*o*lid shows pumpkin on the left and green on the right, and the Ba*c*kground menu on the Page Properties dialog box shows green.

Not to worry. What the Color|S*o*lid box shows you are the **dithered** and solid versions of your choice. The color you chose—the dithered version—is the one that will appear as the background color.

> ❝ *Plain English, please!*
>
> So what's **dithering**? In oversimplified terms, it refers to the process of mixing red, green, blue, black, and white to give the illusion of other colors. Fortunately, you don't need to know anything about dithering to create colors, so we won't go into any further technical explanation here. For our purposes, all you need to remember is that you'll get the color appearing under Color, not the one under Solid and in the Ba*c*kground selection box. ❞

Beyond the basics

Are 48 colors still not enough for you? Do you have the patience and fortitude to explore The Infinite? Then it's time to play with the color matrix box, that large patch of rainbow to the right of the basic colors.

Simply click anywhere in the box with your mouse. The color you selected appears in the Color|S*o*lid box. If you don't like the color, hold down the mouse button and drag the crosshairs. When you see a color you like in the left panel of the Color|S*o*lid box, release the mouse button.

Next, experiment with the luminosity slider to the right of the color matrix to adjust the amount of white your color has. Move the slider up to make the color brighter and down to make it darker.

When you've made a choice, click the OK button to return to the Page Properties dialog box. Your new color appears in the Ba*c*kground selection box. Choose OK to finish the job.

Adding and subtracting custom colors

What if you really, really like one of your custom colors and want to make it available to other web pages? Or you find several custom colors and want to save them all?

No problem. The Color dialog box lets you add up to 14 custom colors to your basic choices. After you've chosen your custom color, click the *A*dd to Custom Colors button instead of the OK button. Editor adds the color to the selections beneath the *C*ustom Colors heading. Once it's there, you choose it just as you would one of the basic colors.

Here are a few tips on adding several colors to the *C*ustom Colors palette:

> If you're adding a group of colors all in one sitting—that is, if you don't leave the Color dialog box between additions—just choose your colors and click the Add to Custom Colors button after each selection. Editor puts each new color in the next box under *C*ustom Colors, column by column.

> If you have closed the Color dialog box and return to add a color, click one of the empty *C*ustom Colors boxes before you choose your custom color from the color matrix box. Otherwise, Editor might replace one of your existing colors with your new one.

> You can replace an existing choice beneath the *C*ustom Colors heading by clicking its box first. When you select your new color and choose *A*dd to Custom Colors, FrontPage replaces the old choice with your new one.

> You can select and use only one custom color at a time for your background. But you can use a different custom color for each web page.

When you create a custom color, it's also available to use with text, hyperlinks, horizontal lines, and tables. We'll talk about the first three later in this chapter; see Chapter 10 for details on adding color to tables.

Q&A Do I have to create a new set of custom colors for each web?

No. Once you've made your selections, the custom colors will be available for all webs, including new ones.

Color me confused

As we've seen, you don't need to know any technical terms to select a color. You just pick a color you like and add it to your palette. But if you're dying to know what some of those terms in the Color dialog box mean, read on.

We'll start with the familiar ones—red, green, and blue. All of the colors on your screen are made of these three colors, mixed in different ratios. Each is assigned a **value** between zero and 255. Solid red, for example, comprises the values 255 for red, zero for green, and zero for blue. The values for aqua are zero for red, 255 for green, and 255 for blue.

Next comes **hue**. This is a value associated with a color's place on the color wheel. Red is zero, green is 80, blue is 160, and everything else falls somewhere in between. So, for example, if your hue is 80 and you change it to 120, your new color falls halfway between green and blue.

Saturation (or Sat in the Color dialog box) tells you how much of a color you're getting. The range of values is zero to 240; the higher the value, the brighter the color.

Finally, **luminosity** indicates how much white the color contains. The higher the luminosity, the whiter the color; the lower the luminosity, the blacker the color.

You can change any of the values described here by typing a new value in the appropriate text box. For example, if you want a hue slightly on the bluish side of green, type 90 in the Hu<u>e</u> text box. FrontPage correspondingly changes the color in the Color|S<u>o</u>lid box and moves the crosshairs in the color matrix.

You might wonder if these values are useful to anyone who isn't a graphic arts professional. For the most part, no—at least, not in your daily work. But the values let you pass a color along to a friend. In general, it's easier to give the person the values of your colors and attributes than it is to say something like, "Well, it's sort of a medium-bright, reddish yellow."

Add texture with background images

A putting green, your uncle's golf pants, and his new Buick might all be the same shade of green, but they evoke different visceral responses. Why? For one thing, texture. Grass, polyester, and metal *feel* different when we look at them.

You can't get much texture from the color options Editor provides. But, with a good paint program or an image editor such as Microsoft's Image Composer, you can create swatches of textured color that you can use as background. If you don't have the right software, you still can download backgrounds from a number of sites on the Web (see the sidebar, "More Background on Backgrounds").

Let's say, for example, that you use Image Composer (see Chapter 9, "Picture This! Adding Graphics to Your Web," for more about the Image Composer) to create a small square of yellow to which you've applied Composer's Sponge art effect (the result of which looks like fresh Hostess Twinkies under a fluorescent light). Here's how to use that swatch for your web's background:

1. Save the swatch as a GIF or JPEG image, using Composer's File, Save Selection As command.

2. Open your web in Editor and choose Format, Background.

3. Click Specify Background and Colors and put a check in the Background Image checkbox.

4. Choose Browse next to the Background Image text box. This opens the Select Background Image dialog box.

5. Since the image is not yet part of your web, click the Other Location panel.

6. Click the From File option and choose the Browse button. FrontPage displays a second dialog box similar to the Open dialog box.

7. Find the image file and double click it. FrontPage takes you back to the Page Properties dialog box, the file name placed in the text box beneath Background Image (see Figure 8.4).

Chapter 8 *Color Me Fun!* **137**

Fig. 8.4
You can turn a GIF or JPEG file into a background image by putting a check next to Background Image and entering the name of the image in the text box.

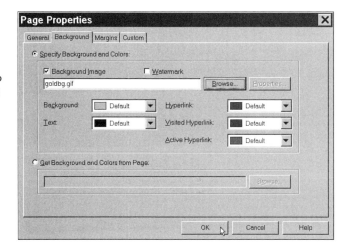

8 Click OK. FrontPage closes the Page Properties dialog box and adds your textured gold as your page's new background.

TIP **FrontPage comes with a collection of background images that you** can play with. To find them, click the Clip Art tab in the Select Background Image dialog box in Step 5 above. Then, choose Backgrounds in the Categories selection box. FrontPage displays a variety of backgrounds such as Gray Gravel and Lava Lamp. Click the image you want to use and choose OK, or double-click the image.

Q&A *What are GIF and JPEG?*

GIF (Graphics Interchange Format) and JPEG (Joint Photographic Expert Group format) are two popular methods used for saving compressed pictures. You must save images you use for your FrontPage web in one of these formats, whether the image is a background, photograph, or graphical doo-dad. You can insert a variety of other types of graphics into a FrontPage web, including BMP, TIF, and PCX files; however, FrontPage automatically converts these files to the GIF or JPEG format. Turn to Chapter 9 for detailed information.

Q&A *My colors appear differently when the web page is viewed with a browser. What's wrong?*

A couple of possible problems. First, some browsers can't display all the colors available in FrontPage. The guaranteed exception is Internet Explorer (not exactly a shock, since both products come from Microsoft). If you want to be sure that your colors will appear in all browsers, then stick to your basic colors. Otherwise, you should check your pages in the two popular browsers, Explorer and Netscape, before you publish them.

The second common problem is hardware-related: not all graphics adapters and monitors are alike. Many older computers cannot display the same number of colors as newer computers can. If you're concerned about accommodating users with older equipment, then, again, don't play with custom colors and stay with the basics.

More background on backgrounds

Would you like instant access to hundreds of backgrounds of every color and texture, free for the taking? Then log on to the Web and visit one of the many collections of backgrounds.

Because web pages come and go, we can't recommend too many specific sites. But you can find a list of sites at **Yahoo!**, one of the Web's more popular search services. Yahoo! has a page of links to background collections, including the ones mentioned below. Go to Yahoo's main page at www.yahoo.com and search for the keyword **backgrounds;** then select **Computers and Internet:Internet:World Wide Web:Page Design and Layout:Backgrounds** under Yahoo Categories. Or you can go directly to the page with the URL **http://www.yahoo.com/ Computers_and_Internet/Internet/ World_Wide_Web/Page_Design_and_Layout/ Backgrounds/**.

Netscape, the company that makes the Navigator browser, has some interesting textured backgrounds on their Background Sampler page (**http:// home.netscape.com/assist/net_sites/bg/ backgrounds.html**). Some of the names will give you an idea of what they look like—red rock, olive-pink marble, red stucco, corrugated metal, and dark raindrops. The site includes instructions on how to download the images to your computer.

You also might want to check out the Netscape page "Controlling Document Backgrounds" (**http:// home.netscape.com/assist/net_sites/bg/**), which provides some information on the HTML tags and attributes that control background color.

Another site devoted to a browser, **Mosaic for Microsoft Windows**, has a page called Sample Background Image Files (http://www.ncsa.uiuc.edu/ SDG/Software/WinMosaic/Backgrnd/). The page includes 40 simple, textured backgrounds, including six good variations of black for that funereal look. The figure shows one of them, black satin.

Finally, visit **Thalia's Guide: The Color Page (http://www.sci.kun.nl/thalia/guide/color/)** for three databases of downloadable background colors, The small (47 backgrounds) and medium (100 backgrounds) databases offer online samples. If you'd rather work offline, the site includes a compressed file with 504 backgrounds that you can download and play with. You'll need to know how to manage ZIP files to do that.

In addition, Thalia's Guide provides a useful FAQ (frequently asked questions page) on background colors and HTML tags and a selected list of links to other pages with background samples.

The color of text

How often have you read a book whose text wasn't black? Probably never. The fact is that black text is easier to read than colored text.

Nevertheless, colored text has its place—if, for example, your background is black (studies show that black on black is difficult to read), you want to highlight a block of text, or you'd like to distinguish a page from its siblings. Also, you can add color to large text—in headings, for example—to add spice to a bland web.

Editor has the tools to make changing text color easy, by the block or page. And you can change your hyperlink colors, too.

Paging all colors

Let's say that you've created a short page of text that contains an important message you want to give extra emphasis. To grab everyone's attention, you decide to give the page a black background with red text. That is, you want to change the default color from white to red. Here's how:

1 Choose Format, Background from the menu bar to display the Background panel in the Page Properties dialog box.

2 Click the arrow next to the Text selection box.

3 Holding down the mouse button, touch the color you want with your pointer, and release the button (see Figure 8.5).

4 Choose the OK button.

Fig. 8.5
You change default text color the same way you do the background; click the arrow next to the Text selection box and click your choice.

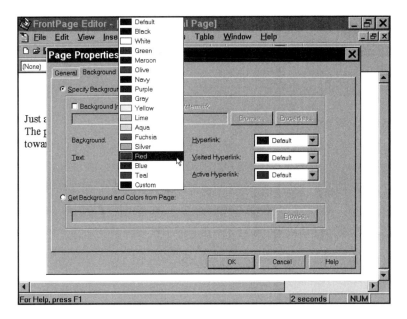

 CAUTION **If you change to a black background before you change your text,** your text vanishes. Don't be fooled into thinking that Editor somehow deleted your text. It's still there, waiting for you to change your text to something other than black. You'll get the same disappearing text if you change your text to white against a white background.

 TIP **You can create and use custom colors for text the same way you** do for backgrounds. Just choose Custom from the Text selection box. Editor displays the same Color dialog box you get when you choose Custom from the Background selection box.

A little daub will do you

 You can change the color of text by the block, too—only this time you can use the Text Color button on the toolbar.

Say, for example, that you want to change a heading to lime green. Select the text you want to change ("To All Members" in Figure 8.6) and click the Text Color button. Editor displays the Color dialog box (refer to Figure 8.6). Click the color you want and choose OK.

Note that custom colors are available in the Color dialog box. If you wish to create a new custom color, click the Define Custom Colors button. Editor expands the Color dialog box to the one that you use when creating custom colors for your background or default text.

Fig. 8.6
To change the color of a few words, select the text you want to change and click the Text Color button on the toolbar.

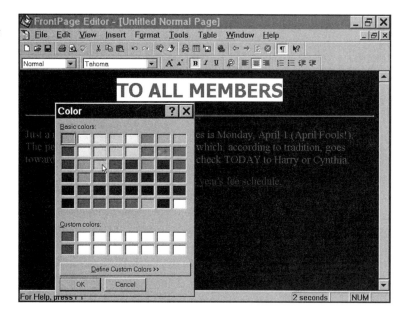

Default is yours

Once you change the color of selected text, the color stays the same, even when you change your default text color in the Page Properties dialog box. This lets you keep your selected-text colors constant, no matter what other color changes you make.

And what if you want to change selected text to conform to the default color? For this, you'll have to go to another dialog box, Font. Take these steps:

1 Open the Font dialog box by choosing Format, Font from the menu bar (see Figure 8.7). Click the Font tab if the Font panel isn't already visible.

Fig. 8.7
How do you change the color of selected text back to the default color? Choose Format, Font from the menu bar and use the Color selection box.

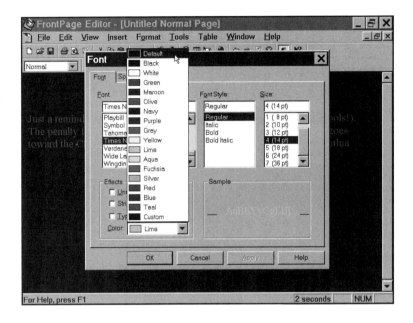

2. Click the right arrow next to the Color selection box and choose Default.

3. Click the OK button.

TIP **Argh! Did you make a color change that you didn't really want?**
Don't forget Editor's handy-dandy Undo command. You can reverse any color change by clicking the Undo button on the Standard toolbar, pressing Ctrl+Z, or choosing Edit, Undo from the menu bar.

The thin blue (or red, or green) horizontal line

There's one other standard page element whose color you can control, and that's the horizontal line. Chapter 9 provides more detail on lines, but here's a simple primer.

You create a horizontal line with the Insert, Horizontal Line command. Lines are gray by default, but you can change their color the same as you can backgrounds and text.

Display the Horizontal Line Properties dialog box using one of two methods. If your insertion point is at the beginning of the line, press Alt+Enter. Otherwise, right-click the line and choose Horizontal Line Properties from the quick menu. In the dialog box, click the arrow next to the Color selection box and pick your color from the menu (see Figure 8.8).

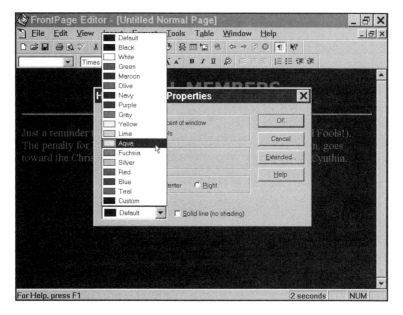

Fig. 8.8
You change the color of a horizontal line by right-clicking the line and choosing Horizontal Line Properties from the quick menu.

As with text and backgrounds, you can choose Custom from the Color menu to create and use custom colors.

I'd like that mauve, please

Despite dizzying technological advances in the modern world, you still have to paint your house one brush stroke at a time. You'd think some enterprising young (and lazy) college student would have figured out a way to paint one side of a house, then automatically fill in the other three sides with the same color.

You can do this in FrontPage. Editor lets you set the background color for one page, then tell any other page to use the same color. You can use the same page to set your text and horizontal line colors, too.

At first blush (or brush), this trick might not seem worth the trouble, since you still have to use the Page Properties dialog box to refer the page you're coloring to the page from which you're copying colors. But the technique has two important advantages.

First, you can change the background color of all your pages simply by changing the color of your reference page. And second, you don't have to remember which color you want for a page. Just tell it to grab the color from the reference page, and Editor takes care of the rest.

How to create your reference page

Your first step is to create a web page whose sole function is to serve as a color reference for your other web pages. Here's how:

1 Press Ctrl+N to start a new page, and choose Normal Page from the New Page dialog box.

2 Set your background color or image.

3 Set the default colors for your text and links.

4 Save the page. Use a page title that describes what the color is for. For example, if you're going to use the color for pages that contain archives, the title might be Colors for Archives; a page that holds colors for schedules might be named Colors for Schedules.

You can have as many reference pages as you need. Make sure that each file has a separate file name; for example, Col-arch.htm for Colors for Archives and Col-sked.htm for Colors for Schedules.

 You can use any page on your web as a reference page, from which other pages can then get their colors. It's not a good idea, though. If you accidentally delete the page, all your other pages that were using it to get their colors will revert to Editor's default colors. You're better off creating a dedicated reference page.

Ready, set, paint!

Next, open the page whose background color you want to change, and follow these steps:

Chapter 8 *Color Me Fun!* **145**

1. Choose F**o**rmat, Bac**k**ground from the main menu to open the Background panel in the Page Properties dialog box.

2. Choose the Get Background and Colors from Page radio button.

3. Click the B**r**owse button. Editor displays the Current Web dialog box, which includes a list of all files in your web.

4. Find the reference page you want. Double-click the file name, or click it and choose the OK button (see Figure 8.9).

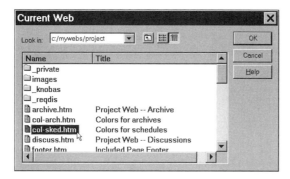

Fig. 8.9
In this web, the page titled "Colors for Schedules" provides the background and text colors for all pages containing project schedules.

5. Editor returns you to the Page Properties dialog box, which will look something like the one in Figure 8.10. Choose OK to close the dialog box. Your web page will reappear with its new background color.

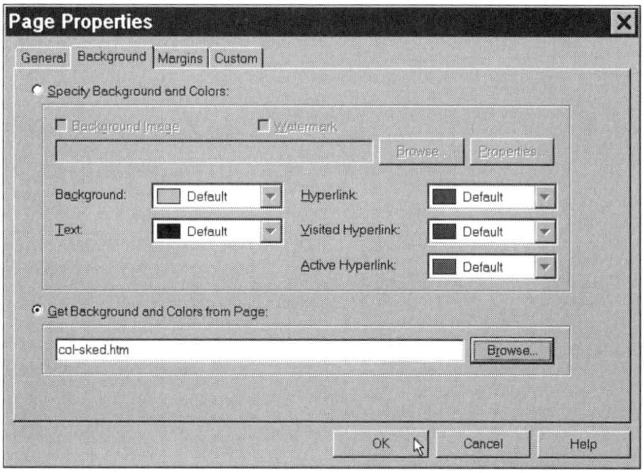

Fig. 8.10
When you've picked a color reference page, its file name appears at the bottom of the Page Properties dialog box.

Q&A *I changed the background color of a reference page, but the background color of my pages that refer to it stayed the same. What's the problem?*

Are both pages open in Editor? Then you might have missed one of two steps. First, make sure you save the reference page after you change the color. If you don't save the page, your other page won't detect the change. Second, after you've saved the reference page, you still must refresh the page that references it. Change to the page and choose View, Refresh.

Which colors are right for you?

OK, you've learned how to select the colors for your web. Now for the hard part—figuring out which colors to select.

You probably don't have much trouble picking colors when you go clothes shopping. You have your favorite colors, and you know which ones go best with your skin, eyes, and hair.

But when you're creating a web, you're essentially becoming a product designer. Trained professionals earn five- and six-figure sums to determine that a detergent box should be red or a magazine logo blue. How can we amateurs sift through the nearly infinite color combinations and pick the one that's right for our webs?

Well, for starters, borrow ideas from other web sites. There's no point in reinventing the color wheel. Find webs that you enjoy reading. What background and text colors do they use? What combinations are effective and which ones make your head hurt?

Also, guidelines for color use exist that you can apply to your web. We've collected a few of them below. These aren't absolute rules, and you'll have to decide if they apply to your needs. But you can use them as a foundation for picking color schemes that will make your web easier for you to design and a more pleasurable experience for visitors:

- Be aware that different colors deliver different messages. Green and blue are soothing, relaxing colors; black provides drama; red and orange excite and enflame. Choose the colors that send the right signals to your readers.

- Cool colors create detachment while warm colors create involvement.

- Use colors that are right for the information you're delivering and the audience you're addressing. A black background might not be the best choice for a florist, but it might be ideal for a site devoted to heavy metal bands.

- Use colors consistently. If your links are red on one page, they should be red on all pages.

- Black is an effective background color when you want to give your page impact, particularly with yellow or red display type.

- However, white or light-colored type against a black or dark-colored background is hard to read in large doses.

- Another combination to avoid is red on blue or vice versa.

- For general purposes, use a light, muted background color and black or very dark text; it's not the most original combination, but it guarantees readability.

- You can get some nicely subtle backgrounds with colors that have high (above 220) luminosity and saturation values. These offer off-whites that provide some color without sacrificing contrast.

- There's nothing wrong with a white background, or even a gray one when combined with appropriate color highlights. Here's an old trick used by magazine designers on low budgets: Spots of bright red in gray boxes on a white page.

- Use background colors to give your reader a sense of where he or she is in a large web. For example, table of contents pages might have light blue backgrounds while pages containing product information might have white backgrounds.

- When you choose a background, make sure all of your hyperlinks, including active and visited, will be visible. If, for example, you use a purple background, you'll have to change the color of your visited hyperlinks, which by default are also purple.

- One bright color draws the reader's eye, but two bright colors compete with one another for the reader's attention. A riot of colors is fine in a bag of M&Ms, but not for a web page. Words to live by: Too much innovation is no innovation at all.

- Color is an effective tool for breaking up a long page of text when used with headings or horizontal lines.

- Color can also effectively direct the reader's eye from one part of a page to another. For example, a spot of red in the upper left corner, middle of the page, and lower right corner moves the reader from one corner to the other.

- One spot of color on a page naturally draws the reader's attention to that spot. This is an important tool if you want to attract readers to a crucial heading or message.

- Break any of the above rules with impunity if you have a good reason to do so.

Picture This! Adding Graphics to Your Web

● **In this chapter:**

- **My page needs some quick art work**
- **Can I import any clip art into my web?**
- **This graphic needs some alterations**
- **There's a library of images on the FrontPage CD?**
- **Customize and create art with the Image Composer**

A web without graphics would be dreary indeed. Whether you make your own or use the ready-made variety, FrontPage has art for every occasion . . . . ▶

The World Wide Web is sometimes called the World Wide Wait, for reasons apparent to anyone who's visited cyberspace. Haven't we all reached for our browser's Stop button before a page was loaded, tired of waiting for the thing to appear?

One reason for bottlenecks on the Web: pages loaded with graphics. Picture files are much bigger than text files, so they take longer to transfer to your PC over the phone lines. A single image can require more transfer time than two hundred pages of text.

Still, travelers in cyberspace wouldn't be satisfied with pages composed entirely of text. Since you'll want to include graphics in your own webs, try to keep them modest in size and number. Smaller, and fewer, images on your pages will keep your visitors from reaching for their browser's Stop button before your work has a chance to appear.

Image formats you need to know about

Just as there are many formats for displaying an image in art, from oil painting to marble statues, computers use various different formats to store and display graphics. Web browsers are designed to support both **GIF** and **JPEG**, which is why most images on the Web are in one or the other format.

The graphics you'll include in your own webs will be in either GIF or JPEG formats. Each has virtues and defects:

- GIF, which stands for Graphics Interchange Format, can handle up to 256 colors. GIF files download relatively quickly, and GIF images are what's most often seen on the Web.

- JPEG, or Joint Photographic Experts Group format, supports over 16 million colors, which makes for richer and crisper graphics. JPEG is the preferred format for photos. Although JPEG files download at a slower transfer speed than GIF, they can also be more compact.

So which format do you use? Both will work, but if you're scanning photos, consider using JPEG for its greater fidelity to the original. For clip art, GIF is the way to go.

Fast art is close to hand

FrontPage comes with its own collection of instant artwork, ready to be inserted into a page. With your web page open, click the Insert Image button on the FrontPage Editor toolbar. Choose the Clip Art tab, shown in Figure 9.1.

Fig. 9.1
Nothing here is exactly of museum quality, but you'll find serviceable artwork nonetheless.

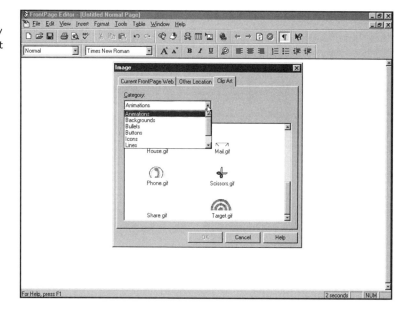

Choose a <u>C</u>ategory in the Image dialog box, then double-click any of the graphics files that appear on the list of Co<u>n</u>tents. That pops the image into your page at the insertion point.

The Animations category shown in Figure 9.1 is a collection of animated graphics of things like cutting scissors, vibrating telephones (really) and moving dots. Inserted in a page in the Editor, they look static; to see the animations come to life, click the Preview in Browser button on the Editor toolbar. You'll be prompted to save the inserted graphic; click <u>Y</u>es, and the page will open in your browser with the animation "animated".

TIP You'll find loads of images to download and insert into your webs at the Microsoft Gallery World Wide Web site, at **http://www.microsoft.com/gallery/files/images/default.htm**.

I want to import JPEG and GIF files into my web

If you don't see anything you like in the FrontPage Clip Art collection, add your own artwork discoveries directly to your web.

FrontPage puts an Images folder in every new web. If you're in the Editor, click the Show FrontPage Explorer button on the Editor toolbar. You'll see the Images folder when you click the Folder View button on the FrontPage Explorer toolbar (see Figure 9.2).

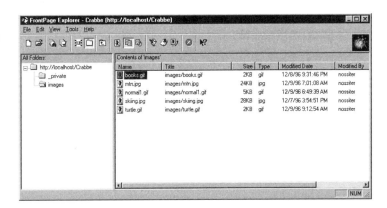

Fig. 9.2
FrontPage throws in an Images folder, gratis, with each new web. Filling the folder, however, is up to you.

You'll find it handy to store a web's graphics in the Images folder. That keeps your graphics files organized in one spot, makes it easier to track links to your graphics, and puts graphics files at your fingertips when you want to insert them in the FrontPage Editor.

Keeping graphics files in the web's Images folder has everything to recommend it, bar one small problem: there are no images in the Images folder until you put them there. You've got to hunt down JPEG and GIF files and stick them in the Images folder yourself. Fortunately, that's easy to do. Just copy or cut your graphic, then paste it into a page in the FrontPage Editor. Save your page, and the Save Image to FrontPage Web dialog box pops up automatically. Type the path of your web's Images folder in the Save as URL text box, and click Yes to save the image.

Don't want to bother typing lengthy paths, bristling with forward slashes? After saving the image, click the Show FrontPage Explorer button on the

Editor toolbar. Now click the Folder View button on the Explorer toolbar. Drag the newly saved image onto the Images folder, release the mouse button, and the image drops into the folder.

Can I import images directly into the Images folder?

For those who don't want to copy and paste images, you can import graphics files straight into a web's Images folder:

1 Open your web and click the Folder View button on the FrontPage Explorer toolbar if it's not already selected.

2 Double-click the Images folder to open it up.

3 Choose File, Import. In the Import File to FrontPage Web dialog box that appears, click Add File.

4 The Add Files to Import List dialog box pops up. Click the Files of type drop-down arrow and select GIF and JPEG(*.gif, *.jpeg).

5 Use the Look in drop-down menu and the Up One Level button to navigate your disk until you track down the JPEG and GIF images you seek (see Figure 9.3).

Fig. 9.3
MS Office users will find JPEG's and GIF's on the Office CD.

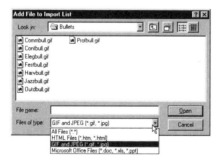

 TIP If you're a Microsoft Office 97 user, insert your Office CD. In the FrontPage Add Files to Import List dialog box, open the CD to the Clipart folder. You'll find JPEG images in the Photos subfolder, and GIF images in the Bullets and Lines folders.

CAUTION **The World Wide Web itself is a treasure house of JPEGs and GIFs.** Using your browser to save those images to disk, and then importing them into FrontPage as we're doing here is the work of a moment. Beware, however, of copyright laws. Images retrieved from other Web pages can't always be republished on your own Web pages without getting permission to do so.

6. Once you locate an image, double-click it. The file name appears in the Import File to FrontPage Web dialog box, as shown in Figure 9.4.

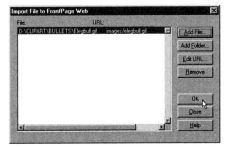

Fig. 9.4
Although it takes some navigating and dialog box opening and closing, importing images into your web saves time in the end.

7. Click OK in the Import File to FrontPage Web dialog box, and after a moment or two you'll see the graphics file appear in the Images folder that you opened in the FrontPage Explorer.

Once imported into your web, graphics files are easy to insert into your web pages. Just open your page and click the Insert Image button on the FrontPage Editor toolbar. Choose the Current Front Page Web tab in the Image dialog box that appears, and double-click the Images folder (see Figure 9.5).

Fig. 9.5
Once the graphics files are in your web, putting them on the page is a snap.

Double-click any of the graphic files in the Images folder to pop the image into your page at the insertion point.

I want to use images that aren't in GIF or JPEG format

You've got a zillion clip art images scattered throughout your hard drive, and none of them are in JPEG or GIF format. No problem: FrontPage will convert them into GIF files automatically. To insert an image that's not in the standard JPEG or GIF format and convert it:

1 Open your web page and click the Insert Image button on the FrontPage Editor toolbar.

2 Click the Other Location tab in the Image dialog box that appears. Either type the full path name of the graphic file in the From File text box, or click the Browse button, locate your image, and double-click it.

3 The image pops into your page. Now you'll want to save it in your web's Images folder. To do that, click the image to select it. You'll see selection handles, in the form of small squares, appear around the image.

4 Click File, Save. The Save Image to FrontPage Web dialog box appears, with the image's file name in the Save as URL text box. Type the path of your web's Images folder if you wish to store the image there, and click Yes to save the image in your web (see Figure 9.6).

Fig. 9.6
Saving to the web the images that you plan to use in your pages keeps your materials where you can find them.

Q&A ***How come I'm getting the Save As dialog box instead of the Save Image to FrontPage Web dialog box?***

If you haven't saved your page first, you'll get the Save As dialog box if you try to save an image to the web. Save your page in the Save As dialog box, and then save the image to the web.

If the saved image doesn't wind up in the web's Images folder, just return to the FrontPage Explorer's Folder View. Drag the image file to the Images folder, then release the mouse button to drop the image into the folder.

How do I get rid of this graphic?

The easiest thing about importing graphics into FrontPage webs is getting rid of them. Click the graphic to select it, then press Delete.

Fit the image to the page

Some pages on the World Wide Web have a jumbled look. Their creators, you get the feeling, didn't pay much attention to the way the various elements on the page coexist. It's as though an absent-minded chef put the spumoni on the same plate with the spaghetti. To avoid similar accidents in your own pages, you'll want to tailor your text and images in a way that makes them look like they belong together. There are two approaches to weaving images into your page in a seamless way:

- Alter the image itself to make it look like it belongs. Move it, resize it—you can even edit the image contents.
- Arrange the text around the images so that all the elements on the page work together.

Not that these approaches are mutually exclusive. Chances are, you'll employ both tactics to design a coherent page.

Moving and resizing your images

There's one thing that all inserted images have in common: they're the wrong size. They might be too small, they might be too big, but they're never just right. FrontPage makes it easy to shrink or expand an image:

1. Click the image to select it. Selection handles, small squares, appear around the image. Depending on the image, the selection handles might be a little hard to see. You'll know the pointer is over one of the handles when it turns into a two-headed arrow.

2. Drag any of the selection handles with the two-headed arrow pointer to resize the image. To prevent your image from becoming distorted when you resize it, drag one of the four corner handles. (See Figure 9.7).

Fig. 9.7
Once you grab the correct handle, resizing images is a simple drag operation.

The pointer turns into a two-headed arrow when it's over a handle.

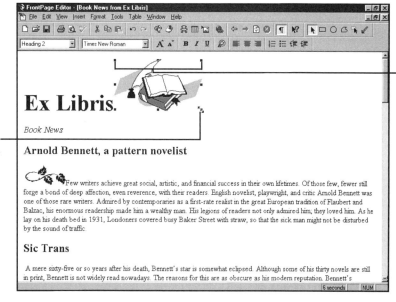

Drag a corner handle to resize the image and keep it in proportion.

Once you've got your image sized correctly, you'll want to move it into position on the page. Just drag the image wherever you like. As you drag, the pointer is joined by a small gray picture frame. A gray outline of the cursor follows the pointer around the page, to let you know where the image will be inserted once you release the mouse button (see Figure 9.8).

Fig. 9.8
Moving graphics is a standard drag and drop, helped by the shadow of the cursor acting as a visual cue.

The gray outline of the cursor moves with the pointer, to let you know where the moved graphic will be inserted.

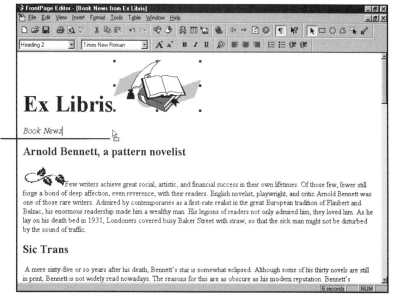

When you release the mouse button, the image snaps into place in the new location.

Q&A *I resized my graphic and chopped off a chunk of it!*

Here's a problem that afflicts certain imported graphics, and for which there's no easy cure. If you lop off a portion of your image when you resize or move it, your best bet is to start over. With the image selection handles still visible, press Delete to get rid of the image. Try inserting it again. If you still run into resizing problems, try opening the graphic in its native program, or, if it has none, in the Windows 95 Paint accessory. Now copy and paste the image to the FrontPage Editor, instead of importing it as a file. You might find that resizing and moving operations are less prone to trouble if the image is copied into the FrontPage Editor.

I want to wrap text around this image

Like certain riders of crowded commuter trains, inserted images shove aside anything that's already there to make room for themselves. Since text is aligned with the bottom of the image by default, that might result in a paragraph of text getting split in two by a space-hogging image (see Figure 9.9).

Fig. 9.9
If a graphic splits a paragraph like this, you can fix the problem without moving the graphic.

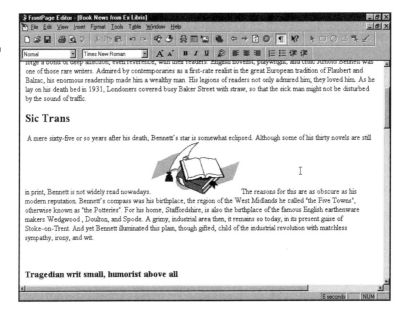

Wrapping text around an image will cure the problem illustrated in Figure 9.9. That places text neatly above, below, or on either side of the image. To get at FrontPage's text wrapping options:

1 Right-click the image and choose Image Properties on the context menu.

2 Click the Appearance tab of the Image Properties dialog box that pops up.

3 In the Appearance tab of the Image Properties dialog box, click the Alignment drop-down arrow, as shown in Figure 9.10.

Fig. 9.10
Here's where you control the way your text and graphics mesh together on the page.

4 Choose an alignment option on the drop-down menu shown in Figure 9.10. Your best bets are the Left or Right options. Left puts the image on the left margin and wraps text against the image's right side. Right puts the image on the right margin and wraps text against the image's left side. The other options give you different text wrapping choices:

- The bottom, middle, and top options align text with the bottom, middle, or top of the image.

- Absbottom and absmiddle align the image with the bottom or middle of the current line of text—the line that held the cursor when the image was inserted.

- Textop aligns the top of the image with the top of the tallest characters in the current line.

5 Click OK in the Image Properties dialog box to save your text wrapping option.

Apart from wrapping text, the Appearance tab of the Image Properties dialog box gives you a few more choices for controlling the way your image and your text coexist:

- If you want more space between the image and your text, enter values greater than zero in the Vertical and Horizontal Spacing text boxes (see Figure 9.10). That'll increase the amount of white space above or below and to the left and right of the image.

- For a border around your image, enter a new value in the Border Thickness text box. By default, it's set to zero, which gives you no border at all.

- If you care enough about the size of your image to want to specify its height and width in pixels, click the Specify Size checkbox and enter new values for Width and Height. Pixels, you'll recall, are the tiny dots of color of which everything on your computer screen is composed. If your screen resolution is set to 800×600, there are 800 pixels across the width and 600 pixels from top to bottom of the screen.

TIP **For precision layout of all your page elements, tables work best.** See Chapter 10, "The Miracle of Tables," for details on tables.

How can I blend my image into a colored background?

The problem: you chose a colored or textured background for your page, and your inserted GIF image, surrounded by white space, sticks out like a sore thumb.

The solution: make the image transparent. Click the image to select it. On the Image toolbar, which appears whenever an image is selected, click the Make Transparent button. Click the image again, and the image background will blend right into the page background.

This trick works with any GIF image, but not on JPEGs. Try to make a JPEG transparent, and FrontPage will offer to convert it to GIF format first. Since the conversion may alter or distort the image, you may not want to go through with it. FrontPage warns you before making the JPEG to GIF conversion, so click Cancel in the message box that appears to back out.

Horizontal lines: add the simplest graphic of all

If you consider simplicity a virtue, you'll approve of FrontPage's horizontal lines. Lines make good page breaks in long web pages, and they're very easy to work with. To add a plain line that spans the width of the editing window, click Insert, Horizontal Line. The line is inserted at the cursor.

To move the line, just drag it to another location on the page. And if all this seems too easy, you can format the line for a custom look. Right-click the line and choose Horizontal Line Properties on the context menu. That pops up the Horizontal Line Properties dialog box shown in Figure 9.11.

Fig. 9.11
For those not content with a simple line, introduce any variations you like right here.

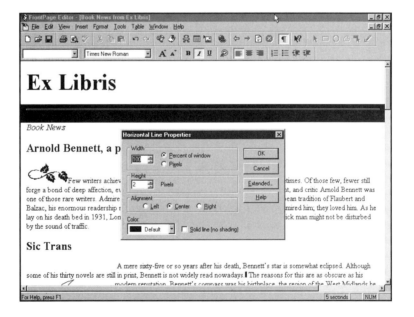

In the Horizontal Line Properties dialog box, change the line height, width, or color. Use the Alignment options to wrap text to the left or right of lines positioned inside a line of text.

Edit images to suit with the Image Composer

Although you can do a lot with an image and its surroundings in the FrontPage Editor, there's not much scope for altering the image contents. FrontPage has another component designed to do just that: the Microsoft Image Composer. The Image Composer has a host of high-powered tools to edit clip art, and to create original artwork. The Image Composer also comes with a large collection of ready-made images that you can pop into webs, either off the rack or after you customize them. The Image Composer is like a paint box, easel, and graphics design studio rolled into one. Since it works (fairly) seamlessly with the FrontPage Editor and Explorer, the Image Composer is worth getting acquainted with.

How do I change the colors in this image?

It could happen to anyone. You've inserted an image into the FrontPage Editor to include in your web, but it's the wrong color. You want a turtle in a soothing, restful shade; instead, the inserted turtle is a lurid green. To adjust the colors, and just about any other attribute, of a FrontPage image:

1. Double-click the image in the FrontPage Editor. That starts the Microsoft Image Composer, which appears in a moment or two with your selected image displayed (see Figure 9.12).

2. Click the Color Tuning button in the toolbox at the left of the Image Composer window (see Figure 9.12). The Color Tuning-Color Shifting tool palette appears. To tone down our livid green, click the Green option button on the Color Tuning-Color Shifting palette, and drag the Brightness control to the left, as shown in Figure 9.13.

3. Click Apply on the Color Tuning-Color Shifting tool palette to see the effects of your tinkering.

TIP Don't hesitate to experiment with the controls in the Image Composer. No alterations you make are permanent until you send the image back to the FrontPage Editor and save it there.

Chapter 9 *Picture This! Adding Graphics to Your Web* **163**

Fig. 9.12
Although it looks complicated, all the tools in the Image Composer are labeled. There's also plenty of online help if you get stuck.

Images are enclosed in a bounding box, whose borders are marked by handles.

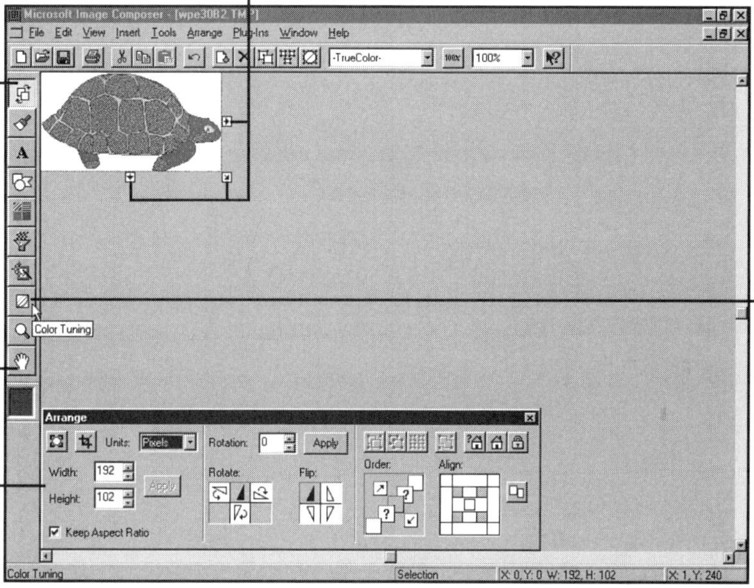

When you click one of these toolbox tools...

The Color Tuning tool

...you get a corresponding tool palette like this one.

Fig. 9.13
Adjusting the brightness and contrast of an image can make it blend into your page.

Negative values mean less of an attribute, positive numbers mean more of the attribute will be applied.

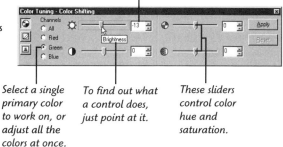

Select a single primary color to work on, or adjust all the colors at once.

To find out what a control does, just point at it.

These sliders control color hue and saturation.

4. Make any other adjustments you like with the Image Composer tools. When you're finished, click File, Send to FrontPage and close the Image Composer (just click the Close button in the upper right corner of the Window). That replaces the image in the FrontPage Editor with your altered version. If it still needs work, just double-click it to run the Image Composer again.

A modest color adjustment like this one is about the least that the Image Composer can do. There are myriad tools for image alterations, and for the creation of original works of art for use in your webs. The best way to get to know the Image Composer's powers is by experimenting. The tools are fun to play around with, and it won't cost you anything except your time.

Q&A *How do I get rid of excess white space around my inserted image?*

Some imported graphics files will have more white space around them than you need. To eliminate the excess space, double-click the image in the FrontPage Editor to run the Image Composer. On the Arrange tool palette, click the Crop/Extend button. Now drag a handle in toward the center of the image. If you choose a handle on the side with the excess space, you'll eliminate the space without affecting the image. Click File, Send to FrontPage and close the Image Composer when you're finished cropping the image.

There's a library of ready-to-use images in the Image Composer

The Microsoft Image Composer comes with a raft of images that you can pop into your webs. They're just not called images—the Image Composer refers to them as **Sprites.** What's a sprite? An image (although the official definition is "A single image object, composed of pixels, whose area is defined by its bounding box"). Why, you might ask, can't we just call them images? A very good question.

Here's another small Image Composer quirk: although you can view a catalog of the program's sprites without it, you'll need to load your FrontPage CD to actually insert a sprite into your web. To view the sprite collection, click Help, Sample Sprites Catalog. In the Help Topics: Sample Sprites Catalog dialog box, click the Contents tab, then double-click Sample Sprites.

Double-click Photos or Web to view the contents of either category. Photos are small pictures of animals, things, buildings—you name it. The Web category of sprites consists mostly of decorative graphics like icons, bullets, and fancy horizontal lines. Figure 9.14 shows samples from the Photos/Animals collection of sprites.

Chapter 9 *Picture This! Adding Graphics to Your Web* **165**

Fig. 9.14
These thumbnails represent images stored on the FrontPage 97 CD.

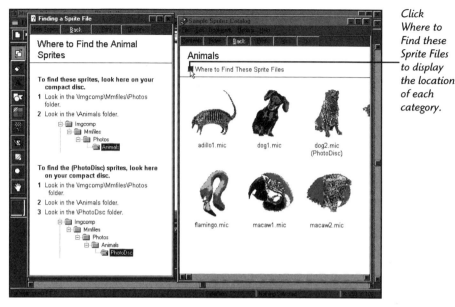

Click Where to Find these Sprite Files to display the location of each category.

When you find a sprite you want, you'll have to hunt it down on your FrontPage CD to insert it into the Image Composer:

1. Load the FrontPage 97 CD into your CD ROM drive.

2. Click the Where to Find these Sprite Files button in the Sample Sprites Catalog window (see Figure 9.14) for the file's location on the CD.

3. Click the Open button on the Image Composer toolbar. In the Open dialog box, navigate your way to the IMGCOMP\MMFILES folder, then open the subfolders shown in the Finding a Sprite File window until you reach your selected sprite file, as shown in Figure 9.15.

Fig. 9.15
It takes a bit of navigating to get there, but all the sprites are just clicks away.

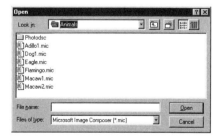

4. Double-click the file you want, and the sprite appears in the Image Composer window.

Now that you've loaded your sprite in the Image Composer window, you can resize it, recolor it, and alter it in any way you like. Or use it as is.

  Once you're satisfied with the sprite, the easiest way to get it from the Image Composer to your FrontPage Editor page is with good old copy and paste. Click the sprite, then click the Copy button on the Image Composer toolbar to copy it. Switch to the FrontPage Editor and click the Paste button on the Editor toolbar to pop the sprite into the page at the insertion point.

Although the sprite started life in the Microsoft Image Composer format (.mic), once inserted into a web page it automatically becomes a GIF file. To save the GIF file to your web, click the image in the Editor, and choose File, Save.

In the Save Image to FrontPage Web dialog box that appears, give your file a name and click Yes.

10

The Miracle of Tables

● **In this chapter:**

- Table setting with a mouse click

- Selecting columns, rows, and cells

- Aligning your cell contents

- The skinny on column widths

- I'd like to delete this row, and add a column here...

- Cells on the move!

- Border line decisions

- Shading: How to change table colors

A FrontPage table is more than just a data receptacle; it's an important tool for designing an attractive web page . . . . . ▶

Mention tables to most people, and you'll be greeted with a shrug and a yawn. Multiplication tables, tax tables, loan tables–what could be more prosaic?

Well, hold on to your hat, because you're about to gain a whole new perspective on the subject. FrontPage tables are more than simply vehicles for presenting data. They're your most important tool for web page design.

Tables give you freedom to arrange the elements of your page. They let you put colors and borders where you want them. Without tables, you're pretty much limited to arranging your text and graphics from top to bottom.

Consider the page in Figure 10.1. It's functional, but hardly eye-catching. With its varying text widths and huge patch of white space, the page is woefully out of balance. And there's not much you can do about it, except perhaps add a background image or play with different paragraph alignments.

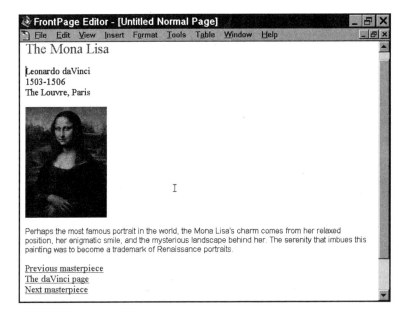

Fig. 10.1
Without tables, you're limited to arranging your page elements vertically.

Now look at Figure 10.2—the same material, only arranged in a table. Here, the graphic takes center stage, with the text more evenly balanced on either side. The table is a pastel yellow set against a light maroon background with bands of pastel blue highlighting the title and the links at the bottom. And the links are arranged to give the reader a visual sense of moving backward

(Previous Masterpiece) and forward (Next Masterpiece), as if he or she were viewing a slide show.

Fig. 10.2
Tables give you the flexibility to arrange your page elements the way you want them.

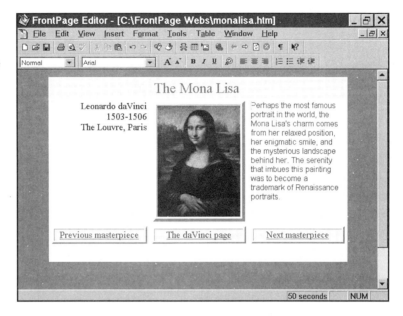

Tables do come with some baggage. They're easy to set up, but Editor doesn't give you a whole lot of tools to fine-tune them. Building a complex table can be a tedious and time-consuming task, and tables sometimes don't look the way you thought they would when you view them with a browser. Still, learning tables is essential if you want to add any design touches to your web.

Turning a table with your mouse

 Editor gives you a couple of ways to create an empty table, but the easiest is to use the Insert Table button on the Standard toolbar:

   1 Click the Insert Table button. A panel of squares representing the cells of your table drops down.

   2 Drag your mouse across and down the grid until you've got the number of columns and rows you want. The dimensions appear at the bottom of the grid. In Figure 10.3, for example, the table will be six rows by three columns. Your grid can have as many as 21 rows and 19 columns. For larger tables—up to 100 columns by 100 rows—choose T<u>a</u>ble, <u>I</u>nsert Table from the menu bar and use the Insert Table dialog box.

Fig. 10.3
The Insert Table button lets you create a table by dragging your mouse across a grid.

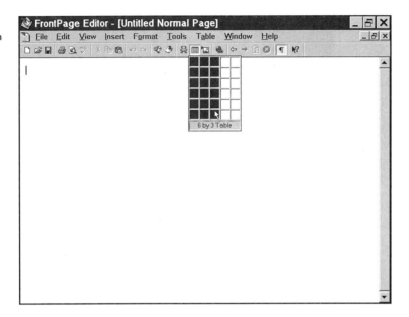

3 Release the mouse button to insert the table. Figure 10.4 shows the results of the process started in Figure 10.3.

Fig. 10.4
Your new table is ready to fill in.

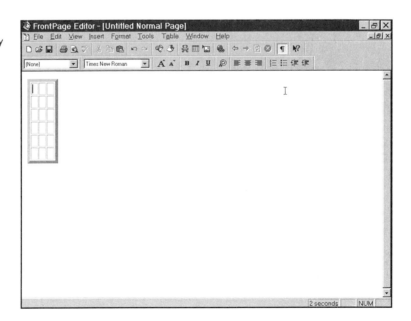

The appearance of your table depends on the settings in your Table Properties dialog box, which we'll talk about later. In this case, the table has a 6-pixel border with no specified column width. You're not stuck with these specifications, and we'll look at how to modify them in a moment.

Are you stuck forever with the number of rows or columns you give your table? No, they're easy to add and remove, as you'll learn in a little while.

Plain English, please!

A table is a **grid** made up of boxes called **cells.** A **row** is a string of cells that move from left to right; a **column** is a string of cells that moves from top to bottom. You can also think of a cell as the spot where a row and column intersect. A **border**, discussed later in this chapter, is a line that outlines your table and its cells. A **pixel**, which is short for **picture element**, is one of the dots that make up your display. The actual size of a pixel depends on the display adapter you've got in your computer. Common displays among PC computers include 640 pixels by 480 pixels and 800 pixels by 600 pixels.

Using the Insert Table dialog box

The Insert Table button is Editor's hacksaw; it's quick and easy, but you'll have to sand and file the table to get it into shape. But Editor also has a jigsaw that lets you shape your table as you make it—the Insert Table dialog box.

Choose T<u>a</u>ble, <u>I</u>nsert Table from the main menu to display the dialog box shown in Figure 10.5. Choose the number of rows and columns, up to 100 for either. Next, configure your table using the Layout and Width options. When you're done, choose OK to insert the table. Figure 10.6 shows the table created with the settings in Figure 10.5.

So what do those esoteric terms in the dialog box mean, and what values do you use? Read on for a quick overview.

Alignment

Alignment determines the horizontal placement of your table; your options are Left, Center, Right, and Default. Left and Right put the table on the left or right edge of the window, respectively. Center puts the table in the middle, with equal amounts of space on either side.

Fig. 10.5
The Insert Table dialog box lets you determine your table's appearance before you create it.

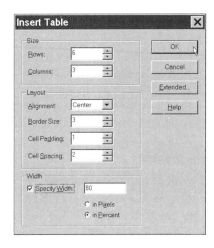

Fig. 10.6
Here's the table created with the settings in Figure 10.5.

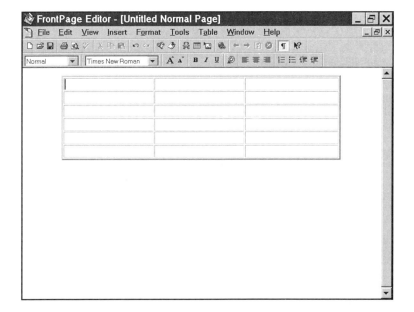

Default tells the table to use the alignment of the text before and after. If the text is centered, Default centers the table.

Order a border

Choose a border width, in pixels, between zero and 100. If you don't want a border, enter a zero. The border appears around your entire table, but also around each individual cell.

http://www.quecorp.com

You use no border when you want to hide the fact that you're using a table; the text and graphics in the table will appear to float on the page when viewed with a browser.

> **TIP** **If your table doesn't have borders, click the Show/Hide** button on your Standard toolbar or choose View, Format Marks from the menu bar. Editor outlines your cells so you can see them. The outline will not appear in a browser.

A little elbow room, please!

Editor offers a couple of tools to make what you put in your tables more readable. You can either change the *padding* within a cell or the *spacing* between cells in your table.

Cell padding is the space between a cell's contents and its borders. You can pad a cell by as much as 100 pixels.

The amount of padding you use depends on the contents of your cells. If your cells are going to be jammed with text, then you'll want some padding to separate the text from the borders. If your cell contains only a few words—a hyperlink, for example—then you might not need much padding.

Cell spacing is the amount of space between cells. Editor shows spacing as a border around each cell. The maximum amount of cell spacing you can use is 100 pixels.

Figure 10.7 shows you some examples of what your cells will look like with different amounts of padding and spacing.

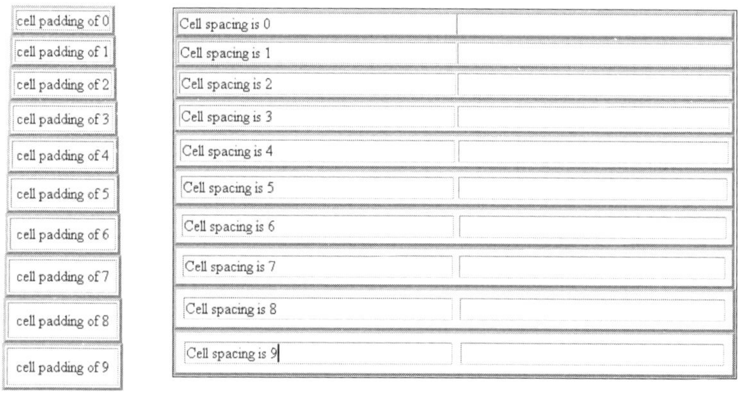

Fig. 10.7
Use cell padding to control the space between the cells' contents and borders; use cell spacing to change the space between cells.

Width or widthout?

Editor lets you specify the width of your table by checking the Specify Width checkbox and entering a value in the text box to the right. You can set your width in pixels or as a percent of the page; click the appropriate radio button below the text box.

Setting your width by the pixel is risky, because different computers have different resolutions. In other words, your screen might be 640 pixels wide, but somebody else's might be 800 pixels wide. Thus, a table that runs from edge to edge on your monitor will float on the other person's monitor.

If you choose a percent, the width of the table will expand in proportion to the width of the entire page. For example, if you choose 80 percent, the table will take 80 percent of the page width.

However you choose your width, be careful that it's enough to accommodate the cells and their contents. If you've got lots of text in lots of columns, a narrow table won't expand to make the text fit better; it'll simply squeeze the text into the available space.

If you don't specify a width, your table makes up its own mind how wide it will be, depending on the cells' contents. This isn't necessarily a bad thing, but if you make changes to your table, it might change its width without your permission.

Remember, your table settings aren't immutable; you can change any of them at any time. So you don't have to plan your table precisely before you set it up. Create the table first, then tinker with it later.

TIP **Tables within tables—it's possible to nest them like Russian dolls.** Why? Well, you might want to format two blocks of text in the same table differently. Or you might want to put a border around a title but not around the text beneath it. Nested tables also offer some interesting ways to layer colors on top of one another. But be careful; nested tables can lead to real formatting problems, some of which won't become apparent until you view the page in a browser. Pay special attention to how you set your table and cell widths. For example, if you set your nested table's width so that it's wider than the maximum width of the cell it's nested in, the tables might look fine in Editor, but the two tables' borders might overlap when opened in a browser.

Tables of content

An empty table is like an empty store, so it's time to look at how you go about stocking the shelves.

You can put just about anything in a table—body text, headings, graphics, hyperlinks, and WebBots. Keep this in mind as you apply what you learned about graphics in Chapter 9, "Picture This! Adding Graphics to Your Web," and as you read later chapters on forms (Chapter 14, "It's Good Form: Letting Your Readers Write Back") and WebBots (Chapter 15, "WebBots and other Web Bells and Whistles"). For now, though, we'll concentrate on text.

There's no trick to entering text in a table. Just place your insertion point in a cell and start typing. If you've set a width for your table, Editor wraps the text to the next line when you reach the right border of the cell, increasing the cell height to fit the text. When you're done typing, you have these options:

- Press the Tab key to move your insertion point to the next cell to the right. The right arrow key also works if you're at the end of the text.

- If you're in the last cell of the table, pressing the tab key adds a row to the table and puts your insertion point in its first cell.

- Press Shift+Tab to move to the next cell to the left. If you're at the beginning of the text, the left arrow key also does the job.

- If you're on the last line in the cell, press the down arrow to move down one cell.

- If you're on the first line in the cell, press the up arrow to move up one cell.

Q&A *Can I create a table from existing text, like I can in Word?*

Unfortunately, no. If you've got columnar material that you want to convert into a table, you've got two options. The long and tedious way is to create the table and manually move the text into the correct cells. The faster way is to copy the text to Word using the Clipboard, create the table using Word's table functions, and copy the table back into Editor. You'll have to tweak the table's properties, but you'll save yourself a lot of busy work up front.

TIP **Editor offers a convenient way to give your table a caption.** Choose Table, Insert Caption from the menu bar. Editor drops your table a line and centers your insertion point above the top row. Type your caption as you would regular text. You can use Editor's formatting tools to align and size the caption. If you want your caption at the bottom of the table, choose Table, Caption Properties and click the Bottom of Table radio button in the Caption Properties dialog box.

Natural selections

Like a chalkboard advertising today's specials at your local diner, a table in a web page can be an ever-changing tablet. How do you update, fix, and rearrange your table once you've finished it? First, you need to know something about selecting columns, rows, and cells.

To select a column, touch its top line with your pointer until the pointer is an arrow pointing down; then click the mouse button (see Figure 10.8).

Fig. 10.8
To select a column, touch the top line with your mouse pointer and click.

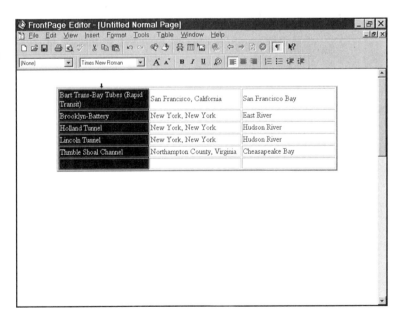

You can select several consecutive columns by clicking and dragging the mouse across the table.

To select several individual columns, hold down the shift key while you click the top line of each one.

You select rows in pretty much the same fashion. Select a row by putting the pointer to the left of the row and clicking once. Drag the pointer down to select several rows.

TIP To select the entire table, move your mouse pointer to the left of the table until it turns into an arrow and double-click. You also can choose Table, Select Table from the menu bar.

Pick a cell, any cell

Editor offers a couple of ways to select a cell. The easiest is to click the cell while pressing the Alt key. You also can move the pointer to the left of the cell until it becomes an arrow and click twice, but you'll feel like you're threading a needle while wearing mittens if you don't have much cell padding. In either case, the entire cell becomes highlighted, as shown in Figure 10.9.

Fig. 10.9
The hard way to select a cell: Move your pointer to the far left until it turns into an arrow and then double-click. Alt+click is easier.

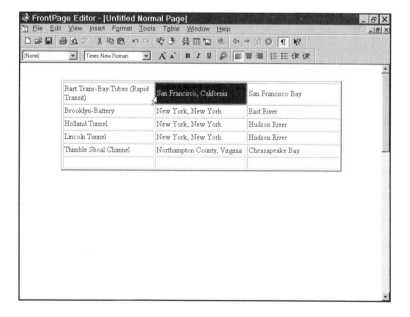

Editor offers some interesting options for selecting more than one cell. You not only can select contiguous cells; you can select several cells that are in different parts of the table.

To select contiguous cells, select the first cell, hold down the Shift key, and drag the mouse pointer across the remaining cells.

If you want to select several individual cells, select the first one and then select the rest by holding down the Ctrl key as you click. Use Ctrl+click to deselect a cell.

It might not be immediately obvious why you would want to select individual cells, but it's a handy trick for changing the properties of several cells in a single stroke, as we'll see later in this chapter.

Selecting just the cell text—what's the difference?

Editor provides a whole different set of tools for selecting only the text in a cell. In Figure 10.9, the entire cell has been selected; in Figure 10.10, only the words in the cell have been selected.

Fig. 10.10
Select the cell contents only when you want to format the contents, not the entire cell.

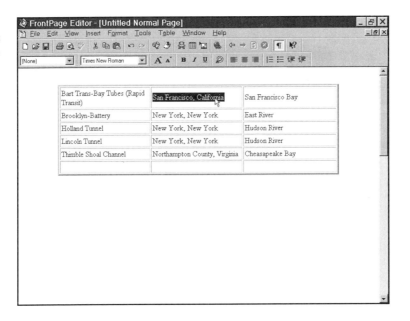

The difference is subtle and usually meaningless, but it's important enough to screw you up regularly if you do a lot of cell and text formatting. For example, the Increase and Decrease Indent buttons on the Formatting toolbar affect selected text but not selected cells, and the three align buttons on the Formatting toolbar get different results (see Figure 10.11).

Fig. 10.11
The top table shows the effects of formatting cells, while the bottom table shows the effects of the same formatting on text. Note the blank lines added in the bottom table.

Formatting actions performed on a cell		
Flush left	Centered	Flush right
San Francisco	San Francisco	San Francisco

Formatting actions performed on text in a cell		
Flush left	Centered	Flush right
San Francisco	San Francisco	San Francisco

You can use the same tools for selecting text in a table as you do for selecting regular text; see Chapter 6, "Editing Tools You'll Learn to Love," for more information. In addition, here are a few extra tools you can use in tables:

- To select the text in a cell, move the mouse pointer to the left of the text until it turns into an arrow and click once. This selects the first paragraph in the cell. If the cell holds more than one paragraph, hold down the mouse button and drag the arrow through the cell.

- Once you've selected the text in a cell, you can select the text in the previous or next cell in the row by holding down the Shift key and dragging the insertion point.

- To select the text in the next cell in the row, press the Tab key.

- To select the text in the previous cell in the row, press Shift+Tab.

TIP You can select a column or row with the right mouse button the same way you do with the left mouse button, only a shortcut menu with common table commands pops up.

Custom alterations

Now that you've learned how to select columns, rows, and cells, it's time to talk about how you can alter the structure of your table. Column widths, inserting and deleting rows and columns, merging cells—these are all tasks that you'll perform routinely as you prepare your table for publication on your web.

Changing your table's properties

Remember that table we created in two seconds with the Table Insert button? It's the one shown in Figure 10.4. Inserting a table this way is fast and simple, but you forego configuring the table the way you do when you set one up with the Table, Insert Table command. How can you retroactively change such options as alignment, width, and cell padding?

The answer: the Table Properties dialog box, shown in Figure 10.12. Right-click the table and choose Table Properties, or choose Table, Table Properties from the menu bar.

Fig. 10.12
Make changes to a table you've already created with the Table Properties dialog box.

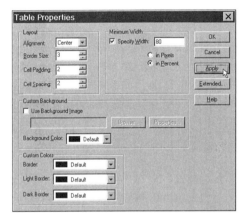

The Table Properties dialog box offers all of the options available in the Insert Table dialog box. (It also includes the functions you need to change colors, which we'll get to in a minute.) Make your changes and take one of these steps:

Choose OK to accept the changes and return to the web page.

Choose Apply to make the changes but keep the dialog box open. This feature is handy when you want to experiment with different values in one of the text boxes or with your colors; just click and drag the dialog box by the title bar to move it out of the way.

Changing your cells' properties

So far, we've talked mostly about changing the look of the entire table. But Editor also lets you change the properties of individual cells, using—no surprise here—the Cell Properties dialog box.

To change the properties of a single cell, right-click the cell and choose Cell Properties from the quick menu. If you've got several cells that you want to change to the same configuration, *don't* do them one by one; the monotony will kill you. Instead, select the cells you want to change, then right-click any of the selected cells to pop up the quick menu.

What exactly can you change about the cell? Give the Cell Properties dialog box in Figure 10.13 a quick look and read on.

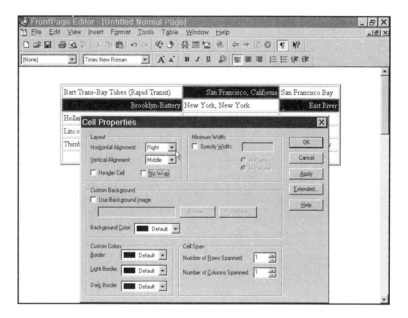

Fig. 10.13
Use the Cell Properties dialog box to change the layout, width, background, and border colors of individual rows, columns, and cells.

Align again, naturally

Cell Properties gives you two ways to set the alignment of a cell's contents—horizontally and vertically.

Click the arrow next to the Horizontal Alignment text box and choose left, center, or right. Left begins the contents at the left edge of the box; center places the contents midway between the left and right edges; and right pushes the contents against the right edge. Figure 10.14 shows an example of each.

Fig. 10.14
Choose left, center, or right alignment in the Cell Properties dialog box to get these three results.

Vertical alignment controls the position of the cell's contents relative to the top and bottom edges of the cell. Again, you have three choices: Top places the contents at the upper edge of the cell, Middle centers the contents between the top and bottom, and Bottom drops the contents to the bottom edge.

Vertical alignment is particularly useful when you're aligning text in adjacent cells that are of different heights. In Figure 10.15, for example, the cells in the first row of each table are higher than the cells in the second row; the three different alignments provide three distinct effects.

Fig. 10.15
Vertical alignment controls the space above and below the contents of a cell.

How to change column widths

A table can start to look pretty ragged if you let each column take whatever space you think it needs. If you think a column needs to be expanded or narrowed, you can do the job with the Specify Width option.

You can set the width of a column from within any cell in that column, but it's not a good idea, as we'll see in a moment. You're better off selecting the entire column and then opening the Cell Properties dialog box. Place a check in the Specify Width checkbox, and then click either the In Pixels or In Percent radio button. Finally, place a value in the Specify Width text box.

Changing column widths is tricky business, and you'll probably have to try different values before you get it right. Here are a few pointers to help you along:

- Set your widths with percentages, not pixels, since you don't know the screen resolution at which your users will view your table.

- Don't set a column width by a single cell. Each cell in a column theoretically can have a different width, but the column will assume the width of the widest cell. Resetting the width of a cell that's narrower than another cell will not have any effect on the column, and you'll waste time trying to figure out why your width setting isn't working.

- Make sure all of your column widths combined don't add up to more than 100 percent. Editor lets you do it, but you might get unwanted results when the page is viewed in a browser.

- Check your finished table in a browser. Tables with set column widths are just plain flaky, and you can't trust what you see in Editor.

TIP Speaking of unpredictable column widths, here's another Cell Properties feature you should use with care: No Wrap. When you check the No Wrap checkbox, the text in a cell will not wrap when viewed with a browser; that is, the browser will show it on one line, no matter what your column and table widths. A long line can expand the cell, column, and table beyond the edge of the screen. You won't see the effects of No Wrap in Editor, so if you use it, make sure you look at the page in a browser before publication.

How to change several columns at once

You can change several column widths at the same time by selecting the columns before opening the Cell Properties dialog box.

TIP Are your column widths all messed up? Can't figure out what's wrong? Sometimes your best bet is to start over. Select the entire table, open the Cell Properties dialog box, and clear the Specify Width checkbox.

Tables, more or less: Adding and deleting cells

A vegetable garden must be planned precisely before you start planting. If you want to add an extra row of beans in the middle of July, you'd better make sure you leave space when you lay out the patch in May.

Editor's tables aren't quite as rigid. You can add and delete rows, columns, and individual cells at any time—although sometimes with unpredictable consequences.

Inserting rows and columns

To insert a row, place your insertion point anywhere in the row that will precede or follow your new row. Choose T<u>a</u>ble, <u>I</u>nsert Rows or Columns from the menu bar. Editor displays the Insert Rows or Columns dialog box shown in Figure 10.16.

Fig. 10.16
Insert as many rows or columns as you need at the insertion point.

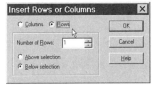

Click the Rows radio button. Then, in the Number of <u>R</u>ows selection box, choose the number of rows you want to add. Finally, choose whether you want the new row above or below the current row by clicking <u>A</u>bove Selection or <u>B</u>elow Selection, and choose OK.

You insert a column the same way you insert a row; simply choose the <u>C</u>olumns radio button in the Insert Rows or Columns dialog box. Your choices for where to put the columns change to <u>L</u>eft of Selection and <u>R</u>ight of Selection.

Cell by cell

You can insert a single cell in your table, as well. Place your insertion point where you want to insert the cell, and choose Insert T<u>a</u>ble, Insert Ce<u>l</u>l from the menu bar.

Editor inserts the cell at the insertion point. If the insertion point is in the middle of your text, then your new cell will split your text. If you don't want that to happen, make sure your insertion point is at the beginning or end of your cell text.

Here's an additional warning: Inserting single cells can lead to unwanted rearrangements of your table. When you insert a cell, Editor moves all cells to the right by one column. That is, the current cell moves into the next column, the cell in that column moves into the next column, and so forth. If you don't like the results, choose Undo to return the table to its former setup.

Why insert a cell?

If you're used to thinking of tables as mere vehicles for tabular data, the ability to insert a single cell might not seem too useful. But single cell insertion can be a valuable tool when you're arranging design elements. Consider the table in Figure 10.17. It's a conventional two columns by four rows. But let's say we want to insert a graphic at the beginning of the first row. Inserting a single cell provides the space, as in Figure 10.18. Insert the graphic into the new cell, and your page has a new design. Figure 10.19 shows the results.

Fig. 10.17
The original table...

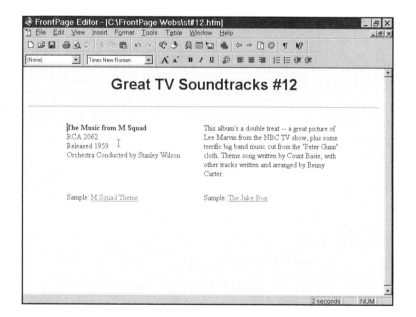

Fig. 10.18
...the table with a cell inserted at the beginning of the first row...

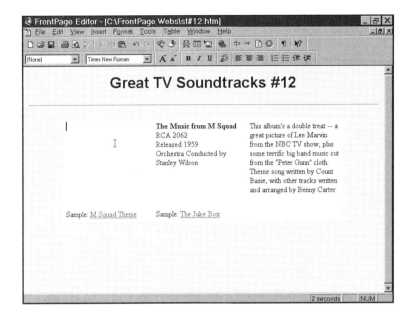

Fig. 10.19
...and the final table with a graphic inserted into the new cell.

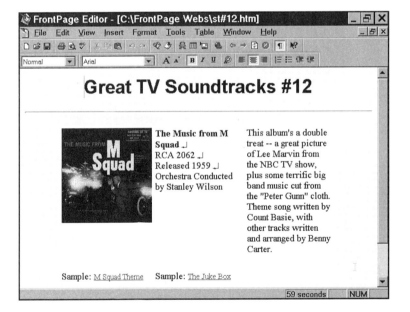

Wipeout! Deleting rows, columns, and cells

Editor's tool for deleting cells is so obvious, it's easy to overlook: the Delete key. Just highlight the row, column, or cells you want to get rid of and press Delete.

Here are a few rules to remember when you're deleting:

- You don't have to select a single cell if the cell's empty; just put the insertion point in the cell and press Delete.

- You can also delete selected cells with the Cut command; click the Cut button on the Standard toolbar, press Ctrl+X, choose Edit, Cut from the menu bar, or choose Cut from the quick menu.

- When you delete a cell, all cells to the right move left one row.

- If you make an accidental deletion, don't forget that Undo is always there to bail you out.

Move it on over: moving rows and columns

Have you ever watched someone move a house? Before they load the house onto a flatbed and drive it to the new site, they have to build a foundation on which to put the house.

Moving rows and columns in Editor is much the same. Unlike Word tables, which let you insert and move in one step, Editor tables require three steps: Insert the new column or row, cut the old one, and paste the old one into the new one.

Say, for example, that we want to move the Waterway column in Figure 10.20 between the Tunnel and Location columns. Here's how:

Fig. 10.20
How do you move the Waterway column to between the Tunnel and Location columns?

Tunnel	Location	Waterway
Bart Trans-Bay Tubes (Rapid Transit)	San Francisco, California	San Francisco Bay
Brooklyn-Battery	New York, New York	East River
Holland Tunnel	New York, New York	Hudson River
Lincoln Tunnel	New York, New York	Hudson River
Thimble Shoal Channel	Northampton County, Virginia	Cheasapeake Bay

1. Insert a column between columns one and two, or, in our example, the Tunnel and Location columns (see Figure 10.21).

2. Select the column to be moved (the Waterway column) and cut it, using the Cut button on the Standard toolbar or one of Editor's other cutting tools.

3. Select the inserted column (see Figure 10.22).

4. Paste the old column into the new column, using the Paste button on the Standard toolbar or one of Editor's other methods for pasting. Figure 10.23 shows the result.

Fig. 10.21
Add the new column first...

Tunnel	Location	Waterway
Bart Trans-Bay Tubes (Rapid Transit)	San Francisco, California	San Francisco Bay
Brooklyn-Battery	New York, New York	East River
Holland Tunnel	New York, New York	Hudson River
Lincoln Tunnel	New York, New York	Hudson River
Thimble Shoal Channel	Northampton County, Virginia	Cheasapeake Bay

Fig. 10.22
...cut the Waterway column and select the new column...

Tunnel		Location
Bart Trans-Bay Tubes (Rapid Transit)		San Francisco, California
Brooklyn-Battery		New York, New York
Holland Tunnel		New York, New York
Lincoln Tunnel		New York, New York
Thimble Shoal Channel		Northampton County, Virginia

Fig. 10.23
...and paste the column into its new location.

Tunnel	Waterway	Location
Bart Trans-Bay Tubes (Rapid Transit)	San Francisco Bay	San Francisco, California
Brooklyn-Battery	East River	New York, New York
Holland Tunnel	Hudson River	New York, New York
Lincoln Tunnel	Hudson River	New York, New York
Thimble Shoal Channel	Cheasapeake Bay	Northampton County, Virginia

You move a row the same way; insert the new row, cut the old row, and paste the old row into the new row.

TIP **You can copy rows and columns with a nearly identical procedure.** Instead of cutting the row or column, copy it with the Copy button on the Standard toolbar or with one of Editor's other Copy tools.

http://www.quecorp.com

Moving and copying cells

Yes, you can move and copy individual cells, too. Follow the same steps you use to move and copy rows and columns. Select the cell. Choose Cut if you're moving it or Copy if you're copying it. Select the destination cell and choose Paste.

Make sure you select the entire destination cell. If you select only its contents, or simply put the insertion point in the cell, Editor inserts the targeted cell inside the destination cell; that is, you'll end up with a cell within a cell.

 Whether you're moving cells, rows, or columns, you must select an equal number of destination cells. For example, if the row you're moving has three cells, the row you're moving it to must also have three cells.

Let's talk about borders

When you decide to hang a picture on your wall, you first decide if it needs a frame. Then you go to the local framery and pick one that's appropriate for the picture. A frame that's right for an old sepia photo of grandpa in his flivver probably won't be the one you choose for your Jimi Hendrix blacklight poster.

Your table's borders are its frame. By default, Editor gives you a generic, $1.99-at-Woolworth's border. But you've got several options for changing the border's color and appearance to meet your needs.

When you give your table a border, you're actually adding two elements: A border around the entire table and separate borders around each individual cell. You can change the width only of the outer border, but you can change the colors of the outside and inside borders.

 Remember, you change the width of your border from the Table Properties dialog box. Choose Table, Table Properties from the menu bar or quick menu, and adjust the value in the Border Size text box.

Both the outer and inner borders consist of two sets of lines, one light and one dark, to give the table a three-dimensional appearance. The contrast is hard to see if you use thin borders. You'll notice it on the outside border if you select a wide border, such as in the 24-pixel border shown in Figure 10.24, and you'll see the contrast in the inner borders if you use colors.

In the outer border, the light lines are at the top and left, while the dark lines are at the bottom and right. The scheme is reversed in the inner borders (see Figure 10.24).

Fig. 10.24
This 24-pixel border reveals that borders by default have light and dark sides.

Most of the changes you can make to your borders are with color, using the Table Properties and Cell Properties dialog boxes. Let's look at some of the options.

Coloring the borders

You change the colors of your borders using three options beneath the custom colors heading in the Table Properties dialog box.

> To change all borders, inside and outside, to the same color, choose a color from the Border selection box.

> To change all of the light borders, choose a color from the Light Border selection box.

> To change all of the dark borders, choose a color from the Dark Border selection box.

Inside borders: setting a different tone

Are you stuck with the same colors for your inside and outside borders? No. You can change the colors of the borders around each cell regardless of what you color the outside border.

First, use the Table Properties box and make your selections beneath the Custom Colors heading. These will be the colors of your outside border.

Next, select the cells whose borders you want different. Open the Cell Properties dialog box, where you'll find the same Custom Colors options available in the Table Properties dialog box. The choices you make here will apply only to the borders of the selected cells and override your choices for the table.

Disappearing borders

You can get some neat effects by removing the inner borders. Technically, you can't actually get rid of them, but you can hide them by changing the appropriate Border color to match the background color.

In Figure 10.25, for example, the borders surrounding the cells in the first row have been changed to white to match the background, giving the titles the appearance of floating above the chart.

Fig. 10.25
The row's first cell borders were changed to white, making them disappear and the headings seem to float.

Tunnel	Waterway	Location
Bart Trans-Bay Tubes (Rapid Transit)	San Francisco Bay	San Francisco, California
Brooklyn-Battery	East River	New York, New York
Holland Tunnel	Hudson River	New York, New York
Lincoln Tunnel	Hudson River	New York, New York
Thimble Shoal Channel	Cheasapeake Bay	Northampton County, Virginia

Shady deals

As you found out in Chapter 8, "Color Me Fun!," or from your own tinkering, you can't give your page more than one background color. But that doesn't mean you can't add new colors wherever you want them. Just create a table and use different backgrounds for the table or the individual cells.

Let's say, for example, that you want to change the table in Figure 10.25 so that the row of titles is red and the rest of the table is gray. First, open the Table Properties dialog box and change Background Color to silver. Then, select the first row, open the Table Properties dialog box, and change Background Color to red.

Part IV: Building Your Web Site

Chapter 11: **The Best-Laid Schemes: Web Planning and Design**

Chapter 12: **Webward Ho! Adding Pages to Your Web**

Chapter 13: **Lights, Action, Click! Hotspots, Video, and Sound**

The Best-Laid Schemes: Web Planning and Design

● In this chapter:

- Do I really need a web building plan?
- I want to avoid common web problems
- What makes a web great?
- How can I tell if my web is structurally sound?

Planning a web is like visiting the dentist. It's more duty than pleasure now, but it's the sure way to prevent future pain.

Unlike, say, a sweet tooth, inability to predict the future is a human failing that can't be corrected. That's why planning of any kind is a headache. Sometimes it's a migraine. On a June morning in 1944, Dwight D. Eisenhower's invasion planning for occupied Europe had to account for hundreds of thousands of American and Allied soldiers, thousands of transport ships and landing craft, and hundreds of warships. We Computer Age types might note that Ike's operation succeeded without the aid of so much as a pocket calculator.

However ambitious, your web planning and design won't involve that many variables, nor is the immediate future quite as uncertain as it was for Eisenhower and his command. Still, as your web expands past a simple home page with a few links, a little preparation beforehand will save time and trouble later. And FrontPage includes some handy tools to help your advance work. As Eisenhower himself liked to say "…plans are useless, but planning is indispensable."

What makes a good Web site?

Although the book publishing industry has been around for hundreds of years, publishers are the first to admit that producing a successful book is more art than science. But how success is measured, at least from the publisher's point of view, is a simple matter of arithmetic. The more sales it racks up, the better the book. Gauging the success of a Web site isn't as straightforward. The most common measure is the number of visitors the site attracts. That's a little like judging a book's success by how many people look at it in bookstores, but keeping a visitor count is the only empirical measure of Web success we've got.

How does a Web site generate traffic? Consultants get paid large fees to answer that question, but perhaps we can come up with a couple of ideas on our own:

Subject matter is any Web site's biggest draw. A compelling topic will bring in the crowds regardless of the quality of the site's design. An obvious point perhaps, but one that many sites, loaded with flashy graphics and special effects at the expense of solid content, would do well to recall. And even if your topic doesn't have universal appeal, content is still king. Not everyone is a butterfly fancier, but if you've assembled the Web's authoritative collection of material on lepidoptera, you'll get plenty of visitors. It's no accident that one of the Web's most visited sites holds more "content" than any other place on earth (see Figure 11.1).

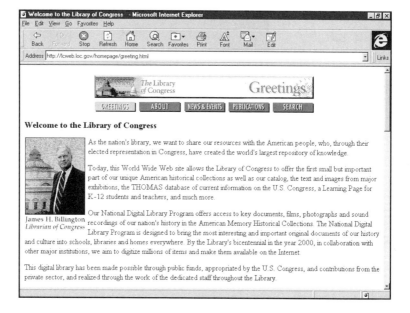

Fig. 11.1
The Web site of the world's biggest library gets millions of visitors each month.

Failing authoritative, or even merely solid, content, some Web sites succeed because they've hit on an appealing theme. When was the last time you gnashed your teeth over the antics of uncivil and reckless fellow motorists? This morning? I thought so. One Web site got a lot of attention for its archive of heartstopping freeway follies, compiled during the site creators' morning commute on Highway 17 in California (see Figure 11.2).

For all the attention that's placed on how Web pages look, what's in the pages is more important. Assemble your content and refine your theme first, and then turn your attention to the web's structure and appearance.

Fig. 11.2
Did you encounter a Jerque du Jour today? This Web site struck a responsive chord in many.

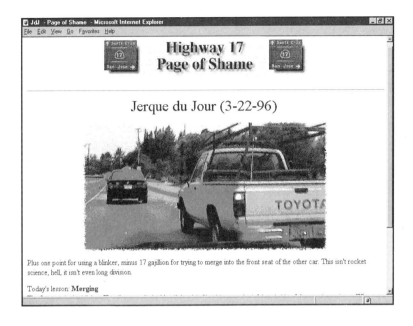

Draw visitors into your web by avoiding Web woes

As the web designer, you want to entice visitors to stop and explore your site, read your pages, and perhaps return as regulars. You can't exactly ensure all these things, but you can help give your work its best chance for success. There are millions of Web pages on the Internet, and though they're all different, many share a handful of annoying characteristics guaranteed to put off potential visitors. You can probably make your own list of Web woes, irritants that drive you away from a site as soon as you get there. The following are the things that make me reach for the browser Back button.

This page loads too slooowly

Pages that take too long to load are intolerable. How long is too long? For me, it's twenty-five seconds or so. If a page takes longer than that to appear, I'm gone. You eliminate the possibility that visitors will leave before they see your work by keeping graphics small in both size and number. Fine, but what if the site must have many large graphics? A Web site for the local historical museum might want to include plenty of scanned photos of the exhibits, for example. If that's the situation, put each graphic on a separate page and link them to a table of contents page. You can even put small copies of the larger images on the table of contents page and link them to their bigger twins (see Chapter 13, "Lights, Action, Click! Hotspots, Video, and Sound," for details on how to do that). Figure 11.3 shows a page with thumbnail images that are links to full-size copies on other pages.

Fig. 11.3
These images are all clickable links to larger versions, and this page only took about twelve seconds to load in my browser.

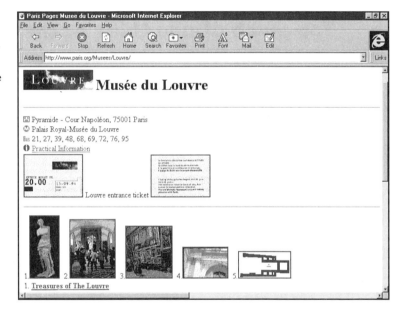

Semi-literacy isn't close enough

Pages burdened with bad writing and poor spelling are certain to drive away visitors. FrontPage has a spell checker to cure the latter problem. *The Chicago Manual of Style*, Strunk and White's *Elements of Style*, and Fowler's *Modern English Usage* all help to eliminate the former affliction. The standards that apply to writing anywhere else apply to writing on the Web. Nobody expects deathless prose or timeless verse, but clarity, brevity, and adherence to the conventions of English grammar are not too much to ask for. Careful proofreading will help produce clean pages. You might try printing your pages as a proofreading aid. Seeing what you've written in the cold light of print often has a salutary, not to say sobering, effect.

An endless loop of links

How many times have you clicked a promising link and waited patiently, only to be greeted by a page with nothing on it except another link? Which in certain egregious cases leads to yet another empty-but-for-a-link page? If you find Web sites like that annoying, help make the Web a better place by not producing one of your own. If visitors take the trouble to load your page into their browsers, give them something more than just another link.

Too much of one thing or the other

Unless it's the subject of the page, avoid large photographs. They leave room for only a sprinkling of text, and you might lose visitors while they wait for the thing to appear in their browsers. Pages of solid, unbroken text are almost as bad. Reading a computer screen is hard on the eyes, but you can relieve the strain with plenty of white space. Some other ideas for breaking up chunks of text to make it more readable:

- Use plenty of headings.
- A horizontal line or two makes an effective page break.
- Pictures aren't always needed to break-up text. One effective page design trick pulls a quotation from the text, and sets it off from the rest of the text with horizontal lines or different formatting (see Figure 11.4 for an example).

Figure 11.4 shows the same text formatted for minimal and for maximum readability.

TIP **Don't want to bother indenting each paragraph to add white space to a page of text?** Click File, Page Properties, Margins. On the Margins tab of the Page Properties dialog box, click the Specify Left Margin checkbox and enter a new value in the text box. You won't get quite the same effect as that shown in Figure 11.4 because FrontPage doesn't let you adjust the right margin.

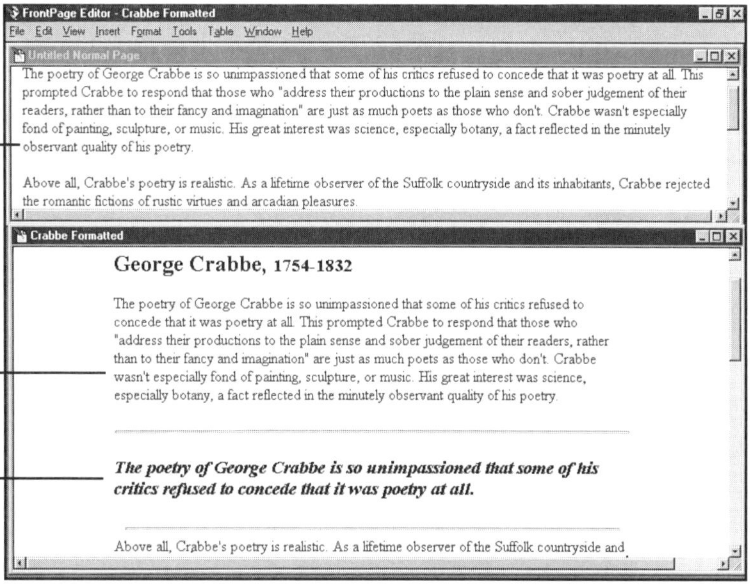

Fig. 11.4
You don't need graphics to make a page of text more inviting to read.

A solid window of text is hard on the eyes.

Indenting each paragraph adds white space.

Quote from your own text, and set it off with lines and bold italics.

What's this page all about?

Just as a good newspaper story gives you the who, why, what, and where in the first couple of paragraphs, Web pages ought to say clearly what they're all about. A good main heading, with a short statement on the purpose and contents of the site parked below it, should be a requirement for any home page. Web surfers, like newspaper readers, are skimmers. They're in a hurry, and they'll be impatient with anything that doesn't tell them what they want to know at a glance.

Newspaper reporters call their first sentences "the lead," and most will spend extra time getting their leads right. A well-crafted lead draws the reader into the story; a dull lead loses the reader fast. Your short introductory statement at the top of the page is your lead, and it's worth all the care you can give it. Writers of all kinds tend to revisit their leads constantly, writing and re-writing until they're sure they've given it their best. Consider the crafting of a lead for an epic novel hundreds of pages long; how on earth do you start such a mammoth enterprise? Herman Melville solved the problem famously with the first line of *Moby Dick*: "Call me Ishmael."

Figure 11.5 shows a Web page with a "lead" that, while unlikely to take its place alongside Melville's, does its job.

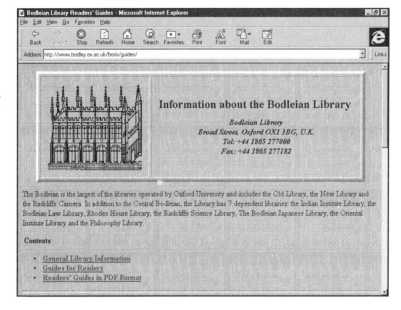

Fig. 11.5
On this Web page, the heading tells you exactly what the page is all about, and the text below the title captures the essence of the page.

Invisible text *is* unreadable text

It seems too obvious to rate a mention, but since so many Web pages are guilty of it, here goes: plan your fonts and backgrounds so that the text on the page is readable. Dark purple text against a black background is atmospheric, and also invisible. Contrast is the watchword when selecting text and background colors. Isn't it surprising how many Web pages ignore this seeming no-brainer? See Chapter 8 "Color Me Fun!" for details on matching background and font colors.

Blinking and scrolling text, though more readable than invisible text, might be just as annoying. The novelty wears off very quickly. Visitors will either ignore it after their first glance, or become irritated and clear out. Chapter 7, "Form and Function: Formatting Text," has some ideas on how to reduce the potential annoyance of text that doesn't sit still.

Consistency is the mother of attention

As you add pages to your web, keep your formatting consistent. Try to stick with a single color scheme and layout for all your pages. Web sites with coordinated interior decorating look better than sites with a distracting jumble of different formatting effects. They also have the practical benefit of reassuring visitors that they're still within the site as they click from page to page.

Planning a structurally sound web

There's a lot to be said for the design of the average book. Turn the pages to go forwards or backwards, glance in the index or the table of contents to find what you're looking for, orient yourself with the page numbers—operating a book is elegantly simple. Web designers would do well to keep the example of the book in mind when they plan their sites.

Just as a book starts with an outline, you might want to begin designing your web with a plan of the site. Pencil and paper, while low tech, work best for this job. Prepare a rough sketch, showing how many pages you plan on including, and what you intend to put in each page. Precision isn't required, but even the roughest draft of the web's design will be helpful as you add and link pages. Bear in mind that a web isn't exactly like a book. Book readers progress sequentially from page to page, chapter to chapter. Web surfers jump around in random fashion.

Still, the aims of both book and web are similar: to be informative, entertaining, easy to navigate, and habit forming. And as with a book, assembling attractive pages is the first step; binding the pages together comes next. Links are the binding of a web, the links that connect the pages within the web, and the links that connect the web to the rest of the network.

Well-forged links make a stronger web

Links, like branches on a tree, tend to grow in number as your web gets bigger. You'll discover relevant links on your trips through cyberspace, and you'll want to add them to your own site. That's fine, because a Web site with many links to related pages is a richer site. You want, however, to start with a logical series of links within your own site. That'll let your visitors get around the site with ease. There are two sets of links that every Web site should include:

- Your home page is a combination book cover and table of contents, in which you'll want to include links to all the important pages in the web. It's common to arrange such a series of links in a bulleted list, an arrangement that's both attractive and practical (see Figure 11.6.) As an alternative to a list of links, many sites use an image map, a collection of clickable images that act as links to other pages (see Chapter 13 for information on creating image maps.)

Fig. 11.6
Web TOCs come in many forms, but bulleted lists and image maps are standard.

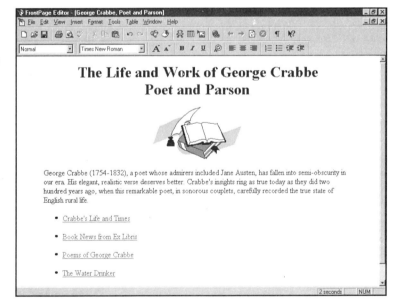

Chapter 11 *The Best-Laid Schemes: Web Planning and Design* **205**

- The web contents, listed and introduced in the home page, are distributed throughout the pages of the web. It makes sense to avoid very long single web pages, since visitors who can't be bothered to scroll will miss important material at the bottom of the page. Instead, break up your material into topics, and give each topic a separate page. Most visitors will find it easier to click a topic heading than to scroll great distances down a page. And with home page links to each topic page, that's exactly what they'll get.

- Visitors clicking their way through a labyrinth of pages in a site can lose their way. To help them reorient themselves, include a link back to your home page on each of the other pages in the web. It's as though you were browsing through a fat reference book and stuck scraps of paper between the crucial pages of the index. Though low-tech, that's an effective way to find your way back along paths that you've already trodden. Links from your other pages back to the home page serve the same purpose.

Once you've established links to your pages on the home page, and links back to the home page on each of the other pages in the web, check your work. Click the Hyperlink View button on the FrontPage Explorer toolbar to see the structure of your web, as shown in Figure 11.7.

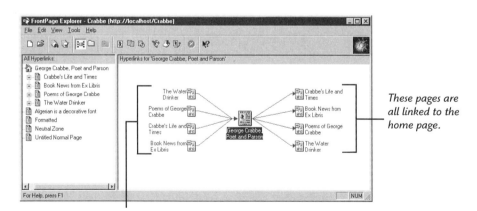

Fig. 11.7
The Explorer's Hyperlink View shows the skeleton of the web, free from the clutter of the pages themselves.

These pages are all linked to the home page.

Each page has a link back to the home page.

No matter how many other links you add, a basic structure like the one shown in Figure 11.7 makes it easy for your visitors to get around the site.

Put your web to the test

A new web is like any new invention; you don't know if it works until you try it out. Set aside some time to test your web before allowing visitors in. You'll want to make sure that all the links work as advertised, and that the formatting looks the way you intended it to look.

You can't test your web until you publish it (see Chapter 19, "This Web Is Suitable for Publication," on publishing webs). Once it's actually up and running on your internet service provider's server, give it the treatment. Click each link and time the downloading of each page. Although the FrontPage Editor displays the approximate download time of web pages, "real world" times may be quite a bit longer. If possible, view your web in different browsers. Pages that look fine in the Microsoft Internet Explorer may not look as fine in the Netscape Navigator. Whenever you make changes to the web, test it again.

There's no reason to think that all won't work as planned. But since the best-laid schemes can go awry, make comprehensive testing part of your web building plans.

12
Webward Ho! Adding Pages to Your Web

● In this chapter:

- How do I add a page to my site?
- Ties that bind: creating hyperlinks
- Link first, build the page later
- How to import pages
- Can I import a page from the WWW?
- How to link to audio/graphic files
- Linking with Bookmarks
- How to insert text files and non-HTML documents

A few pages here, a few hyperlinks there—and pretty soon you've got a full-fledged web on your hands . . . . ➢

One flyer advertises an old refrigerator. Another seeks a roommate. A third announces next week's church rummage sale. Welcome to the community bulletin board, that time-honored news service that graces a wall of nearly every Laundromat, library, and corner store.

In many respects, the World Wide Web is like a bulletin board. Thousands of simple, single-page webs provide news and views on an endless variety of subjects. Perhaps your web is one of them, a humble leaflet stapled to the cork of cyberspace.

So what happens if you've got more than a few words to say? Perhaps your flyer has expanded into a brochure, or even a book. You can cram everything onto one web page, just as you can tape a bunch of flyers end to end and hang them from the Laundromat ceiling. But long, endlessly scrolling pages are unwieldy to read—and, not incidentally, take longer to load into a browser. It's time to add pages to your web.

Chapter 11, "The Best-Laid Schemes: Web Planning and Design," covered how to plan your web, so we won't spend much time in this chapter discussing organizational issues. We'll assume that you've got ideas on what you want your web to look like. Now it's time to get down to the nitty-gritty—adding pages and binding them together with hyperlinks.

Paging all webs!

Let's start with the basics—a single-page web to which we're going to add a second page. You start by opening the web in FrontPage Explorer and then opening the home page in Editor. Next, choose File, New from Editor's menu bar or press Ctrl+N. Editor opens the New Page dialog box, shown in Figure 12.1.

Fig. 12.1
The New Page dialog box lets you choose from a number of templates and wizards, preformatted and ready to fill in.

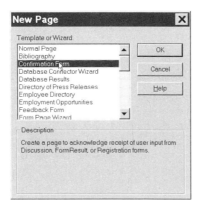

Remember how Explorer provided templates and wizards to set up a web? Well, Editor provides the same, 30 in all, to set up new pages. Use your arrow keys to scroll through the list; as you highlight each, a description of the template or wizard appears in the Description box below.

Most of the templates become useful only after you've learned about hyperlinks, since you have to modify them for your own needs. But you also can teach yourself something about hyperlinks and bookmarks by loading and studying the templates.

For now, we'll use the Normal template, which creates a blank web page. Either double-click Normal Page twice or select it and choose the OK button. Editor opens the page in a new window.

 TIP To open a Normal page without going through the New Page dialog box, click the New button on the Standard toolbar.

How do I move from page to page?

Once you've got two or more pages open, you'll want to move among them. Editor offers several tools.

You can get a list of open pages by choosing Window from the menu bar. In Figure 12.2, for example, three pages are open: Home Page, an untitled page, and Tullie. Switch to any page by clicking it or pressing the number that precedes it.

Fig. 12.2
Use the Window command to move quickly to any open page.

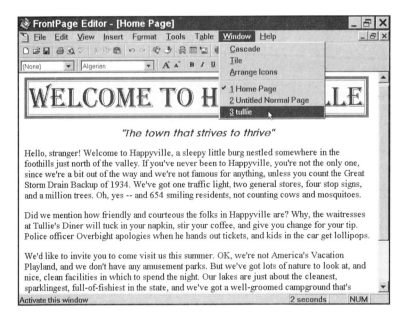

You can cycle among your open pages by pressing Ctrl+F6. Editor opens windows in the order in which they appear on the Window menu.

Editor also keeps a history of pages you've displayed, in the order in which you've displayed them. You can move through this list by clicking the Back and Forward buttons on the Standard toolbar.

Save it now!

Save yourself some headaches by saving your new page immediately. You risk making critical mistakes if you wait, particularly when you've got lots of new pages open and you try to exit Editor before saving the pages. (Editor won't even prompt you to save a page if it's new and you haven't put anything in it.) Also, the purpose of your new page will be fresh in your mind, and you'll be sure to give it a meaningful name. Chapter 1, "Read All About It: FrontPage Essentials," explains how to save and close Editor pages.

Closing pages

Editor will let you open a page even if the web to which it belongs is not open. However, it won't let you save the page. Make sure you save and close your pages in Editor *before* you close the web (or open a new web) in FrontPage Explorer.

If you accidentally close your web first, Save won't work, and the OK button in the Save As dialog box will be grayed out. To fix the problem, go to Explorer and reopen the web. Then return to Editor and save the page.

 Q&A *Don't my pages have to be linked first before they become part of my web?*

No. An unlinked page can still be a part of your web; it just won't be accessible from any web page in your site. (Someone can, however, load the unlinked page if he knows the URL.) Thus, you can work on a page until it's done before you actually hook it up to the rest of your web.

Reopening pages

Let's say you've created a page, saved it, and closed it. Now you want to reopen the page to work on it some more. Do you have to open the web's home page first?

No. Once you've opened the web in Explorer, you can open any page in the web and work on it individually, using one of three methods.

First, you can double-click the page in Explorer.

Second, you can choose File from the menu bar and check the list of recently opened files at the bottom of the menu. If the page is there, click it or press its corresponding number.

 Finally, you can click the Open button on the Standard toolbar or choose File, Open. Editor opens the Open File dialog box and displays the Current FrontPage Web panel. Click the file name of the page you want to open and choose OK.

Editor also lets you open a page from a hyperlink by right-clicking the link and choosing Follow Hyperlink from the quick menu.

Linking your pages

We've created a web with a home page. We've created a second page for the web. So what do we have? Two separate pages, unattached, sitting side-by-side like shy lovers in a movie theater. It's time we got our pages to hold hands. In other words, we want to connect the two pages with a hyperlink.

Assume that we want visitors to be able to jump from the home page to the second page. In Figure 12.3, for example, the hyperlink might be the text "Great Storm Drain Backup of 1934," starting at the end of the third line and continuing on the fourth line. When the user clicks this link, his or her browser will display the second page, which has been stored as a file called Backup.htm. We'll also assume, for a moment, that both pages are open in Editor. Here's how to create the link:

Fig. 12.3
You can hyperlink any text in your document. In this case, we're going to hyperlink the phrase "Great Storm Drain Backup of 1934," starting at the end of line 3.

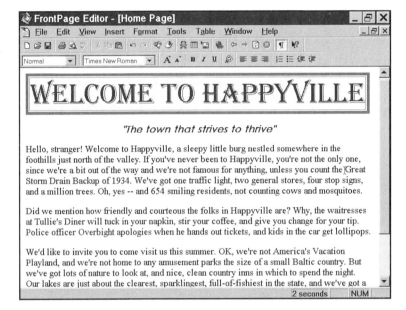

Creating the link

1 Select the text that will make up the link.

2 Click the Create or Edit Hyperlink button on the Standard toolbar or press Ctrl+K (you also can choose Insert, Hyperlink or Edit, Hyperlink from the menu bar). Editor opens the Create Hyperlink dialog box shown in Figure 12.4.

http://www.quecorp.com

Fig. 12.4
The Open Pages panel of the Create Hyperlink dialog box lets you choose another open page as the destination page for your link.

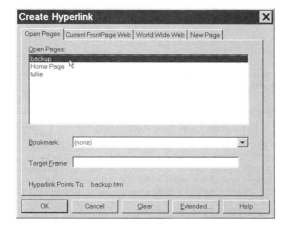

3 Click the Open Pages tab if the panel isn't displayed already.

4 Under Open Pages are the titles of the pages Editor has open. Choose the page you want to link to (in this case, Backup). Notice when you select the page that its file name appears at the bottom of the box, after Hyperlink Points To.

5 Click OK to create the link and close the dialog box.

When you return to the page, click anywhere in the document to deselect the linked text; you'll see that the link is now underlined (see Figure 12.5) and in a different color (usually blue, unless you've changed the colors of your links with Format, Background). And if you touch the link with your mouse pointer, the file name of the linked page appears in the status bar at the bottom of Editor's window, as shown in Figure 12.5.

 TIP **Not convinced that your hyperlink works? Right-click the hyperlink** and choose Follow Hyperlink from the quick menu. Editor switches you to the targeted page. If the page isn't open, Editor opens it for you.

Fig. 12.5
Links are easy to spot—they're dark blue and underlined.

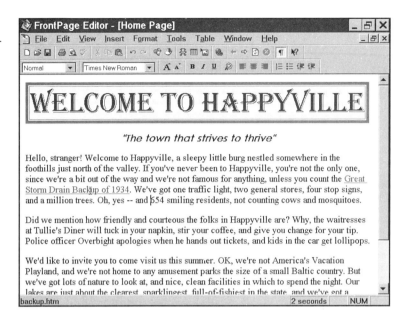

 Q&A *Can I create more than one link to the same page?*

Go right ahead. You can have links in many pages that all point to the same page, or you can have several links on the same page that point to the same page.

 Q&A *What happens if I delete a destination page or change its file name?*

Bad things. The link has no way of knowing that the destination page isn't there anymore. So when someone clicks the link in his browser, he'll get a rude message that the page doesn't exist, leading him to wonder why you didn't check your links more carefully.

How do I get rid of a link?

Want to unlink a link and convert it back to plain text? If you just created the link, you can use Undo. Otherwise, click anywhere in the link and choose Edit, Unlink from the menu bar.

You can unlink many links at the same time. Just select enough text to cover the links you want to change and choose Edit, Unlink.

Bringing new pages into the fold

Can you link to a page that you've created but haven't saved? Yes and no. You can create the link, but Editor must save the unsaved page first. Luckily, Editor does this automatically.

Follow the steps described above. When you click the OK button (Step 5), you'll get a message box asking you if you want to save the page being linked. Choose the Yes button. Editor opens the Save As dialog box; give the page a title and choose OK. Editor saves your new page and creates the hyperlink.

Do I have to open a page before I link to it?

As you add pages to your web, it's likely that you'll want to create links to web pages that aren't open in Editor. Opening and closing pages just so you can link to them becomes tiresome. Conveniently, the Create Hyperlink dialog box lets you link to web pages that aren't open.

Select the text to be linked and open the Create Hyperlink dialog box (click the Create or Edit Hyperlink button or press Ctrl+K). Choose the Current FrontPage Web tab instead of the Open Pages tab, and click the Browse button.

Edit displays the Current Web dialog box (see Figure 12.6). Double-click the file name of the target page, or click it once and choose the OK button. Editor returns you to the Create Hyperlink page, with the file name inserted in the Page text box. Click the OK button to finish the job.

Fig. 12.6
Choose the Current FrontPage Web panel to link to a page that's part of your web but isn't open in Editor.

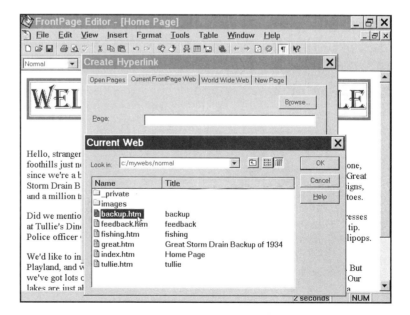

TIP A large web can become a confusing tangle of pages and links, and you'll sometimes find yourself wondering what pages have been linked to where and what pages are still unlinked. Use FrontPage Explorer, in Hyperlink view, to get a snapshot of your web's organization. You can go to FrontPage Explorer at any time by clicking the Show FrontPage Explorer button on the Standard toolbar or using Windows 95's taskbar. Remember that changes to your web pages in Editor don't show up in Explorer until you save the pages.

Q&A *I need to change a link. How do I do it?*

The same way you created the link in the first place. Put your insertion point anywhere in the link and click the Create or Edit Hyperlink button on the Standard toolbar or press Ctrl+K. Editor displays a dialog box called Edit Hyperlink, but it's the same as the one called Create Hyperlink. You can change the destination page or create a new page, or even remove the link by clicking the Clear button.

Build a link, and the page will come

At first glance, FrontPage seems to require a great deal of planning and discourages seat-of-the-pants web design. It assumes you know exactly what hyperlinks you're going to include and have the linked pages already in place.

But where's the fun in that? Like teachers, attorneys, and Jean-Claude Van Damme, web designers should be able to brainstorm as they go along. You shouldn't need an existing page every time you get an idea for a hyperlink—and you don't.

Editor lets you create a hyperlink to a page that doesn't yet exist. After you've created the link, you can create the destination page immediately, or you can tuck the page away for a rainy day.

Links for procrastinators

Let's say, for example, that the words "country inns" in Figure 12.7 inspire a thought: How about a link to a directory of country inns in the Happyville area? Compiling the directory will take some time, but there's no reason why the hyperlink can't be created now. Here's how:

Fig. 12.7
Link first and create the destination page later with the New Page panel of the Create Hyperlink dialog box.

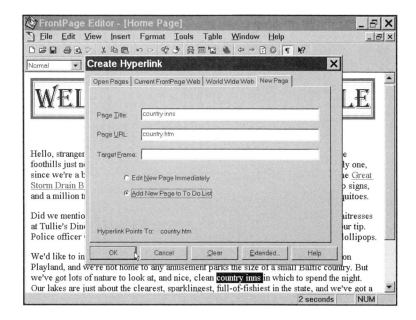

1 After selecting the text, open the Create Hyperlink dialog box (click the Create or Edit Hyperlink button on the Standard toolbar or press Ctrl+K).

2 Choose the New Page tab (see Figure 12.7).

3 Enter a page title and URL if necessary.

4 Click the Add New Page to To Do List radio button and click OK.

5 Editor displays the New Page dialog box; choose a template or wizard and click OK.

When you're done, Editor creates and saves a file for your new page (in Figure 12.7, it's Country.htm) but doesn't open it. At the same time, Editor adds the task to your To Do list.

 TIP If you want to work on the page right now, click the Edit New Page Immediately radio button. Editor opens the page. Edit and save it as you would any other page in your web.

So much To Do

When you log a page in your To Do List, you should open it from the To Do list rather than with Editor's Open command. You'll be able to track your progress as you finish pages and lessen the chance that you'll let an empty page slip through the cracks.

Display the list by clicking the Show To Do List button on the Standard toolbar. The advantage of the To Do List becomes more apparent when you finish and save your new page. Editor displays a message box asking you if you want to mark the task as completed. If you choose Yes, Editor removes the task from the To Do list.

The page that came in from the cold

So far, we've stayed within the comfy confines of our growing web, adding pages and hyperlinks as we need them. But most of us aren't hermits, and most webs aren't cabins hidden in the woods. Eventually, the chances are you'll need to add a web page from another location—one that's in another web, for example, or is a lone wolf that you nurtured outside of the pack.

Bringing in a page from outside your web is called **importing**. Editor offers some convoluted ways to import a page, but FrontPage Explorer, bless its soul, has an actual Import command that's much easier to use.

TIP Keep in mind that a hyperlink can point to a page anywhere on the World Wide Web, in which case you don't need to make the page a part of your own web site. You can create a link that will take the user to the location of the target page. We'll talk about how to do this in a minute.

Q&A *Can I create Web pages singly, without creating a web for them first?*

Sure. Open Editor, and create and edit your page. When you save it, choose As File in the Save As dialog box (the OK button will be grayed out). Explorer opens a Save as File dialog box. Choose a folder from the Save In selection box, choose HTML Files in the Save as Type selection box, enter file name, and choose Save. Your single, swingin' web page is ready for importing. If you create a lot of unattached pages, create a special folder so they're easy to find when you need them.

Importing pages into your web

Picture a web page that comprises a directory of the company's management team. Each job title is a link to a page that includes information about the position and its holder. You've just added a new title to the list, and the page to which you're going to link the title is somewhere on your hard drive. Here's how to import the page:

1 Open the web in Explorer.

2 Choose File, Import from the menu bar; Explorer opens the Import File to FrontPage Web dialog box.

3 Click the Add File button. Explorer opens the Add File to Import List dialog box.

4 Find the file on your hard drive and double-click it. For example, in Figure 12.8, the file is bio.htm, and it's in the folder C:\temp. Explorer takes you back to the Import File dialog box, which looks something like the one in Figure 12.9.

Fig. 12.8
Bring pages into your web from other locations using the Import command.

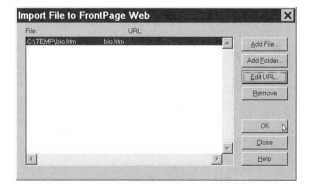

Fig. 12.9
The Import File to FrontPage Web dialog box lets you edit the URL—that is, rename the file—of your new page before you bring it into your web.

5. The Import File dialog box lets you rename the URL, or file name. You'll want to do this if you're using a system for naming your URLs. For example, bio.htm in Figure 12.9 might become jobdesc8.htm to conform to the names of other job descriptions.

6. Click the OK button to add the page.

Once your new page has been added to your web, you can return to Editor and link to the page following the steps described earlier.

Q&A When I import a file, what happens to the original file?

Nothing; it's still there at its original location. Explorer's Import command copies, rather than moves, the file to your web. To avoid clogging your hard drive with duplicate files, delete the original with Windows Explorer (unless, of course, you might need the original for some other purpose).

Other import duties

The Import Files to FrontPage Web dialog box has several options that you can use to manage imported files more efficiently:

You can add several files to your import list; just keep clicking Add File and follow the above steps. Explorer adds each new file to the list in the Import File dialog box.

If you're adding several files that are in the same folder, you can select them at once. In the Add File to Import List dialog box, select multiple files by pressing Ctrl as you click each one. You can select a block of contiguous files by clicking the first file name and then clicking the last one while holding down the Shift key.

To add all files in a folder, use the Add Folder button in the Import File dialog box. Explorer lets you find and select the folder in a Browse for Folder dialog box.

Click Close in the Import Files dialog box to return to Explorer without adding files to the web. Explorer maintains the list of files in the Import Files dialog box, and you can return to it at any time by choosing File, Import from the menu bar.

You can add one, several, or all of the files in the Import File dialog box to your web by using the same keyboard-mouse combinations you use to select files in the Add File to Import List dialog box.

Remove files from your list by selecting them and choosing the Remove button.

Live from the World Wide Web!

Can you import a page from the World Wide Web? Sort of. But first, you have to copy the page to your hard drive from your browser. Once you've saved the file locally, you can import the page with FrontPage Explorer.

There's also a clever way to open the page directly into FrontPage Editor. This isn't exactly importing, but it does the same thing in fewer steps:

1 Log on to the Web.

2 Switch to Editor and choose File, Open. Editor opens the Open File dialog box.

3 Click the Other Location panel and click the From Location radio button.

4 Type the URL of the page you want to open and choose OK. Editor downloads the page straight from the Web.

5 Save the new page.

CAUTION   **There's a word to describe people who pull pages off the World** Wide Web and publish them as their own: Thieves. Publishing someone else's electronic work is a copyright violation, no different from Xeroxing pages from the latest Tom Clancy novel and reprinting them in your own book. That said, it is ok to download pages for your own use. This is a good way to teach yourself web design; you can find pages on the Web that you like, pick them apart, and incorporate the ideas into your own web.

Language barriers

As we discussed briefly in Chapter 1, web pages are written in HyperText Markup Language (HTML). FrontPage Editor automatically inserts the appropriate HTML codes—called **tags**—as you create your pages.

The tags Editor supports are only a subset of the complete HTML library. Serious web authors who use industrial-strength web authoring programs have many other HTML tags available to them. You don't have to worry about these as long as you create your webs entirely with FrontPage. However, if you import pages created with other programs, the chances are Editor eventually will run into an HTML tag that it doesn't understand and can't translate.

Fortunately, Editor will recognize that it's a tag of some sort and inserts a special icon to alert you to the tag's presence. It's called the Unknown HTML placeholder icon, and it looks like this:

A page dotted with these icons can be intimidating, but you don't have to panic. In most cases, you can work around the icons without affecting the page. Make whatever changes you want, leaving the icons alone. When you save the page, FrontPage preserves the unknown HTML tags, and they'll work as before when a user views the page in a browser.

Unknown HTML tags—what can I do with them?

Here are a few other pointers that might help you manage these placeholder icons:

- You can view the contents of the tag by right-clicking the icon and choosing HTML Markup Properties from the quick menu. Editor opens the HTML Markup dialog box, which will display a string of text between two angle brackets, such as this:

    <IMG DYNSRC="bowling.avi">

- While you can edit the tag in the HTML Markup dialog box, do so only if you understand HTML code.

- You can delete, copy, and paste placeholder icons. Click the icon and use your regular editing tools (see Chapter 6, "Editing Tools You'll Learn to Love," for more information). Needless to say, you shouldn't perform any actions on an icon unless you know what the results will be.

- You can use unknown HTML tags to learn more about HTML programming. Get yourself a good book on HTML and look up the tag to see what it does.

Q&A *Some of my placeholder icons have exclamation points instead of question marks. Are these tags, too?*

These tags contain comments—usually notes the programmer included to provide information about the page or surrounding HTML tags. Comments do not show up in a browser. If you look at the tag (right-click the icon and choose HTML Markup Proerties from the quick menu), you'll see that it starts with the string <!-- and ends with the string -->. You can edit comments if you wish; just make sure you edit only the text between dashes. Also, you can delete comment icons without affecting your page's appearance.

Linking to non-HTML files

Libraries hold more than just books. Flip through the card catalog and you'll find myriad recordings, pamphlets, and audio tapes. Some libraries even let you check out paintings for your walls.

Likewise, your web can contain a variety of different types of files. For example, you might include spreadsheets, plain-text documents, audio files, and graphics. You can link to any of these files just as you would a web page.

But before you start importing your entire sound effects library, keep this thought in mind: these are *not* HTML pages. Your user won't be able to use a file unless he or she has a browser that recognizes the format and knows what to do with it. In many cases, the user needs extra software, too.

For example, if your page includes an audio Christmas message from the kids, grandpa can listen to it only if he's got the right audio software, a sound card, and speakers. Similarly, he won't be able to read your family newsletter that you created in Word unless he's got Word on his computer.

You import a non-HTML file almost the same way you do a web page:

1 Choose File, Import from Explorer's menu bar and click Add in the Import File dialog box.

2 In the Add File to Import List dialog box, choose a file type in the Files of Type selection box. In addition to HTML files, you can choose two types of graphics files (GIF and JPEG) and three types of Microsoft

Office files—DOC (Word), XLS (Excel), and PPT (PowerPoint). If the file you want to import is none of these, choose All Files.

3. After you've selected a file type, find and import the file as described in the "Importing pages into your web" section above.

Once the file is in your web, you can go to Editor and create a hyperlink to it the same way you do a web page. But, again, remember that visitors to your web might not be able to use the file if the file isn't in a format their browsers and computers can handle.

Going by the bookmark—linking to the middle of a page

Imagine a dictionary in which every entry gets its own page. The Oxford English Dictionary would weigh in with well over 600,000 pages, and Webster's 10th Collegiate—well, with 160,000 entries, it wouldn't exactly be bathtub reading.

A web becomes equally unwieldy if you devote a single page to every piece of information. Directories and glossaries are much easier to compile and manage when you gather them into larger documents. For example, if your web includes one-paragraph biographies of your company's top executives, putting each biography on a separate page is wasteful when they'll fit easily in a single document.

But when you create a hyperlink, it takes you to the top of the targeted page. How do you create a hyperlink to an individual entry in the middle of the page?

Section by section—creating the bookmark

The job isn't as tough as you might think. Editor provides a tool, called a *bookmark*, that lets you link to any part of another document.

In essence, a bookmark is a name that you give to a part of the destination page. When you create a hyperlink to that part of the page, you link to both the page and the bookmark. And when a user clicks a bookmarked link, his or her browser opens the page to the spot where the bookmark was added.

http://www.quecorp.com

In Figure 12.10, for example, each job title in the table links to a page called Bios, shown in Figure 12.11. In addition, each link targets a bookmark in Bios (Editor shows the links as dashed underlines under each heading; these dashes are not displayed when your user views the page in a browser). Clicking the Chief Executive Officer link in 12.11 opens the Bios page to Hyrem Sackum's entry, clicking the Executive Chief Officer link opens to Noah Vale's entry, and so on.

Fig. 12.10
Each of these links points to the same page but to different spots, or bookmarks, on that page.

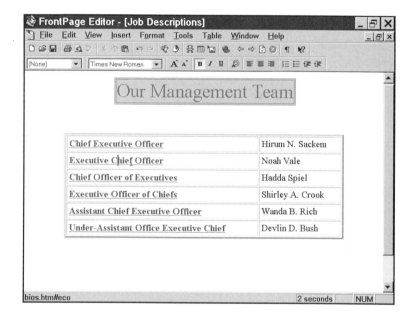

Creating bookmarked links starts with inserting the bookmarks into the targeted page. Chapter 5, "Text Typing Tips, Tricks, and Traps," provides details; basically, you select some text at the beginning of the section you want to bookmark and choose Edit, Bookmark.

Linking to the bookmark

With your bookmarks in place, you can go to the page from which you're linking and create your hyperlinks. The steps you take are the same as for creating a link to a page, with one added step.

1. Select the text that will be the hyperlink and open the Create Hyperlink dialog box (click the Create or Edit Hyperlink button or press Ctrl+K).

2 Choose the Open Pages tab and select the page that you're linking to; in this case, Bios.

3 Here comes the extra step: Click the down arrow next to the Bookmark text box and select the bookmark you want.

4 Choose OK.

Fig. 12.11
You can identify text that has been bookmarked by its dashed underline.

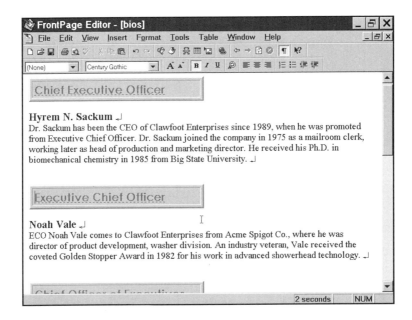

When you're done, notice in your Create Hyperlink dialog box that the name of the hyperlink target, after Hyperlink Points To at the bottom of the dialog box, includes the bookmark, separated from the URL by a pound sign. You'll see the same name when you touch the hyperlink, as in Figure 12.10.

 **You can change the name of a bookmark by highlighting it,** choosing Edit, Bookmark, and typing the new name in the Bookmark dialog box. However, any hyperlinks that pointed to the old bookmark will no longer work; you'll have to modify the hyperlinks to include the new bookmark.

Inside moves

Those scrolls the ancients used before books were invented look like lots of fun, but they had one drawback—if the address for Wizards 'r' Us was somewhere in the middle, you had to unroll practically the entire scroll to find it. The long web page offers a similar problem (it's not an etymological coincidence that the process of moving a page through your browser window is called *scrolling*).

Bookmarks offer a ready solution. You can bookmark entries on the page, and then jump to them via a hyperlinked index at the top of the page.

Figure 12.12, for example, shows the top of a page that contains an entire corporate telephone directory. Clicking one of the hyperlinked letters takes the user to that section of the directory. Thus, clicking the hyperlinked letter B in the list at the top takes you to the bookmark named sectB, which is the large B that heads the B section (see Figure 12.13).

Creating a hyperlink to a bookmark on the same page is almost the same as creating any other hyperlink. Select the text that will be your link, open the Create Hyperlink dialog box, and choose the Open Page tab. Then, simply choose the bookmark from the Bookmark list.

TIP One of the more common uses of internal bookmarks is to give the user a way to get from any section of the page back to the top of the page. In Figure 12.12, for example, the title of the page, Telephone Directory, is a bookmark named Top. In Figure 12.13, the hyperlink Back to Top is linked to the Top bookmark.

Fig. 12.12
Use an index to jump to sections of a page; for example, clicking the letter B takes you to the B entries.

Click a letter in the index...

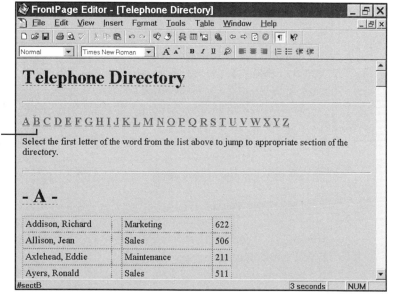

Fig. 12.13
Clicking the Back to Top links transports the reader back to the index at the top of the page.

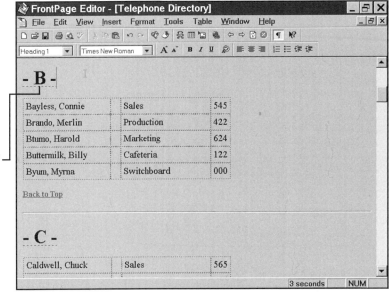

...to jump to that section of the Web Page.

Links to the World Wide Web

Perhaps you have a list of favorite Web sites you think everyone should visit. Or maybe you know of sites that provide more information on the topic your own web covers. Then why not include a directory of these sites in your web? In fact, why not make each directory listing a hyperlink to the site itself?

As usual, FrontPage has several ways to skin the proverbial cat. You can convert existing text to a link using the Create Hyperlink dialog box. Or you can copy a link into your document via the Clipboard. In fact, you can even create a hyperlink simply by typing it.

We'll look at how to convert existing text first.

Doing it by hand

Let's say you already have the destination site in a list in your browser (the list is called Favorites in Internet Explorer and Bookmarks in Netscape Navigator). Open your browser and jot down the site's URL. Then, return to Editor and follow these steps:

1. Select the text that will make up your link and open the Create Hyperlink dialog box. (Click the Create or Edit Hyperlink button on the Standard toolbar or press Ctrl+K.)

2. Click the World Wide Web tab.

3. Choose http:// from the Hyperlink Type drop-down list. This is the protocol for a web page in HTML format (other protocols in the list, such as ftp and gopher, are for other types of Internet services).

4. Editor inserts the string http:// in the URL text box. Type the rest of the destination address immediately after. Be careful not to put a space between the slashes and the address, and make sure you copy the address exactly as it appears in your browser's favorites list.

5. Choose OK.

Find me a link

Don't know the URL of the destination site? Then let Editor do the work. You can browse the Web for the site from Editor, and Editor will insert the URL for you.

1. Follow Steps 1 and 2 in the previous section and then click the Browse button; Editor opens and switches you to your browser.

2. Connect to the Internet if you aren't already, and find the page you're linking to.

3. Switch back to Editor and the Create Hyperlink dialog box. The URL of the page that's open in your browser will have magically appeared in the URL text box.

4. Click OK.

Q&A *I've already got my browser running, and I've found a Web page to which I want to create a link. How do I insert the destination page's URL into the Create Hyperlink dialog box? Do I still have to follow one of the two procedures described above?*

FrontPage is one step ahead of you. In Editor, just select the text you're using for your hyperlink and open the Create Hyperlink dialog box. You'll discover that the URL of the page loaded into your browser has automatically been inserted into the URL text box.

Save time; use the Clipboard

We usually think of the Clipboard as a tool for copying or moving parts of documents, but you can use it to copy URLs, too. This trick can sometimes save you the work of going to a lot of Web sites simply to gather their URLs.

Say, for example, that you've got the Lycos home page loaded into Internet Explorer, as in Figure 12.14. Display the address, if it isn't already, by clicking the Address button. Right-click the address in the selection box and choose Copy (refer to Figure 12.14). Follow the same steps in Netscape Navigator.

Fig. 12.14
Want to link to a Web site you've got open in your browser? Just copy the link and paste it into an open page in Editor.

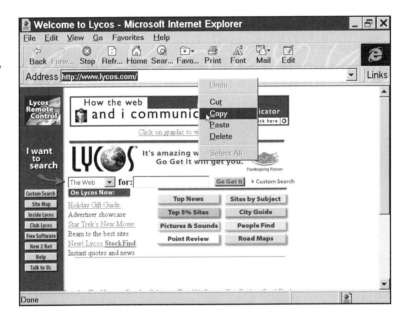

The address is now on Windows' Clipboard. Return to Editor and place your insertion point where you want to insert the link. Click the Paste button on the Standard toolbar or press Ctrl+V. The Clipboard inserts the hyperlink.

The link initially appears as plain text. To finish copying the link, press the Enter key or the Spacebar. When you're done, the link will look something like the one in Figure 12.15.

Fig. 12.15
Editor automatically creates a link when you paste it from the Clipboard.

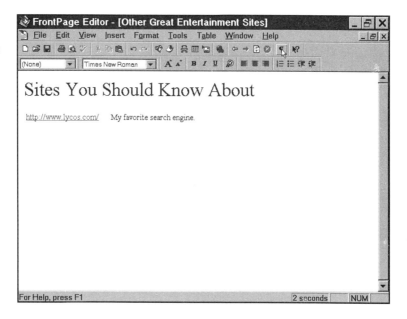

It's likely that you'll want your hyperlinked text to be something a little more descriptive. Go ahead—edit it. Changing the text that represents the link does not affect the link itself.

Copy, copy, copy

You can copy and paste links in many other ways, as well. For example, Navigator and Explorer both let you copy a link that appears on a web page, and both have tools that let you copy the URLs of the sites that appear in their respective Favorites and Bookmarks lists. Refer to your browser's documentation for more info on how to copy.

 TIP In fact, you can paste a link from just about anywhere, even if it's plain text in a word processor's document. As long as the link begins with a protocol that Editor recognizes (such as http:// or www), Editor converts the text into a link.

Type your links

There's one other quick-and-dirty way to create a link—just type it into your web page. As soon as you press Enter or the Spacebar, Editor converts the text into a hyperlink.

CAUTION You can insert any hyperlink you want into your web page, but Editor has no way of knowing if the link is to a valid destination. Proofread your links accurately after you type them.

Q&A *Can I create a link to a graphic on the World Wide Web?*

Yes. The graphic appears to users as if it were a part of your own web. However, there's one significant drawback. To open and edit the page that contains the link, you must to be connected to the World Wide Web. Otherwise, FrontPage dumps you into Explorer and displays an error message.

Open page, insert here

The world (and your hard drive) is filled with fragments of information, some in HTML documents, most not. As you flesh out your web pages, one of your tasks is to bring these fragments together into a whole.

We learned earlier how to import HTML files into your web and create links to non-HTML files. But these tools don't go far enough. How do you merge several web pages? Drop a paragraph from a Word document into a web page? Or create a new web page from an Excel spreadsheet?

Editor provides several tools that let you combine all of your documents, no matter what their original formats.

At the top of the list is Editor's Insert command, which lets you insert an entire file into an open web page. You can use Insert to merge several HTML files or to bring in a file from another program.

When Insert doesn't work, you can fall back on Windows' famous, fabulous Clipboard.

Open page, insert file

First, what's the difference between importing and inserting a file? When you import a file, you bring it into your web intact; it's the same file, only now it's nestled in your web. When you insert a file into an open page, you're combining the file you're inserting with the page that's opened.

Inserting an HTML page is simple, so we'll step you through the process and then move on to the tougher task of inserting non-HTML files.

Put your insertion point where you want to insert the page and choose Insert, File from the menu bar. Editor opens the Select a File dialog box. Make sure the Files of Type text box lists HTML Files. Using the Look In box, find the folder that contains the file, and double-click the file. That's it; Editor closes the dialog box and puts the file in your web page.

TIP If you make a mistake and decide you don't want to insert the file, choose Undo.

Q&A *What happens to the file I'm inserting?*

Nothing. The file remains on your hard drive in its original location. Thus, you can insert the same file many times into different web pages.

ASCII and ye shall receive

Inserting a text (or ASCII) file involves an extra step. Remember, a text file is nothing but numbers, letters, and characters, which means you have to tell Editor how to format the file before inserting it.

Open the Select a File dialog box using the Insert, File command. If your text file has a txt extension (which is the extension Windows NotePad and many other text editors use), choose Text Files in the Files of Type selection box. If the file has another extension, or if you don't know the extension, choose All Files. Find the file and double-click it.

Now comes the extra step: Editor opens the Convert Text dialog box shown in Figure 12.16, where you'll have to make one of four choices on how you want the text file to appear in your page:

Fig. 12.16
When you insert a text file, you'll usually chose to convert it into Editor's Normal style.

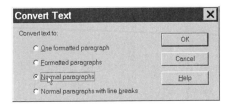

One Formatted Paragraph inserts your text as a single paragraph in the Formatted style. Formatted style is a monospace font, like the one most typewriters use. Also, whereas the text of your original file wrapped from one line to the next, this option puts a line break at the end of each line. For more information on Formatted style, see Chapter 7, "Form and Function: Formatting Text."

Formatted Paragraphs is the same, except that separate paragraphs in the original file will be brought into the inserted text.

Normal Paragraphs inserts text using the Normal style, which means that it appears in a proportional font such as Times New Roman or Arial. Text wraps from line to line, and all text is incorporated into a single paragraph. Again, refer to Chapter 7 for a refresher on styles.

Normal Paragraphs with Line Breaks, as you might guess, is the same as Normal Paragraphs except that line breaks in the original file are included.

Make your choice and click the OK button.

Inserting DOC, XLS, and other non-HTML files

Earlier in this chapter, we talked about how you can import documents that are not in HTML format. For example, you might add a Word document or Excel spreadsheet to your web. But also recall that users can't view these non-HTML files unless they have the right software on their computers.

So do we live in a world in which everyone has to own Word and Excel? Not yet (although Bill Gates is working on it). Editor lets you insert many types of non-HTML documents, converting them into HTML in the process.

Or, at least, it tries to convert them. Editor won't convert formats not supported by HTML; tabular material created with tabs, for example, or oversize fonts. And once you step outside Microsoft's family of co-dependent software, you're on your own.

 TIP **While FrontPage Explorer's Import command lets you import a** non-HTML file, it won't convert the file to HTML. But you can in essence import such a file with Editor's Insert command. Create a new web page, and then insert the file into the empty page. Editor converts the file as you insert it. When you save your new page, Editor saves it in HTML.

Let's try it!

Here's how to insert a non-HTML file in Editor:

1 Choose Insert, File, from the menu bar to open the Select a File dialog box.

2 Choose the appropriate file type from the Files of Type selection box; in the example in Figure 12.17, Word 6.0/95 for Windows & Macintosh.

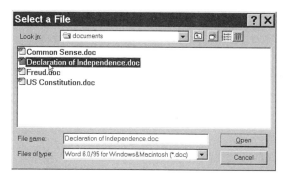

Fig. 12.17
To insert a non-HTML file, change the file type as appropriate; in this case, the file type is Word 6.

3 Use the Look In box to find the folder that contains your file. Click the file name (Declaration of Independence.doc in Figure 12.17) and choose Open or double-click the file name.

4 Editor displays an Open File As dialog box (see Figure 12.18). Click the RTF radio button and choose OK.

Fig. 12.18
Choose RTF in the Open File As dialog box. The other two options will open your file with a lot of useless formatting codes.

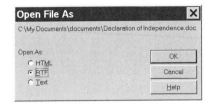

Figure 12.19 shows a Word document that contains two versions of the same chart, the top one formatted with a table and the bottom one with tabs. Figures 12.20 and 12.21 show the results of converting the file. Editor converted the table faithfully, including several colors, although the heading lost its small caps and border. The tabular material didn't fare as well; since Editor doesn't recognize tabs, it ran the columns together.

Fig. 12.19
Two versions of the same chart, one created with a table and the other with tabs. Guess which one stays formatted when it's opened in Editor?

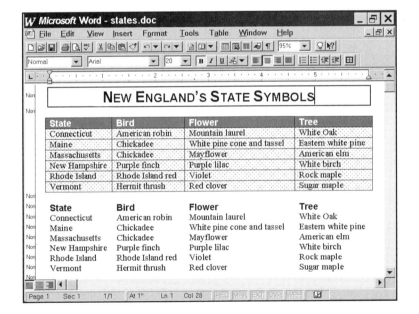

Fig. 12.20
The table remains intact, although Editor rejects the heading's small caps and border.

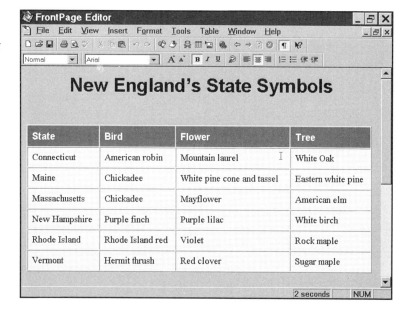

Fig. 12.21
Editor can't digest the tabs in the second version. The result: A table that's going to take a lot of work to get into shape.

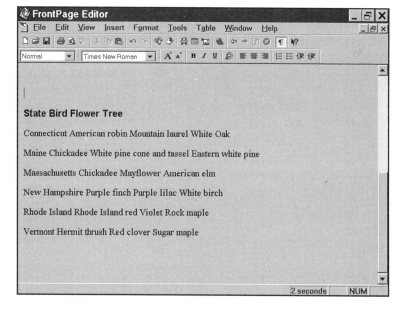

What other formats will Editor convert?

Editor's Select a File dialog box offers a variety of file formats in its Files of Type selection box. Not surprisingly, the bulk are formats used by Microsoft software, including Excel, Works, and various versions of Word. But you also can convert two popular non-Microsoft file types, Lotus 1-2-3 and Word-Perfect.

Q&A *What's RTF?*

RTF (Rich Text Format) is a universal format that many programs use to simplify converting documents from one program to another. What really happens when Editor opens a Word document is that Word is converted to an RTF document, which is then converted into an HTML document.

If you you've created documents in a format that Editor doesn't recognize, check to see if you can save the document in RTF. Then, open the file in Editor using its RTF option.

My program isn't listed! Now what?

If your program isn't listed in the Files of Type selection box, all is not lost; you might be able to save the file from its native program in a format Editor recognizes.

Run the program and open the file you want to insert. Execute whatever command the program uses to save a file to a different file name (usually Save As). If the Save As dialog box has a selection box similar to Editor's Files of Type, open it and look for an RTF option.

If the program doesn't support RTF, look for another file type that you know Editor can handle. For example, most word processors can save files in text format.

Be prepared to lose some of your document's special formatting when you save to another file type.

TIP **Attention, Office 97 users! You're in luck—Office programs can** save their files in HTML format, ready for insertion. Check the programs' help files for more information. Note, however, that you still can't use formats not supported by HTML.

Using the Clipboard

Some programs, particularly older ones, simply aren't going to be insert-friendly. No matter what tricks you pull, you won't be able to get their files into a format Editor can translate.

Enter the Clipboard, Windows' version of the universal remote. When all else fails, you often can copy the document from the recalcitrant program to the Clipboard and paste it into Editor.

The copy-and-paste method also is useful when the file you want to bring into the web already is open in its application. For example, you might be online, reading an e-mail that you want to drop into a web page. The Clipboard is much faster and more convenient than saving the message as a file and then trying to find the file on your hard drive when you need it.

Select, copy, paste!

Start in the program that contains the document you're copying and by select the document. Copy the selection to the Clipboard using the program's copy command (if it follows Windows conventions, Ctrl+C will work).

Switch to the destination page in Editor. Click the Paste button on the Standard toolbar or press Ctrl+V. Editor places the selected document into the new page.

Figures 12.22 and 12.23 show the results of copying and pasting a small Excel spreadsheet (Figure 12.22) into a new page (Figure 12.23). Editor translates the spreadsheet into a table, converting the formula results in column O to text and even picking up the column's flush-right alignment.

Fig. 12.22
This small spreadsheet is ideal for copying to the Clipboard...

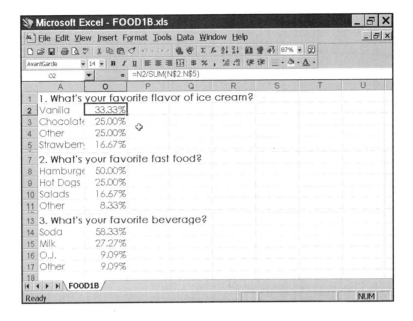

Fig. 12.23
...and then pasting into a new page in Editor. Along the way, Editor conveniently converts the spreadsheet into a table.

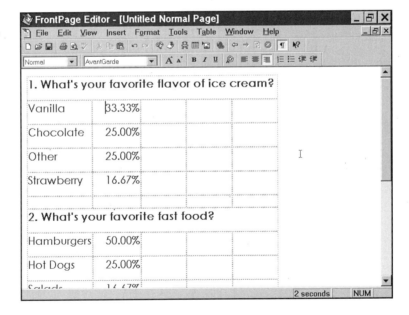

13 Lights, Action, Click! Hotspots, Video, and Sound

● **In this chapter:**

- I want to use this image as a link
- What's a hotspot?
- How can I put together a web menu in pictures?
- This web needs video and sound

A colorful image makes an inviting link. In webs that include sound and video, an image link is an invitation to a multimedia spectacle. . . . .

Sometimes technology takes us backward. The pages of the *Utrecht Book of Hours* in the National Museum of the Netherlands glow with rich decorations and miniatures. Created over 500 years ago, the magnificent volume's gilt lettering and ornaments make it difficult to tell where the text leaves off and the art work begins. In the many decorated dropped capital letters, the text *is* art.

Nobody produces works like the *Utrecht Book of Hours* nowadays, but the melding of words and pictures is as modern as the Internet. You've seen these hybrids on your travels through cyberspace; whenever you click an image that takes you someplace else, you've encountered a text address embedded in a picture.

FrontPage gives you all the tools you need to create your own image links. Take any graphic, turn it into a link, and you've got the modern equivalent of an illumination. It's even easier to insert sound and video, for a page that really comes alive. And although it's unlikely that your work will be around 500 years hence, you'll have finished it much quicker than the creator of the *Utrecht Book of Hours*.

I can see my links in pictures

The average hyperlink has much in common with white bread. It's essential, it can lead to almost anything (buttered toast or smoked salmon sandwiches come to mind), but in itself, it's pretty dull. Hyperlinks are blue and underlined; useful, and boring. Considering that hyperlinks are the fabric that holds your web together, you might be tempted to do something more exciting with them. You can, and without putting yourself to any great trouble. Instead of the standard link, you can use an image instead. And instead of the standard menu of hyperlinks that appears on most home pages, turn several images into links and create an image map. Figure 13.1 shows one example of an image map.

The image map shown in Figure 13.1 is an appealing substitute for the usual menu of text links. Adding an image map of your own to your web is a snap, as you'll see in this chapter.

http://www.quecorp.com

Fig. 13.1
Here's the Web at its best: The Netherlands National Library site is full of fascinating history and art.

For anyone interested in art and the history of books, the hundred highlights exhibition of the Netherlands National Library is a must.

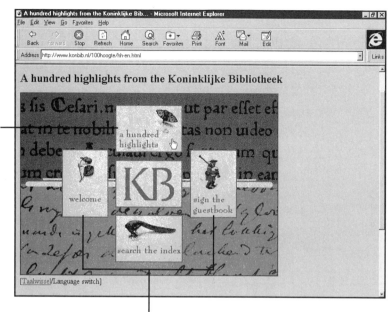

Each of these images is a clickable link to pages in the site; the images together form an image map.

Hotspots turn images into links

Secret doors cut into fake bookcases, so often seen in movies, so rare in real life, look like part of a solid bookcase until they're activated. Pull out the right book, and they open to the underground laboratory or the dungeon or whatever, depending on the movie. FrontPage's **hotspots** work like those secret doors. You draw a hotspot onto an image, then link the hotspot to a web page or bookmark. Although you determine the size and shape of the hotspot, it's invisible, indistinguishable from the rest of the image, just like a secret door.

To turn an image into a link with a hotspot:

1 With your page open in the FrontPage Editor, click the image you want to turn into a link.

2 The selection handles pop up around the image, and the Image toolbar appears.

3. Depending on the shape of your image, click either the Rectangle, Circle, or Polygon buttons on the Image toolbar. These three buttons let you draw your hotspot onto the image. You want to try to match the shape of the hotspot to the shape of the image, but the match doesn't have to be perfect. In Figure 13.2, the image is circular, which makes the choice of the Circle button logical.

Fig. 13.2
The Image toolbar tools are used to draw hotspots of different shapes onto the selected image.

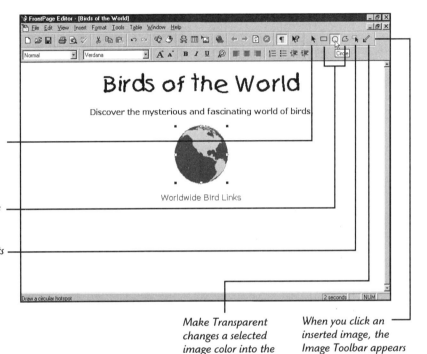

Click Select to select additional images on the page.

Choose a hotspot shape to suit your image.

Click Highlight Hotspots to hide the image and show only the hotspots you've drawn.

Make Transparent changes a selected image color into the color of the page background.

When you click an inserted image, the Image Toolbar appears automatically.

 Q&A *The Image toolbar disappeared on me!*

If the Image toolbar vanishes, it's because you clicked outside an image and deselected it. Just click the image again to make the toolbar reappear.

4. To create the actual "hotspot," point at the center of the circular area where you want your hotspot, and drag in any direction. A circular, aquamarine-colored frame follows the pointer, as shown in Figure 13.3.

Chapter 13 *Lights, Action, Click! Hotspots, Video, and Sound* **245**

Fig. 13.3
Drawing a hotspot onto an image is a simple drag operation.

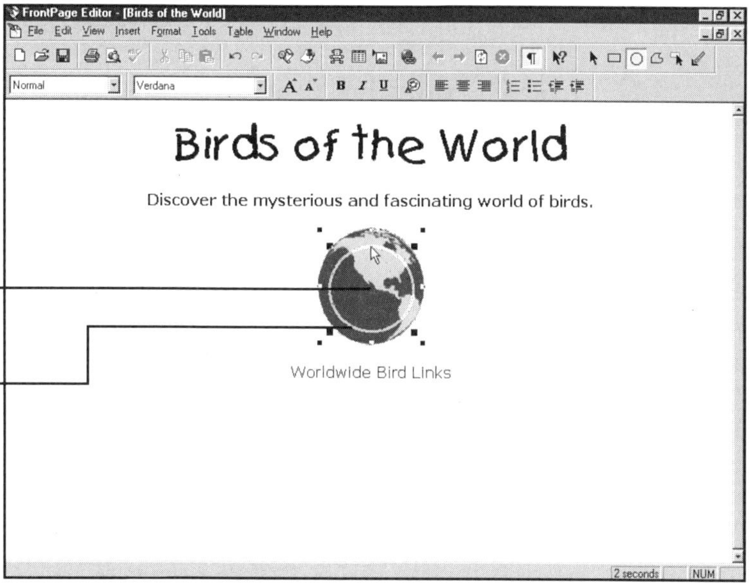

Start at the center of the hotspot-to-be.

Drag in any direction to enclose the image in the aquamarine frame.

5. Release the mouse button when you've framed the area of the image you want for a hotspot, and the Create Hyperlink dialog box pops up. Depending on the target of your link, choose the appropriate tab in the Create Hyperlink dialog box and enter the target address. Figure 13.4 shows the Current FrontPage Web tab selected, with a page in the current web entered in the Page text box.

Fig. 13.4
This hotspot will be linked to another page in the current web, but you can link hotspots to other Web sites or bookmarks as well.

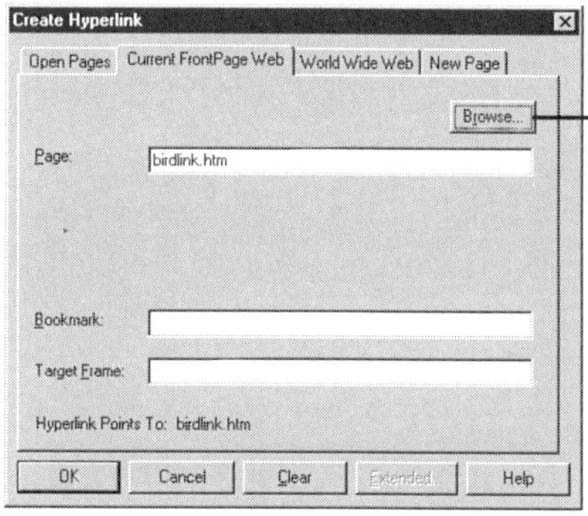

Click the Browse button and select the target for the link if you don't want to bother typing it.

> **66 Plain English, please!**
>
> The **target** of a hyperlink is the page, Web site, or bookmark where you'll wind up when you click the link. **Bookmarks** are named areas on the current page which can serve as hyperlink targets. See Chapter 12, "Webward Ho! Adding Pages to Your Web," for details on hyperlinks and bookmarks. **99**

6. Click OK in the Create Hyperlink dialog box, and the hotspot is created. As long as the image is selected, the hotspot frame will be visible. Click outside the image, and the frame disappears.

I need a rectangular (or polygonal) hotspot

If your image doesn't fit neatly into a circular hotspot frame, use the Rectangle and Polygon tools on the Image toolbar to create hotspots of different shapes.

For a rectangular hotspot, point at the upper left corner of the image, or section of the image, that you want to make a hotspot. The pointer turns into a little pencil; drag to the lower right corner of where you want your hotspot.

Polygonal hotspots are a little trickier, but handy if your image is irregularly shaped. To create a polygonal hotspot:

1. Click the Polygon button on the Image toolbar. Point at any corner of the image area you want to turn into a hotspot. Drag to the next corner and release the mouse button.

2. That creates the first side of the polygon. Now drag from the second corner to the next corner of the polygon. If you're creating a triangle, you're done. If the area you're turning into a hotspot has more than three sides, continue dragging to each corner, releasing the mouse button when you arrive at the next corner.

3. When you close the polygon, the Create Hyperlink dialog box pops up (see Figure 13.4) and you can establish your link.

Moving hotspots

If you're the kind of golfer who sinks every putt, you can skip this bit. For the rest of us, enclosing the exact image area we want for a hotspot on the first try might not always be possible. That's not a big deal, because hotspots are easily moved. Just click the hotspot; the selection handles pop up. Now drag the hotspot frame until you've got it properly positioned.

To expand or shrink the hotspot, click to select it. Now drag any of the selection handles with the two-headed arrow pointer until the hotspot encloses the area of the image you want (see Figure 13.5).

Fig. 13.5
Drag a hotspot handle with the two-headed arrow pointer to change the hotspot area.

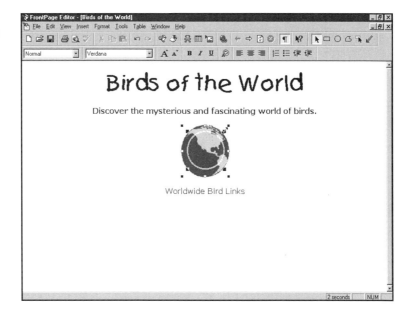

How do I edit this hotspot?

Like any hyperlink in the FrontPage Editor, you can't activate a hotspot link by clicking the hotspot. Instead, right-click the hotspot and choose Follow Hyperlink on the context menu.

Followed the hyperlink to the wrong place? You'll have to change the link's target. Just right-click the hotspot and choose Image Hotspot Properties on the context menu. That pops up the Edit Hyperlink dialog box, in which you can change the target address.

I need to get rid of this hotspot

To delete a hotspot, click it and press Delete. That gets rid of the hyperlink and the hotspot frame, but the image itself isn't affected.

Replace that menu with an image map

Anyone who's ever gotten lost in a big museum knows the relief those handy "you are here" maps provide. They're like a visual guide to the place, and a great comfort to the strayed visitor. An image map on a web page serves the same function, with the added advantage that a click of the map takes you directly to the page represented by the image. If museums could offer that service, museum feet would be stamped out forever.

Image maps are simply collections of hotspot images grouped together. Since each image represents a web page, you'll want to choose graphics relevant to the content of the pages. You can then use the Microsoft Image Composer to assemble your graphics into a single image. Once that's done, export your creation to the FrontPage Editor, add hotspots to each part of the image, and your image map is ready.

An image map example

The Microsoft Image Composer included with FrontPage is a powerful graphics editing program. The FrontPage CD contains a large collection of ready-to-use images (see Chapter 9, "Picture This! Adding Graphics to Your Web," for details on the Image Composer and FrontPage's art collection). Together with the FrontPage Editor, you've got all the tools you need to create a quick image map.

To whip up a quick image map:

1. Insert the FrontPage CD and click the Show Image Editor button on the FrontPage explorer toolbar.

TIP If you press Shift as you insert the FrontPage CD, you'll disable the CD's autoplay feature and avoid the CD's opening screen.

2. In the Microsoft Image Editor, click Insert, From File. The Insert From File dialog box appears. Click your way to the IMGCOMP/MMFILES/ PHOTOS folder in the FrontPage CD.

3 Double-click any images you want to use, and they'll pop into the Image Composer window.

TIP If you want to use several images from the same folder, click the first image file, then Ctrl+click each additional file. Click OK in the Insert From File dialog box, and all the selected images will load into the Image Composer window at once.

CAUTION The more images you stick in your web page, the longer the page will take to load in a browser. You don't want to lose visitors before they've had a chance to see your image map, so try to keep your images small in size and number.

4 Move and resize the images you've inserted until they're arranged the way you want them for your image map.

5 Now group the images into one unit. Click the first image, then Ctrl+click each additional image until they're all selected. Click the Group button on the Arrange palette to group the images together, as shown in Figure 13.6.

Fig. 13.6
Grouping images puts them together in a single unit, simplifying exporting, moving, and resizing maneuvers.

The Group button

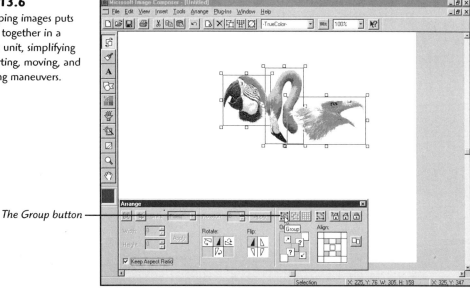

6. With the grouped image selected, click the Copy button on the Image Composer toolbar. Switch to the FrontPage Editor, and click the Paste button on the Editor toolbar to insert the image into the page.

7. In the FrontPage Editor, click the inserted image to select it. Use the Circle, Rectangle, and Polygon buttons on the Image toolbar to add hotspots to each section of your image. The different sections will represent different pages in your web, so link them accordingly (see Figure 13.7).

Fig. 13.7
I needed a hexagon, created with the Polygon tool, to frame the flamingo in a hotspot.

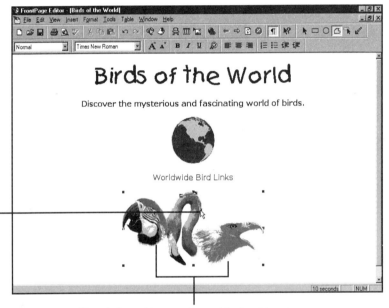

Draw your hotspots over the sections of the different graphics that make up the image.

Hyperlinks in this example would take visitors to pages about the macaw, flamingo, and eagle.

8. Click the Save button, and give your image map a file name in the Save Image to FrontPage Web dialog box that pops up.

I can't see my hotspots!

It's not always easy to spot the hotspots in an image map. With several images sandwiched together, you might not be able to see those aquamarine hotspot borders.

If that's the case, click the image to select it. Now click the Highlight Hotspots button on the Image toolbar. That hides the image, revealing the outlines of the hotspots (see Figure 13.8).

Fig. 13.8
When your view of the hotspots is for the birds, hide the image away.

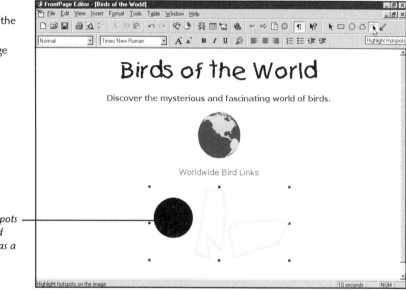

In Highlight Hotspots view, the selected hotspot is shown as a filled shape.

With your hotspots visible again, you can select them, edit the hyperlinks, and move them with ease.

Action! Adding video and sound to a page

Technology prophets tell us that Internet surfers will soon be downloading their choice of full length feature films, in stereo of course, right into their browsers. Maybe. In the meantime, it *is* possible to download short movie clips from the World Wide Web, but the procedure is akin to Dr. Johnson's dog walking on its hind legs: "It is not done well, but then, one is surprised to see it done at all." It takes a very long time to download very short bits of blurry movies with scratchy sound.

Still, you can stick bits of video and sound into your own web pages for others to download if you want to. Bear in mind that a simple 25-second animation might require a one megabyte-sized file and take 10 to 20 minutes for a visitor to download. Sound files, while smaller than video, also slow the crucial time it takes for your page to appear in a visitor's browser.

You probably don't want to include either sound or video files on your home page, or the page you intend as the introduction and table of contents for your web. The slow download times would drive away visitors faster than you can say "Click the Back button." Instead, put sound and video files on their own pages, and add links to them on your home page. Visitors who want to invest the time it takes to download the files can; those whose idea of fulfilling pastimes does not include twiddling their thumbs don't have to.

How do I put a sound in my page?

If you want your visitors to hear sounds when they open one of your web pages, add a **background sound** to your web. Background sounds run automatically when the page is displayed in a browser. FrontPage supports all the standard sound files, including Wave (.WAV) and Midi (.MID) files.

To add a background sound to the active page, click Insert, Background Sound in the FrontPage Editor. In the Background Sound dialog box that appears, choose the Other Location tab. Type the name and location of your sound file in the From File text box, or click Browse and locate the file on your disk (see Figure 13.9).

Fig. 13.9
If you know the type of sound file you're looking for, select it on the Files of type drop-down menu.

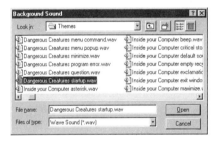

Once located, double-click the sound file to insert it in the current page. Disconcertingly, you won't see any evidence that it's in the page. Nor will you hear it in the FrontPage Editor; to play the sound, click the Preview in Browser button on the Editor toolbar.

To change or delete the sound file, choose File, Page Properties. Click the General tab in the Page Properties dialog box that pops up. Here's where you can exercise some control over how the sound behaves on your page (see Figure 13.10).

http://www.quecorp.com

Fig. 13.10
Although you can't see the background sound file on the page, you can control it with the Page Properties dialog box.

Enter a new value to have the sound play more than once when the page is opened.

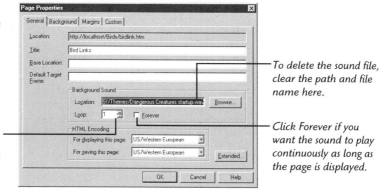

To delete the sound file, clear the path and file name here.

Click Forever if you want the sound to play continuously as long as the page is displayed.

 **CAUTION** Although the status bar in the FrontPage Editor provides a clue about how much extra time a page with a background sound will take to download, you can't tell how slow the page will actually be until you put the web on the server and try downloading it yourself.

When you save the current page, you're prompted to save the inserted background sound to the web as well.

Web video for those who insist on it

FrontPage supports the Video for Windows video file format (.AVI), and it's easy enough to toss an .AVI file into a web page:

1 In the FrontPage Editor, choose Insert, Video.

2 In the Video dialog box that appears, click the Other Location tab. Either type the path and file name of the video and choose OK in the Video dialog box, or click Browse and double-click the video clip once you locate it. Either way, the video is inserted into the page.

3 The first frame of the video is displayed on the page as a placeholder. Like an inserted image, you can click the video to select it, drag to move it, and simply press Delete to get rid of it.

 You'll be prompted to save the video to your web when you save the current page. To see the video run, click the Preview in Browser button on the FrontPage Editor toolbar.

Part V: Beyond the Basic Web Page

Chapter 14: **It's Good Form: Letting Your Readers Write Back**

Chapter 15: **WebBots and Other Web Bells and Whistles**

Chapter 16: **Inducting Your Page into the Hall of Frames**

Chapter 17: **Templates: Professional Pages, Painlessly**

Chapter 18: **Let's Talk! The Fine Art of Web Conversation**

14 It's Good Form: Letting Your Readers Write Back

● **In this chapter:**

- What's a form, and how does it work?

- At play in the fields of your form

- Text boxes: One line or many?

- Controlling what your user can type

- Getting the drop on your drop-down menus

- How do I save the information I collect?

Now that you've reached out with your web and touched someone, let them touch you back with a response form .

Sometimes it seems as if everyone in the world wants to get information from you. Want a credit card? Fill out a form. Need a driver's license? Fill out a form. Getting married? Fill out a form.

Now that you've got a web, it's your turn to ask the questions. Maybe you want to build a mailing list for your company, or poll readers on their favorite fast-food hamburger, or simply solicit feedback on how great your web is. Whatever the information you're seeking, how are you going to get it? By having people fill out a form, of course.

FrontPage offers a variety of tools to create forms. You can let people type comments into a form just as they would a word processor. Or you can ask them to select a response from a list, like a multiple choice quiz. Once they fill out their forms, you can store the information in a format that will let you peruse and use it at your leisure.

First things first: how do forms work?

You don't need to know a lot of technical details to design forms, but you should have a general idea of what goes on when someone fills out a form and submits it.

The user's browser is responsible for presenting your form and collecting his or her input. When the user finishes the form and submits it, the browser sends the information to a form handler on the server for processing. The form handler saves the information to a file, from which you can later retrieve it.

You have to designate the form handler and the file, and your choices will depend partly on the capabilities of the server. You can't use one of FrontPage's Bots to handle forms unless your server has the FrontPage Server Extensions installed. If you're concerned about whether your server will be able to handle your forms, you should ask your Internet service provider for information.

For now, we're going to concentrate on how to create your form.

Let's begin with a few basic definitions.

A **form** is a section in a web page that you designate as the area in which you're going to gather information. For example, an address form might include places in which the user can type her name, address, city, state, and Zip code.

You can always tell where a form is: it's contained within a box of long dashes. In Figure 14.1, for example, the form is all of the material from Name through Zip, while the heading sits outside of the form.

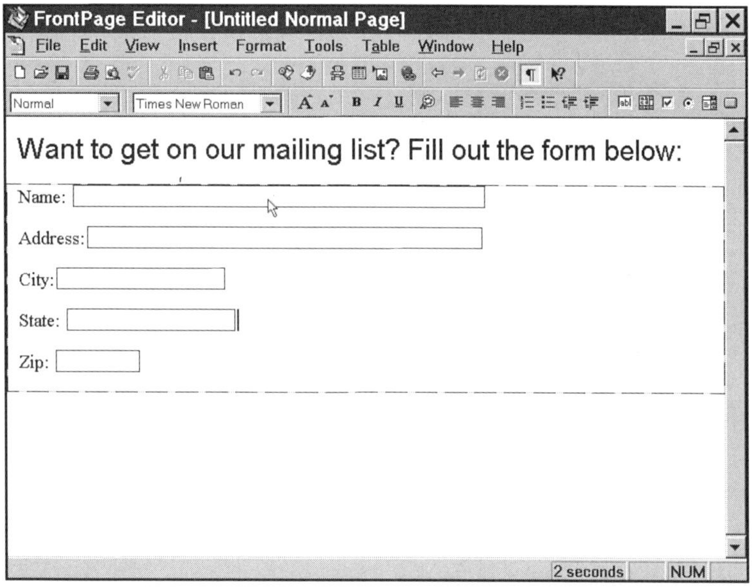

Fig. 14.1
Editor creates your form, outlined by a dashed box, when you insert your first field, such as the one next to the Name heading.

A **form field** is the specific place in which the user enters or selects a piece of information. In Figure 14.1, Name, Address, City, State, and Zip is each a form field.

You don't have to actually create a form; all you have to do is insert a form field anywhere on a web page. Editor automatically creates the form as it inserts the field.

Make sure you insert each additional form field inside the dashed lines. Should you insert a field above or below the dashed lines, Editor starts a new form.

Q&A *Can I put more than one form on a page?*

Sure—but remember that the user has to fill out and submit each form separately. Putting forms on separate pages will result in fewer user errors.

Form fields: a quick introduction

Your forms would be pretty limited if the only type of field you had available was the one in Figure 14.1. You'll be happy to know that Editor provides six fields, each of which can be modified in different ways. Check out Figure 14.2 for simple examples of each field type.

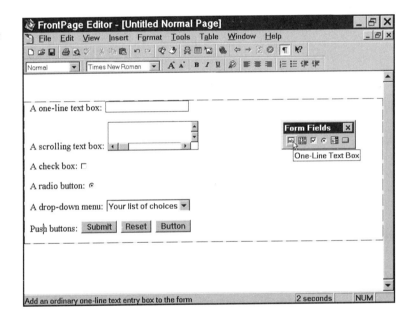

Fig. 14.2
You can create any of six types of fields by clicking one of the buttons on the Form Fields toolbar.

Before we go any further, you might want to know how to actually insert a form field. The easiest way is with the Form Fields toolbar, which you display by choosing View, Forms Toolbar. Put your insertion bar where you want the field and click the appropriate button.

Here's a quick rundown of each form field type and what it does:

 The One-Line Text Box lets the user type a single line.

A Scrolling Text Box lets the user type entire paragraphs, as if he were in a mini-word processor.

 A Check Box lets the user check or uncheck a choice in a list. Unlike radio buttons (see below), each checkbox in a list can be selected and deselected individually.

 A Radio Button also lets the user select a choice in a list, but only one radio button can be pushed; selecting a radio button deselects the previously selected radio button.

 A Drop-Down Menu lets the user select from a list of choices you put into the menu.

 A Push Button lets the user perform an action on the form. Three buttons are available—Submit, which submits the form; Reset, which clears the form; and Normal (labeled Button by Editor), which you can customize to perform some other action.

 TIP To float your Form Fields toolbar as in Figure 14.2, click a space in the toolbar with your mouse and drag it into the document window.

A few field notes

It's time to look at each field type in a little more detail. As you play along on your computer, keep these tips in mind:

Each field type has a different properties dialog box in which you can change the appearance and function of the field. Display the dialog box by right-clicking the field and choosing Form Field Properties from the quick menu.

Your fields won't work in Editor. To get a better sense of how your fields will look and behave, preview the page in your browser with the Files, Preview in Browser command. Remember: after each change, you must save the page in Editor and refresh the screen in your browser.

Goof up? You can reverse any action with the Undo command.

Text—by the line or by the box?

I just flew in from L.A. and boy are my arms tired. (Rim shot.)

A priest, a minister, and a rabbi are on a plane over the ocean. Suddenly, one of the engines catches fire. A flight attendant comes up and says...

Sorry, don't have time to finish the second joke. But here's the idea: the first joke is a one-liner; the second, a story. If you decide to collect one-line gags at your web page, Editor's One-Line Text Box might be all you need. On the other hand, if you're gathering tall tales or bawdy limericks, you'll want to opt for the Scrolling Text Box.

The One-Line Text Box is good for short answers: names, addresses, favorite movie stars, and the like. The Scrolling Text Box is best when you're giving the reader a chance to spout off—for instance, comments on your web or suggestions on what the Boston Red Sox need to do to win a World Series.

When the One-Line Text box appears in a browser, the user clicks the box and types whatever information you're asking for. By default, the length of the text is not limited to the length of the box; if the user goes beyond the right edge, the text scrolls from right to left. The Scrolling Text Box works the same way, except text wraps each time the user reaches the left border and scrolls up when he or she reaches the bottom of the box.

The two types of text boxes are similar in many respects, so we'll cover options for both in one stroke.

Sizing up your text boxes

Both text boxes are 20 characters wide by default. To change the width, first select the box by clicking it. Small, black squares, called size handles, appear at various points along the edge. Stretch the box by touching a size handle on the right end with your pointer until the pointer turns into a double-headed arrow, as in Figure 14.3. Click the mouse button and drag the end to its new position. Shorten the box by clicking and dragging either end in the other direction.

You also can change the depth of the Scrolling Text Box (the default is two lines). Grab a size handle on the bottom edge and pull down, like a window shade.

Fig. 14.3
You can widen a One-Line Text Box by clicking and dragging the right edge.

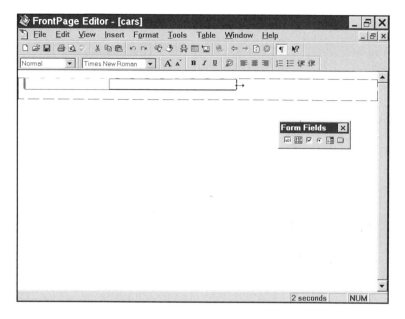

 TIP If you've got a precise width or depth in mind for your text box, you can enter it in the field's properties dialog box. Enter a Width in Characters value for either type of box, or a Number of Lines value for a scrolling text box. You can enter any number from 1 to 999 inclusive.

Start me up

Your text box doesn't have to be empty. You can include some starter text, which the user can then either accept or delete. For example, if people are filling out a form for a Studebaker rally, then a question on what cars they drive can have "Studebaker" already in place (see Figure 14.4). The ones who also own Dodge Darts can add their second car to the list.

You can place text in both One-Line and Scrolling text boxes. Open the properties dialog box by right-clicking the field and choosing Form Field Properties. Type the text in the Initial Value text box, as in Figure 14.5, and choose OK.

Fig. 14.4
This scrolling text box already has a value inserted when the user views it with his browser. He can delete "Studebaker" or keep it and add his own choices.

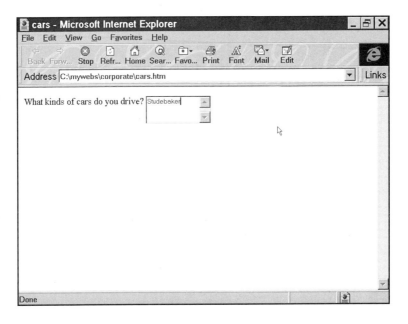

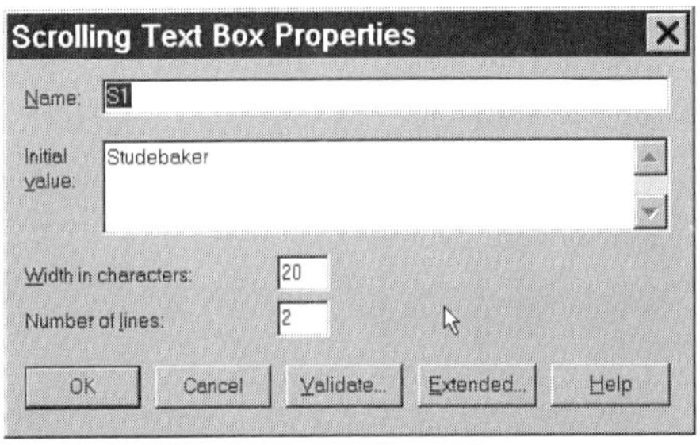

Fig. 14.5
Insert an initial value for either a one-line or scrolling text box in its properties dialog box.

* * * * * * * * * * * *

You know how little asterisks appear when you type a password to start Windows 95 or log on to a computer? You can give users the same feature in a One-Line Text Box, shielding sensitive information from inquisitive on-lookers.

Open the Text Box Properties dialog box and click the Yes radio button next to Password Field.

This option is not available for a Scrolling Text Box.

The name game—renaming your field

What's in a name? Not much, if it's the one FrontPage assigns your fields. Your first Scrolling Text Box, for example, is called S1; the next one, S2; and so on. These appear in the field's properties dialog box, as in Figure 14.5.

A name like S1 is just fine—until you try to read the forms after users have submitted them. Should you choose to include the field name with your data (we'll discuss your save options later), the data file will contain something like:

```
S1    Studebaker
```

Not too useful, is it?

Also, if you choose to display a confirmation after the user submits his form, the user will see the same cryptic field name.

You're better off changing the field names to correspond to the field's content: "Name" for a name field, "Zip" for a Zip code field, and so on.

Hey! You can't type that!

How would you like to force your user to enter only two characters, both letters, in a State field? Or exactly 12 digits, no spaces allowed, in a User ID field? Or at least a gross in an Order Quantity field?

You can do any of these, and a whole lot more, in the Text Box Validation dialog box.

In the Scrolling Text Properties dialog box (see Figure 14.5), click the Validate… button (see Figure 14.6). You also can go directly to the Text Box Validation dialog box by right-clicking the field and choosing Form Field Validation. Here's a rundown of your most important options. The One-Line and Scrolling text boxes have identical Validation dialog boxes, and all of this information applies to both.

Near the top of the dialog box is a selection box called Data Type. The options you use depend on which of four data types you choose: No Constraints, Text, Integer, and Number. We'll look at each data type in a minute, but first, let's talk about the options that are available to you with all data types.

Fig. 14.6
The Text Box Validation dialog box can limit the user to entering letters or numbers, as well as define how much text the text box will accept.

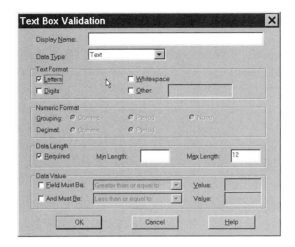

This line can contain no more than 44 charac

The Data Length heading is self-explanatory; its options control the length of your data.

- Check the Required checkbox if you want to force the user to put data in the box. In other words, he can't submit a form if the field is empty.

- In the Min Length box, enter a minimum number of characters the user must type. For example, you can set a Zip code field to a five-character minimum. If the user doesn't meet the minimum, he gets a reproachful error message.

- In the Max Length box, enter a maximum number of characters. This is useful when you don't want some wise guy typing his life story into your two-character Postal Code field; his browser won't let him type more than the maximum you've set.

TIP If you want your user to type a precise number of characters, such as a User I.D. number that's always 12 characters long, set the minimum and maximum to the same number.

CAUTION Pop quiz: What do you think happens if your minimum length is higher than your maximum length? Can you compel your user, for example, to type at least 12 characters but no more than 6 characters? Strangely, FrontPage actually lets you set these incompatible parameters, but the result

http://www.quecorp.com

is that the user won't be able to enter any data without getting an error message when he or she tries to submit the form.

Value added fields

Use the Data Value options to limit the value your user can enter in the field. Say, for example, that you're building a form in which people can order your home-made yogurt-coated radishes, and the minimum order is 12. You'd click the Field Must Be checkbox, choose the data value limit Greater Than or Equal To from the selection box, and enter 12 in the Value box.

The selection box includes six data value limits. The following table explains what each one does if the value is 12:

Data value limit is:	The result is:
Less than	The user must enter a value less than 12
Greater than	The user must enter a value greater than 12
Less than or equal to	The user must enter a value that's 12 or less
Greater than or equal to	The user must enter a value that's 12 or more
Equal to	The user must enter 12.
Not equal to	The user can enter any value except 12.

The data value limit can control letters as well as numbers. For example, you might want your user to enter a selection between the letters X and Z. Your choices would be Greater Than or Equal To and X in the Field Must Be line and Less Than or Equal to and Z in the And Must Be line. Note, however, than alphabetic values are case-sensitive. In this example, the user must type an uppercase letter; his browser won't accept a lowercase x, y, or z.

Q&A *How does the user know what characters he can type into a field?*

You should tell him. But if he's not paying attention and types an invalid entry, his browser displays an error message that tells him what characters he can enter.

What type of data do you prefer?

Let's return to the Data Type selection box at the top of the Text Box Validation dialog box (see Figure 14.6).

By default, your text box's data type is No Constraints, meaning exactly what it says—the user can type just about anything he wants, without guilt or remorse. If he types JIMI LIVES in the Zip code field, it's your own fault.

You can limit a field to text or numbers by choosing one of the other three options. You then can define further limits under the Text Format and Numeric Format headings, respectively.

Limiting your field to text

Choose Text as your data type if you want to limit the type of text the field will accept. FrontPage gives you four choices under Text Format:

- Clicking the Letters checkbox lets the user type only letters; the browser will reject numbers, spaces, and symbols.

- Clicking the Digits checkbox lets the user type numbers, as well. If the Letters checkbox is unchecked, the user is restricted to numbers only.

- Clicking the Whitespace checkbox lets the user include spaces between characters. If Whitespace is the only box checked, then the browser accepts only spaces (although we can't think of a practical use for this option).

- Clicking the Other checkbox lets you specify text the user can type. Use this option when you need to include an exception to the other items checked under Text Format. For example, if the user is submitting part numbers that are always preceded by a pound sign (#), then put a pound sign in the text box next to Other.

Numbers only, please

The Integer and Number data types are similar—they both restrict the user to entering numbers. The options, however, are somewhat different.

Both let you decide if the user can use commas (for example, 123,456) or periods (3.14), or whether he has to enter a whole number (5, 34, 123456). Select the radio button next to the appropriate Grouping option. Note that if you choose comma or period, the user doesn't *have* to use commas and periods; you're just giving him the option.

If you choose Number in the Data T̲ype selection box, you also can choose which punctuation, a period or comma, the user can use as a decimal point. If you choose Comma next to De̲cimal, the user can insert a comma as a decimal point; 3,14, for example. If you choose the Period radio button, then the decimal point must be a period.

May I have the check?

Windows dialog boxes are full of checkboxes, so you should be familiar with them by now. They let you check and uncheck options in a list. Unlike radio buttons, checkboxes let you check as many options as you want. In Figure 14.7, for example, Studebaker and Falcon are checked, but the user can check as many or as few as apply.

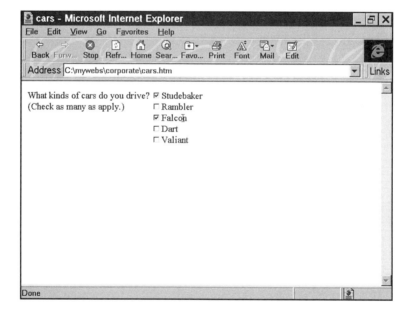

Fig. 14.7
Use checkboxes when users can choose more than one option from a list.

Open the Check Box Properties dialog box by right-clicking the check box and choosing Form Field Properties from the quick menu. The box offers few options, but they're important ones. First, Editor lets you enter a value in the V̲alue text box. As we explained in our discussion of text boxes, you should change this value to something that describes the option, so that the information makes more sense when you read the data file later.

Also change the Value, which is On by default, to one that will be more descriptive when you look at the data file later. In Figure 14.8, the Check Box Properties dialog box for the Studebaker field shown in Figure 14.7, the value has been changed to Yes. If a user checks Studebaker, the data file includes the line Studebaker=Yes, letting you know that this person owns a Studebaker. If the user does not check Studebaker, then the browser doesn't save any information about the field.

Fig. 14.8
Whatever you enter in the Value text box is what will appear in the data file when the user checks the field.

Next, you can decide if the browser will display the box with or without a check. Click the Checked or Not Checked radio button next to the Initial State heading. You might want a checked box, for example, next to a box asking if the user wants more information about a product. The user has to uncheck the box to avoid getting your brochures.

Radio buttons

Remember 8-track tapes (ka-*chunk*)? The music was split among four tracks; to play a track, you pressed the appropriate button on your player. You could listen to only one track at a time (although, if you owned a really cheap player, you'd sometimes hear another track faintly in the background).

Radio buttons work along the same lines. The user has several choices, but he can select only one. In Figure 14.9, for example, the user must choose a favorite car; he can't choose Studebaker and Rambler. So, if the user clicks Rambler, it clears the radio button next to Studebaker.

The radio buttons in a group have a collective name, which appears in the Group Name text box in the Radio Button Properties dialog box. Change the name to reflect the content of the question. For example, if the question is, "Are you married?," the group name might be "marriage status."

Like a checkbox field, a radio button field has a value, which you also set in the Radio Button Properties dialog box. By default, the values are sequential within the group: for example, V1, V2, V3, and so on. Change the value to something that describes the choice. For example, the value of one button in a group might be "yes" and the value of another button, "no."

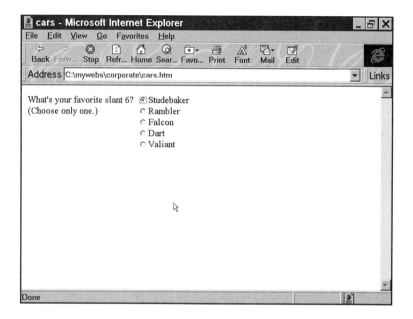

Fig. 14.9
A radio button limits the user to selecting one choice in a list.

The Radio Button Properties dialog box also lets you decide which button will be selected when the user looks at the form in his browser; click Selected or Not Selected next to the Initial State heading. You can pick only one button in a group to be selected; if you try to select a second one, Editor automatically clears the first one.

The war against ambivalence—make a choice, dang it!

Sick of people waffling? Do you want to force them to choose an option? You can do it in the Radio Button Validation dialog box.

Right-click any button in the group and choose Form Field Validation from the quick menu. In the Radio Button Validation dialog box, put a check next to Data Required. Enter an optional name for the group in the Display Name text box; this is the name that the browser displays in the error message if the user doesn't make a selection.

Drop down and give me five (or maybe fifty)

Back in the days when vacationers got their kicks on Route 66 at 22 cents a gallon, the postcard album was a favorite souvenir. It looked to be the size of a single card, but when you took off the cover, voila! Oklahoma's scenic wonders unfolded like an accordian.

That's what a drop-down menu is like. It ostensibly is similar to a One-Line Text Box, but when you click the box of the down arrow, sacre bleu! A menu of wondrous length cascades down your screen.

Figure 14.10 shows a typical drop-down menu as it might appear in a browser. Click it and it becomes the menu in Figure 14.11. The user touches his selection with the mouse pointer (Miami in Figure 14.11) and clicks. If the menu is too long for the menu window, the user can move down the menu with the scroll bar.

Fig. 14.10
A drop-down menu lets you pack a long list of selections into a small space.

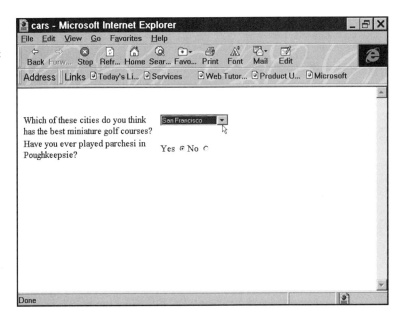

The Drop-Down Menu Properties and Validation dialog boxes offer a riot of options. But first things first—putting the items into your menu.

Fig. 14.11
The menu drops, the user clicks, and the world is saved.

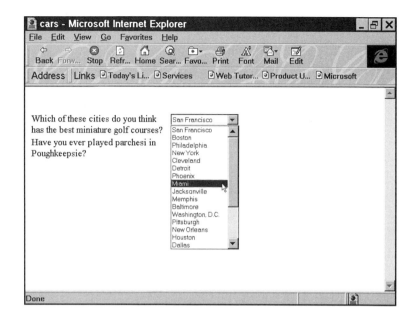

TIP You can resize a drop-down menu as you do a text menu—click it and drag one of the size handles.

Add, type, OK; add, type, OK; add, type, OK...

Adding entries to your menu is like dropping coins in a piggy bank; there's no other way to do it except one at a time. Create your menu by clicking the Drop-Down Menu button on the Form Fields toolbar to open the Drop-Down Menu Properties dialog box, and follow these steps:

1 Click the Add button; Editor opens the Add Choice dialog box (see Figure 14.12).

2 Type your entry in the Choice text box.

3 By default, the server software that saves the form's data uses the menu choice as the value. To refresh your memory, the value is what is stored in the data file when the user selects the entry. If you want a different value, select the Specify Value checkbox and type the value in the text box beneath.

4 Choose the Selected button under the Initial State heading if you want the browser to display the menu choice as selected.

5 Choose OK.

Fig. 14.12
Building your list of drop-down menu items is (almost) as easy as clicking the Add button and typing.

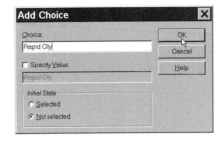

When you return to the Drop-Down Menu Properties dialog box, your new entry appears at the bottom of the Choice display box, along with whether it's been selected and the value, as in Figure 14.13. You can rearrange the order of your menu choices with the Move Up and Move Down buttons.

Fig. 14.13
The drop-down menu options as they appear in the Drop-Down Menu Properties dialog box.

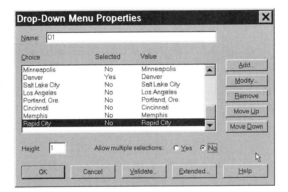

Want to change the options you chose for a menu choice? Select the item in the Choice selection box and choose the Modify button. Choose the Remove button to delete the choice.

 TIP You can have more than one menu choice appear in the browser as selected. In the Drop-Down Menu Properties dialog box, click the Yes radio button next to the Allow Multiple Selections heading.

 TIP As with other types of fields, you should give your drop-down menu a descriptive name in the Name text box of the properties dialog box.

But wait—there's more

If you want to require the user to make a choice, you can do so in the Drop-Down Menu Validation dialog box. Right-click the field and choose Form Field Validation from the quick menu, or click the Validate button in the Drop-Down Menu Properties dialog box. Put a check next to Data Required.

In the Display Name text box, you can enter a new name for error messages. Otherwise, the browser uses the name entered in Name text box of the Drop-Down Menu Properties dialog box.

If you chose Yes next to Allow Multiple Selections in the Drop-Down Menu Properties dialog box, the Validation dialog box includes Minimum Items and Maximum Items text boxes. Enter a value if you want to require the user to select a minimum or maximum number of items, respectively, from the drop-down menu.

TIP One space-saving trick some web designers use is to put directions for a drop-down menu in the first line of the menu itself. If you decided to go this route, check Disallow First Item in the Validation dialog box, which prevents the user from choosing the first line.

Push-button technology

Just as your computer's Enter key lets you finish computing tasks, the Submit button lets the user finish a form, sending the data to the server for storage.

You insert a Submit button in your form by clicking the Push Button icon on the Form Fields toolbar. The button is labeled "Submit" by default. You can change the label to something else—for example, "Send Form" or "I'm Done!"—in the Push Button Properties dialog box. Right-click the field and choose Form Field Properties from the quick menu. Enter the new label in the Value/Label text box of the properties dialog box.

Editor also lets you change the button to a Reset button, which resets all the form's fields to their default settings. A Reset button lets the user start over with a clean slate if he decides he filled out the form incorrectly. Choose the Reset radio button in the Push Button Properties dialog box.

Q&A *What's the Normal button?*

The Normal option lets you define your own special push button. You determine the actions of the button by writing a **script**. "Script-writing" is a nice way of saying "programming;" the topic is beyond the scope of this discussion, but you can get an idea of the process by right-clicking the button and choosing Script Wizard from the quick menu. When Editor opens the Script Wizard dialog box, choose Help for more information.

Add text and stir

The form in Figure 14.14 includes all six of the fields we've talked about. It's short, simple, and easy to fill out. Still, it lacks something, a certain quality that might elevate it from a mere form to a form with a purpose.

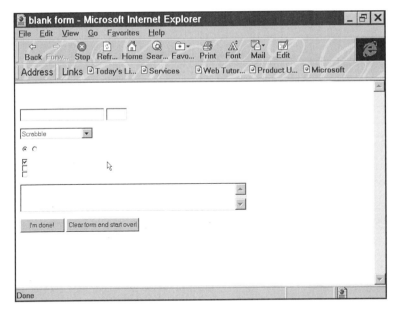

Fig. 14.14
The minimalist form: Interesting, but not too functional.

Oh, right—it doesn't have any text. Does Figure 14.15 look any better?

You insert text into a form the same way you do in any Editor document. All of Editor's formats and attributes are available. You can choose colors and backgrounds, too. And don't forget tables; a well-designed table can do wonders for a form's layout.

Fig. 14.15
A few judicious words do wonders. Add and format type the way you would in any web page.

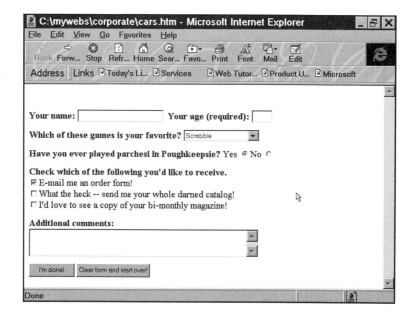

There's no mystery to selecting form fields, laying them out, and adding text. You'll get a feel for what works best as you experiment. But a few basic principles are worth keeping in mind.

Simply marvelous, marvelously simple

Direct marketing firms spend zillions of dollars a year designing those annoying mailings that engorge your mailbox every January. But no matter how fancy the marketers get with all those four-color brochures, endorsements from Dick Clark, and cornball letters from satisfied customers, there's one piece they don't mess with: the order card. Businesses want to make it as easy as possible for you to say "yes" (or, more accurately, "Yes! Yes! Yes!"). So they design the card to be simple, direct, clear, and easy to use.

A FrontPage form is similar in many ways. So why not borrow some ideas from the Big Boys? You get the benefits of their expertise while they pay the tolls:

> **Keep your form short**. A one-screen form is ideal; anything more than two screens is asking too much. Remember, the user who chooses to fill out your form is doing you a favor, so don't pepper him with a lot of irrelevant questions.

Keep your form simple. The user should be able to fill out your form in a matter of seconds without a lot of distractions. Don't add graphics and sound unless they make the form easier to use. And avoid convoluted instructions like, "Go to question 4 if you answered Yes to question 1, unless you answered 'Maybe' to question 2, in which case go to question 5 before you answer question 4 (Ohio residents excepted)."

Give clear directions. Can users enter only letters? Can they choose several options from a list? Add brief instructions if there's a chance the user might make a mistake.

Finally, be friendly. Let your user know that she's responding to a human being, not a computer.

Gathering your nuts

Every big college has a mailroom. If you've got a letter to deliver, you hand it to a mailroom clerk, who puts it in the appropriate mail box. Eventually, the owner of the box comes to the window and retrieves your letter.

On the Web, your server is the mailroom. When a user delivers a form, she gives it to the server's version of the mailroom clerk, called a **form handler**. The form handler then puts the form into the proper mail box, or data file, from which you eventually retrieve the information.

Unfortunately for us, different servers have different form handlers. You have to know what the handler is and specify it as part of your form's configuration. You pick the handler in the Form Properties dialog box, which you display by right-clicking the form and choosing Form Properties from the quick menu. (You also can display this dialog box as you create a push button; choose the Form button in the Push Button Properties dialog box.)

Choosing a handler

Choose a handler from the Form Handler selection box (see Figure 14.16). The first (and default) choice is Custom ISAPI, NSAPI, or CGI Script. Explaining these scripts in detail is beyond the scope of this book; they're handlers that you or someone else has written and placed on the server. If your server doesn't have FrontPage's handlers, then this is the option you'll select.

Fig. 14.16
The WebBot Save Results Component passes submitted forms to a data file on servers that have the FrontPage Extensions.

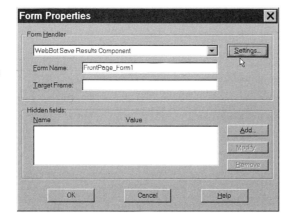

If your server has the FrontPage Extensions, then you'll most likely want to use the WebBot Save Results Component as your form handler. Enter a form name (it's optional) if you don't like the default FrontPage provides in the Form Name text box. Next, you'll need to configure the handler; click the Settings button to open the Settings for Saving Results of Form dialog box.

The Results tab

Start by clicking the Results tab and entering a name in the File for Results text box (see Figure 14.17). This is the name of the file in which the handler stores data from submitted forms.

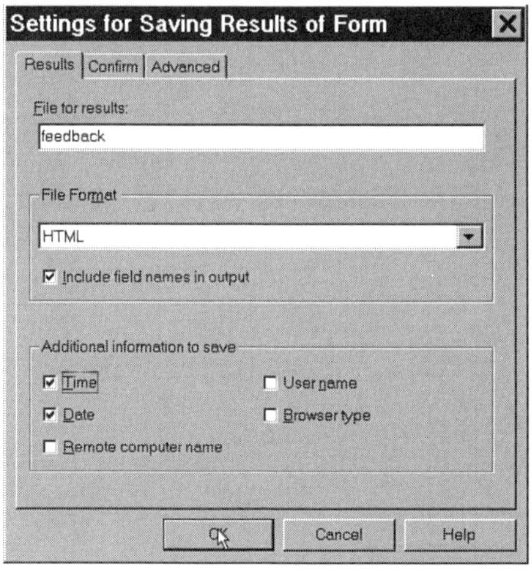

Fig. 14.17
You can tell the handler if you want your file saved for reading in a browser, editing in a word processor, or storing in a database manager.

Next, in the File Format drop-down box, choose the format in which you want the file. The format you choose depends on how you plan to look at or use the data.

The first four options save the data in HTML format, so you can view the data file in your browser, FrontPage Editor, or another program (such as Word 97) that recognizes HTML. Figure 14.18 shows what a data file saved with the HTML option might look like in Editor. The bulleted list option puts bullets in front of each field, while the definition list option puts the responses underneath the field names. If you choose Formatted Text Within HTML, the information appears in the Formatted style, as in Figure 14.19. (See Chapter 7, "Form and Function: Formatting Text," for information on styles.)

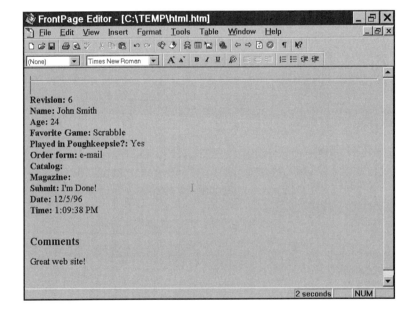

Fig. 14.18
Saving your forms file in HTML format lets you view the data in your browser or in FrontPage Editor.

The formatted text option saves your forms file in plain text, so you can view it in a word processor. Figure 14.20 gives you an idea of what your forms file will look like in Windows Notepad.

The three text database options let you save the forms file in a format that a database manager or spreadsheet program can read. Entries are saved in rows, one row per form, with the names serving as headings for the rows. The form handler puts quotes around each heading and entry, with either a comma, tab, or space separating the entries.

Fig. 14.19
You also can choose to view your data as formatted text in an HTML file.

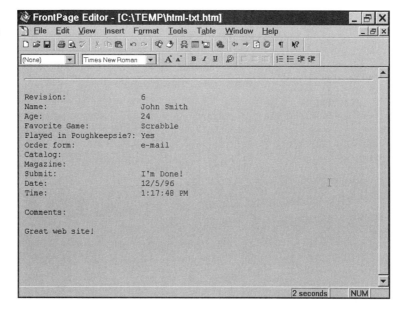

Fig. 14.20
The formatted text option lets you look at a forms file in your word processor.

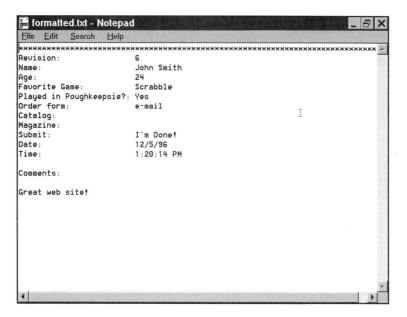

Figure 14.21 shows you what a forms file saved with comma separators looks like in Notepad, while Figure 14.22 shows what the same forms file looks like when it's opened in Microsoft Excel.

Fig. 14.21
Saved as in database format, a forms file doesn't look like much in a word processor...

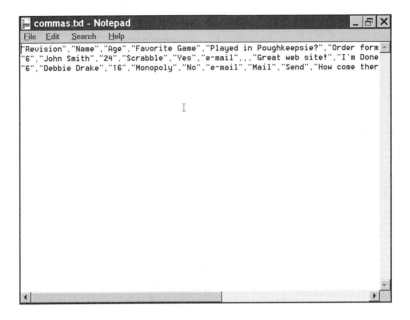

Fig. 14.22
...but it looks great as a spreadsheet.

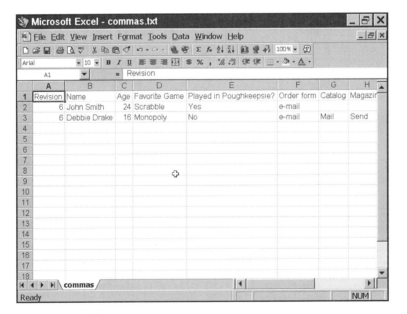

As you can see, a forms file converted into a spreadsheet offers endless possibilities. You can create a membership in alphabetical order, or sort the list by a particular category, or even do statistical analyses of numerical data.

If you don't want field names saved with the user's responses, do not check Include Field Names in Output.

Finally, choose any of the options under Additional Information to Save heading. For example, if you want to keep track of when each form was submitted, check Time and Date.

I'd like to confirm this

The Confirm tab (see Figure 14.17) lets you set up a confirmation page that shows the user what he or she has submitted. Figure 14.23, for example, displays a confirmation page for the form shown in Figure 14.15. The form does not let the user return to the form to correct it.

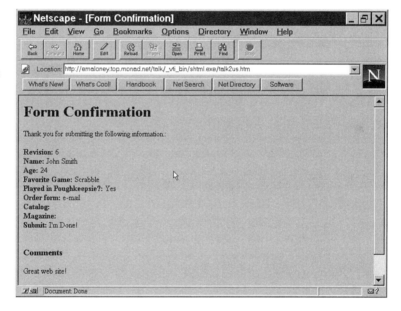

Fig. 14.23
A confirmation page lets the user know that his form has been submitted and tells him what information he provided.

The confirmation form that displays the page in Figure 14.23 was automatically generated by FrontPage. But you can create your own confirmation form with a template.

Choose File, New from Editor's menu bar and choose the Confirmation Form template in the New Page dialog box. After you save the page, enter its name in the Confirm panel's URL of Confirmation Page text box. FrontPage sets up a confirmation page automatically if you don't create one.

You also can set up a validation failure page, which displays a message when the data in a field is not valid as defined in its Validation dialog box. Again, if you don't create your own page, FrontPage will do it for you.

I'll have seconds

The Advanced tab lets you create a second data file with its own format. Create a second file if, for example, you'd like your data saved in HTML for viewing in your browser and in text database format to import into a spreadsheet. Put the name of the file in the Second File for Results text box and choose a format from the Format of Second File drop-down menu.

The Advanced panel has one other option, the Form Fields to Include text box, that lets you define the order in which the handler saves your fields in the results file. Thus, you can create a form in which the fields appear in one order but are saved in another. If you leave the text box blank, the handler saves the fields in the order in which you set them up in Editor.

Secret messages

The Form Properties dialog box has one other option worth mentioning: Hidden fields. These are fields you create that the user can't see in her browser but are stored in the data file. You might include a revision number (such as in the form in Figure 14.18), the author of the form, or some other piece of information that might be useful to you when you review the data.

You create a hidden field by clicking the Add button next to the Hidden Fields text box. Editor displays a Name/Value Pair dialog box (see Figure 14.24). Type a name for the field in the Name text box and its value in the Value text box, and choose OK.

Use the Modify and Remove buttons in the Form Properties dialog box to change or delete a field you've selected in the Hidden Fields box.

Fig. 14.24
Create a hidden field if you want to save information with each submitted form but don't want users to see the field. See Figure 14.18 to view an example of the resulting forms file.

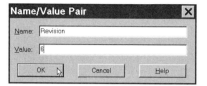

15
WebBots and Other Web Bells and Whistles

● In this chapter:

- Just what is a WebBot?

- How do I add a search feature for my web visitors?

- Instant table of web contents? Just what I needed

- I'm selling advertising space on my web

- ActiveX? What's that all about?

Like those household appliances that we'd prefer not to be without, WebBots add labor-saving convenience to web pages........................... ▶

Robots have been a big disappointment. All these years we've been waiting for humanoid machines to cook dinner, wash the car, and teach the kids French. Instead, we get contraptions that look like Meccano set projects and that do only repetitious chores of interest to very few—auto assembly line welding, for example. Robots do specific jobs very well, to be sure, but when you wanted a genius and a mechanical moron shows up, it's hard not to feel let-down.

FrontPage's WebBots, like their robotic cousins on the assembly lines, are designed to do one web chore each. They do that chore—it could be date stamping a web page every time it's updated—automatically, unerringly, and uncomplainingly. They're easy to insert into webs, and they need little in the way of maintenance.

But they're not those clever robots we've always wanted.

What are WebBots?

You're looking for some specific information in a big Web site loaded with pages of text and graphics. Right at the top of the home page is a link that reads "Search." You click the link, enter a few key words, click the Search button, and your information appears in moments.

Adding a search feature like that to a web used to require fancy programming; FrontPage's Search WebBot (or Bot for short) creates a search feature for you automatically; no programming needed. Or take a mundane chore like displaying the date when your page was last updated. You could insert the new date by hand each time you change the page, or you can have the Timestamp WebBot do it for you. WebBots, in short, are prefabricated bits of programming code that do useful things. Once inserted, they run automatically when a page is opened, or updated, or when a button is clicked. Like a garage door opener, each WebBot does a particular chore for you that you'd otherwise have to do yourself. If you hate getting out of the car to open the garage, you'll like WebBots.

Before inserting WebBots, make sure that the server to which you're planning to publish your web has the FrontPage Server Extensions installed. FrontPage Server Extensions are helper programs that allow servers to display and use FrontPage's special functions and formatting. Without the

FrontPage extensions, WebBots won't work (see Chapter 19, "This Web Is Suitable for Publication," for more on FrontPage extensions). Both the FrontPage Personal Web Server and the Microsoft Personal Web Server have the FrontPage extensions installed, so your WebBots will work perfectly on your own system.

Make your web user-friendly with a Search Bot

Even if your web isn't a vast labyrinth of pages, users will be grateful for the chance to search for what they need without having to examine the whole site. Unlike good novels, webs are not designed to be read from start to finish. For the browsing multitudes, a search feature is their best friend. The Search Bot lets readers search your web for strings of text.

The Search WebBot is not your chance to compete with Web search services like Yahoo; the Search Bot allows searches only within the web where it's been installed. It's a useful addition to any web nevertheless.

How do searches work?

Computers are especially good at brute force jobs. One such job is scanning pages of text for matches with criteria set by the user. And that, in a nutshell, is how computerized searches work. You enter words or phrases—they're called **text strings** or **key words**—to search for, and the computer rifles through its files looking for matching strings of text. If it finds any, the computer displays the number of matches and their location. Depending on the search program (sometimes called a **search engine**), the computer can even score each match on how close it comes to the original text string.

That's pretty much what happens when you search the tens of millions of World Wide Web pages with services like Excite or Alta Vista. If you use the same text string with different services, you'll notice that you get different results. That's because (at least in part), the search services don't actually search the Web each time you run a search. Instead, they use programs called **spiders** that comb the Web automatically, compiling vast indexes of key words found on the millions of web pages. When you run a search, you're searching through these indexes rather than the Web itself. Because each index is different, you get different results even with the same text string.

To insert a Search Bot in your web:

1. In the FrontPage Editor, open the page where you want the search form to appear. Click the Insert WebBot Component button on the Editor toolbar, and the Insert WebBot Component dialog box appears (see Figure 15.1).

Fig. 15.1
FrontPage's WebBot collection is a handy assortment of automated gadgets for your web.

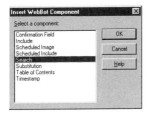

2. Double-click Search in the Insert WebBot Component dialog box, and the WebBot Search Component Properties dialog box shown in Figure 15.2 pops up.

Width is the size of the search form text box.

Fig. 15.2
WebBots are automated right from the start; these default settings work perfectly well as they stand.

Check these boxes if you want the search results to display this extra information.

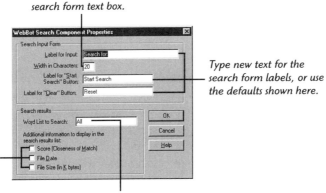

Type new text for the search form labels, or use the defaults shown here.

The default All searches all the pages in your web. For searches that cover only a discussion group, enter the name of your discussion group directory.

3. Make any changes you like, or accept the defaults in the WebBot Search Component Properties dialog box. Click OK when you're done.

4. A search form is inserted at the cursor on the active page, complete with text box and buttons. Add text above or below the form if you like. You can also move the form around the page: click inside the form and drag to move it. Figure 15.3 shows the inserted Search WebBot component with text added.

Fig. 15.3
This is a working search feature, but not in the Editor; preview the page in your browser to test the Search Bot.

Add text above or below the form.

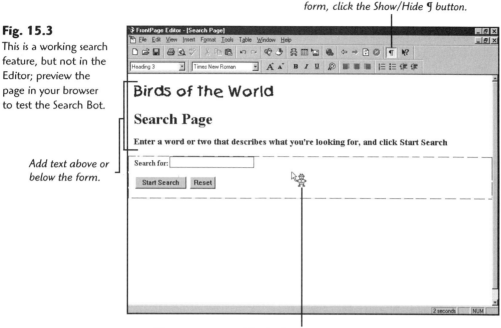

If you don't see the border around the form, click the Show/Hide ¶ button.

The pointer is joined by this little robot when you point at a WebBot component; drag the form to move it around the page.

Although the inserted search feature really works, you'll have to preview the page in your browser (click the Preview in Browser button) to see it in action. In the FrontPage Editor, clicking the Search Bot just selects it.

To change any of the Search Bot properties, the label text for example, right-click the form and choose WebBot Component Properties on the context menu. And to get rid of the Search Bot, click it and press Delete.

Get a web header with the Include Bot

The Include WebBot component inserts a page from your web into other pages in the web. Why would you want to do that? Web page headers might be one good use for the Include Bot. Headers repeat text on every page of a document, and often include a logo, the document title, or the author's name. Although there is no headers feature in FrontPage, you can put header text on its own page, use the Include Bot to insert the page throughout your web, and get exactly the same effect. If the header text needs to be updated, you'll only have to edit the one page that holds it. The other pages where you've inserted the text with the Include Bot will get the updated text automatically.

Part V *Beyond the Basic Web Page*

To create header-like repeating text with the Include Bot:

1. In a new FrontPage Editor page, type and format your text. See Figure 15.4 for one idea.

2. You don't want visitors to open the actual page that contains the text, since they'll be reading the text throughout the web anyway. Save the page, therefore, in the web's Private folder. Click the Save button on the Editor toolbar. In the Save As dialog box that appears, type a title in the Page Title text box. The page's file name appears automatically in the File path within your FrontPage web text box; position the cursor before the file name and type _private/, as shown in Figure 15.4.

Fig. 15.4
Files saved in the Private folder are available to you, but can't be accessed by web visitors.

Don't forget to type the underscore character in _private/—it's part of the folder name

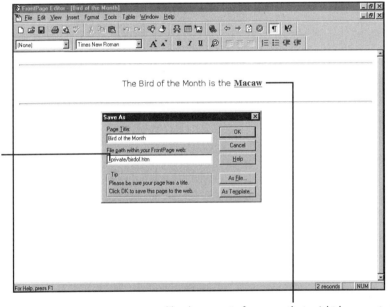

Here's one sort of message that might be repeated throughout a web with the Include Bot. This page will be inserted into the page where the Include Bot is installed

FrontPage creates the Private folder as a place to store material that you need but don't want others to access. The Private folder can be used with other WebBots besides the Include Bot. And if you don't want to bother typing the path to the Private folder when you save pages, just save them to the web in the ordinary way. Switch to the FrontPage Explorer, click the Folder View button, and drag pages into the Private folder to store them there.

3 Click OK in the Save As dialog box to close it. Open or switch to the page where you want to insert the Include Bot, position the cursor, and click the Insert WebBot Component button on the Editor toolbar.

TIP

To speedily switch between open pages in the Editor, press Ctrl+F6.

4 The Insert WebBot Component dialog box appears. Double-click Include, and the WebBot Include Component Properties dialog box pops up. Click Browse, double-click the _private folder, then double-click your file. The file name and path appear in the WebBot Include Component Properties dialog box, as shown in Figure 15.5.

Fig. 15.5
Include any file you like, as long as it's in the current web. The Include Bot doesn't work with files stored outside the open web.

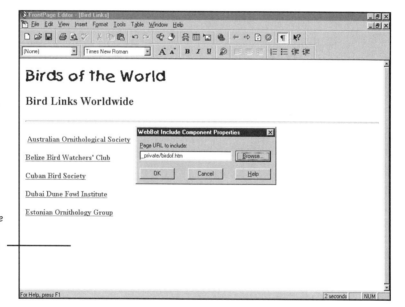

The file named in the Include Component Properties dialog box will appear at the cursor on this page.

5 Click OK in the WebBot Include Component Properties dialog box, and the included file appears at the cursor.

Insert other Include Bots throughout your web if you like. Although useful, the Include Bot has limitations: it only works with pages in the current web, and you have to insert the whole page—you can't include a selection from a page.

Selling ads? Try the Scheduled Bots

Buy a classified ad in the newspaper, and, after taking your text over the phone, the paper inserts your ad for the number of days you've paid for. If you're selling ad space on your web, you can be your own classified advertising department with the Scheduled Image and the Scheduled Include Bots. They both work the same way. The Scheduled Image Bot inserts an image from your web for a specified time; the Scheduled Include Bot inserts any page from your web for a specified time.

All you do is store your advertiser's page or image in your web, and insert either one with the Scheduled Bots. Not that you have to use them for advertising. You might have seasonal pictures that you'd like to rotate in and out of your web at intervals, or a timely page that you wish to display for a limited period.

The Scheduled Image Bot

To insert an image for a period you specify, call on the Scheduled Image Bot:

1 Import the image to your web Images folder, if it's not already there.

2 Open the page where the image is to appear and click the Insert WebBot Component button on the Editor toolbar.

3 In the Insert WebBot Component dialog box that pops up, double-click Scheduled Image. The Scheduled Image WebBot Component Properties dialog box appears. Type the name and path of an image in your web, or click Browse and select the image (see Figure 15.6).

Fig. 15.6
Set your starting and ending times and dates, and the scheduled image will be displayed only in the specified period.

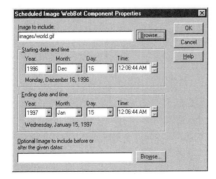

4 Enter the Starting and Ending dates and times for the image. If you have two rotating images, select another image and enter it in the Optional image to include text box. The second image will replace the first image after it expires.

5 Click OK in the Scheduled Image WebBot Component Properties dialog box, and the image will be inserted at the cursor whenever your specified starting time begins.

When the Scheduled Image Bot's ending time is reached, an [Expired Scheduled Image] message appears in the FrontPage Editor. The message won't display in browsers; instead, the image will simply vanish from the page.

The Scheduled Include Bot

If you've got a page of time-sensitive material, rather than an image, use the Scheduled Include WebBot Component. It works precisely the same as the Scheduled Image Bot, right down to an identical dialog box.

Insert an instant TOC with the Table of Contents Bot

Most word processors have a handy feature that produces an automatic table of contents for you. The Table of Contents WebBot Component does the same thing for your web. It produces a bulleted list of all the pages in the web, in the form of links to each page. And as you add or edit pages, the Table of Contents Bot can be configured to automatically update your TOC to reflect the changes.

To insert an automatic table of contents in a web page:

1 Click the Insert WebBot Component button on the Editor toolbar, and double-click Table of Contents in the Insert WebBot Component dialog box that appears.

2 The WebBot Table of Contents Properties dialog box pops up. For a TOC that covers all the pages in the web, accept the default Page URL for Starting Point of Table. The default is your home page, INDEX.HTM, as shown in Figure 15.7.

Part V Beyond the Basic Web Page

These options are checked by default, and you'll have no reason to change them.

Fig. 15.7
Like most of the Bot Properties dialog boxes, this one comes already filled-in with defaults that you probably won't need to change.

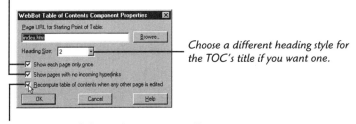

Choose a different heading style for the TOC's title if you want one.

If you want the TOC to update automatically when you add or edit pages, check this option.

  3. Click OK in the WebBot Table of Contents Properties dialog box, and a dummy TOC is inserted at the cursor. It's just there as a place-holder; you can't edit it or change the links. To see the actual TOC, click the Preview in Browser button on the Editor toolbar. Figure 15.8 shows a windowed view of the Editor's dummy TOC and the corresponding actual TOC in the Browser.

Fig. 15.8
The Table of Contents bot inserts a dummy TOC in the Editor; to see the real thing, view the page in your browser.

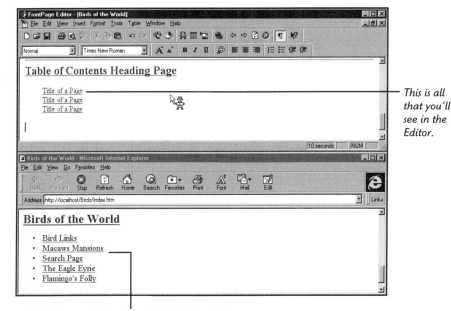

This is all that you'll see in the Editor.

The browser displays the list of links to all the pages in the web that make up your TOC.

http://www.quecorp.com

If you checked the Recompute table of contents option in the WebBot Table of Contents Properties dialog box (see Figure 15.7), your TOC will update automatically. Not in the Editor though. That dummy table is all you'll see. Double-clicking the table just pops up the WebBot Table of Contents Properties dialog box, so don't try to edit the dummy text.

Q&A **How do I change the formatting for my Table of Contents Bot table?**

Apart from changing the heading style of the table's title, you can't change the formatting of a Bot-generated TOC. Sorry. If you want a table with a different look, create one manually by listing links to all your web pages in the format of your choice.

Keep your pages fresh with a timestamp

Web surfers like to be assured that they're viewing the very latest. They might also like to know if anything's changed since their last visit. To keep your visitors happy, use the Timestamp WebBot Component to automatically insert the date with a page was last edited.

To date your page, click the Insert WebBot Component button on the Editor toolbar and double-click Timestamp in the Insert WebBot Component dialog box that appears.

The WebBot Timestamp Component Properties dialog box pops up; just click OK to insert the date when the page was last edited. The Timestamp Bot will change the date the next time you save the page.

TIP **The Timestamp Bot inserts the date, or the date and time, but** that's about it. If you want to add text before the date, "This page was last updated on" for example, just type the text before the inserted date.

ActiveX controls? Java applets? Plug-ins? Explain, please

If you've investigated the Insert, Other Components command in the FrontPage Editor, you'll have noticed that FrontPage lets you insert ActiveX controls, Java applets, and Plug-ins into your web pages. Which is fine, providing you know what these things are.

Like WebBots, FrontPage's Other Components are small programs that extend the capabilities of a web page. Java applets, ActiveX controls, and Plug-ins of many types can be downloaded from the World Wide Web and inserted into your pages. If you go deeply enough into the subject, you can write your own; Java and ActiveX are both programming languages in wide use among web site developers. Java was created by Sun Microsystems, and ActiveX was developed by Microsoft. Both languages have their adherents, and many of the fancy effects you'll see on the World Wide Web were created with one or the other.

Plug-ins, short for Netscape Plug-ins, are helper programs that let browsers and web sites do things like show movies. RealAudio is a popular plug-in, for example, that stores and plays sound files over the Internet.

A good place to start exploring the possibilities offered by these other components is Microsoft's Web Gallery page, at **http://www.microsoft.com/gallery/default.htm** (see Figure 15.9).

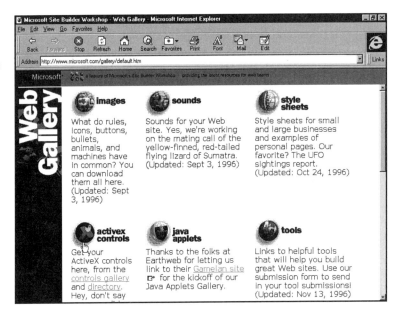

Fig. 15.9
The Microsoft Web Gallery has many small programs you can insert into web pages. If you're looking for images or sounds to download, you'll find those too.

You can download Java applets, ActiveX Controls, and Plug-ins from the Web Gallery pages, and insert them into your own FrontPage webs. Why would you want to do that? Depending on what kind of web you're creating, you'll find plenty of ideas to help make your web a livelier place. For example, one ActiveX control grabs data from a specified Web site and displays it, stock ticker fashion, in your own pages. Other plug-ins, controls, and applets are used for animations, to display heavily formatted documents, and for other effects.

Not all browsers support these other components, and they add considerably to the size of your pages. That, as we never tire of repeating, can make for slow page loading times for your web visitors.

16 Inducting Your Page into the Hall of Frames

● **In this chapter:**

- **The secrets of framed pages revealed!**

- **How do I create a framed page?**

- **The size of it: Rearranging your framed page**

- **Click a link *here* and open the page *there***

- **How to convert your existing web**

Frames are the latest craze in page design. Find out how they can help you organize your pages, and give them some extra pizzazz, to boot . . . .▸

Have you ever used one of those travel guides that includes a fold-out map? As you search the listings for your next roadside stop, the map lies ready to give you instant directions, saving you the trouble of having to flip back and forth between pages.

A framed web page works much the same way. The user's browser window is divided into smaller windows, each with its own content. One frame can hold a table of contents, logo, or user guide that always remains visible, while another frame displays the different pages the user selects.

In Figure 16.1, for example, the browser window includes three frames. The top one displays a menu that is continuously available to the user. If the user clicks one of the links in this frame, it opens the linked page in the left frame. The left frame, in turn, contains a table of contents; click one of the links, and its linked page pops up in the right frame.

FrontPage lets you arrange frames just about any way you want. Using a wizard or building from the ground up, you can devise interesting and creative ways to make your web's contents available to your visitor.

How do frames work?

At the heart of a framed page is the **frame set**, a web page that contains information on how your page will look and behave in a browser. In addition, FrontPage sets up a separate web page for each frame. Thus, if the page contains two framed windows, your web actually sets up three pages.

The frames can work together or separately. A frame might contain a logo or menu that's always visible. Or it might include links that, when clicked, display a page in another frame (the second frame is called the **target frame**). In other words, a frame can function like a permanent billboard on the side of the road, or it can work like one of those rotating signs you see at ballparks.

Anatomy of a framed page

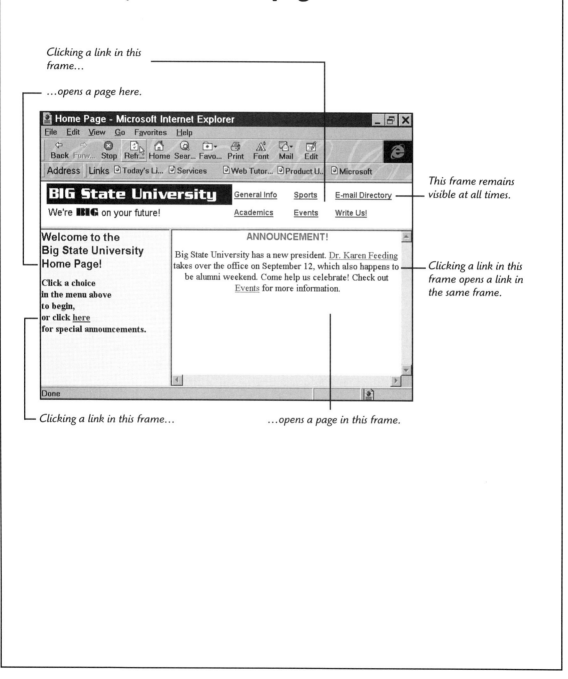

CAUTION A framed page can be loads of fun to design but not much fun to use. Too many frames clutter a screen and display text in frustratingly small parcels. Remember, too, that many users have 14-inch monitors and lower-resolution screens, which combine to make a framed page a very unpleasant experience. Even as few as three frames can overcrowd a browser. Also, keep in mind that many users are accustomed to using their browser's Back and Forward buttons to get around a web site. These buttons don't always take the user where he wants to go when he's navigating a framed web. The bottom line: if your frames don't make your page easier to use, you're better off using the full browser window.

Start from the beginning!

You're probably wondering how to change your current web into one that uses frames. Yes, it can be done, and we'll talk about it a bit later. But adapting an existing web can be a tricky process, involving renaming files, redesigning pages, and perhaps changing links. Learning about frames will be a much less frustrating experience if you first set up a framed page from scratch, even if it's just a mock page that you'll use for instructional purposes only. And you'll have an easier time reframing your existing web.

As we explain how to make a framed web, we'll also assume that you want the framed page to be your home page; that is, the framed page will be index.htm. There's certainly nothing wrong with giving your framed page a different name and linking to it from another page; but if you're going to go through the not inconsiderable bother of using frames, you might as well trot them out front and center.

Now that we've gotten the caveats out of the way, let's begin. Create a new web in Explorer, using the Normal Web template. The new web contains a single, empty page, index.htm. Switch to Editor by clicking the Show FrontPage Editor button on the Explorer toolbar.

If you're new to frames, there's no better way to create a framed page than with Editor's Frames wizard. The wizard can set you up with the most popular types of framed pages—the ones you see at many sites across the Web. It does most of the dirty work for you, configuring the number, size, and location of your frames. The resulting frames are flexible enough so that you can fine tune the page when you're done. Once you've learned the elements of a framed page, you can create your own.

Let's run through the steps, exploring some of your options along the way.

Frame wizardry

Choose File, New or press Ctrl+N to open the New Page dialog box. (Do not press the New button; you'll get a Normal page, and a framed page is anything but normal.) Choose Frames Wizard and click OK; Editor opens the Choose Technique window of the Frames Wizard (see Figure 16.1).

Fig. 16.1
Choose Pick a Template to create a framed page using one of the Frames Wizard's six preset layouts; choose Make a Custom Grid if you want to create a framed page to your own specifications.

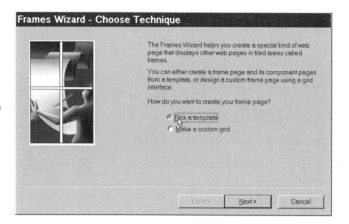

You've got two options here: Pick a Template and Make a Custom Grid. The second option gives you more flexibility in setting up your frames, but templates are easier to use, and modifying your page is a simple task. We suggest that you experiment with the templates first, and then give the custom grid option a try.

Choose the Pick a Template radio button and click the Next button. The wizard opens the Pick Template Layout window (see Figure 16.2), where you can choose among six layouts in the Layout selection box.

Select a layout to preview it in the box to the left and get a description down below. In Figure 16.2, for example, you can see that selecting Banner with Nested Table of Contents produces a page with one horizontal frame and two vertical frames. When you've found one that's close to what you have in mind, choose Next.

Fig. 16.2
The Frames Wizard lets you choose among six common framed page layouts.

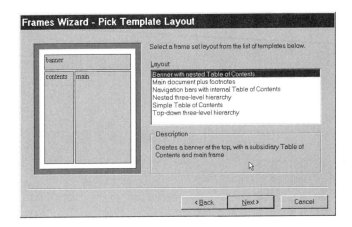

For those without frames

The wizard's next window, Choose Alternate Content, lets you specify a page for people whose browsers don't support frames. If, for example, you have an old homepage, just drop its URL in the Alternate Page URL text box. Who can't display framed pages? Mostly, people who still use old browsers. But the latest versions of the most popular browsers are frame-friendly and free, so the number of users who can't view frames is dwindling rapidly.

Keep in mind, too, that an alternate page is one more page you have to maintain and update. Use an alternate page if you have one convenient or if it's critical that you reach everyone in the universe.

Time to save the page

The next window, Save Page, lets you give your framed page a title and file name (see Figure 16.3). Use a descriptive title, such as Home Page, that's different from the default provided by the wizard; you'll have an easier time identifying your pages as you build the web. And if the framed page is going to be the home page, as is the case here, give it the URL Index.htm. The wizard asks you if you want to replace the current Index.htm; choose Yes.

Fig. 16.3
The URL of your framed page is index.htm if the page will serve as your home page.

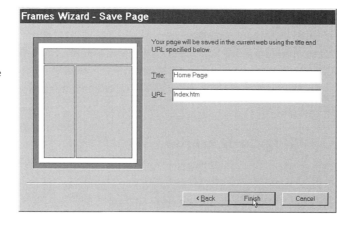

Wait a minute—nothing happened!

When the wizard is done, it returns you to Editor—which mysteriously remains blank. Did FrontPage actually do anything?

Switch back to Explorer to find out. You'll see that the wizard was quite busy; it not only saved your home page, but created several other pages in the process. For example, for the Banner with Nested Table of Contents layout (refer to Figure 16.2), the wizard created three linked pages, shown in Figure 16.4.

Fig. 16.4
The wizard creates your framed page—in this case, Home Page—plus a page for each of the page's frames.

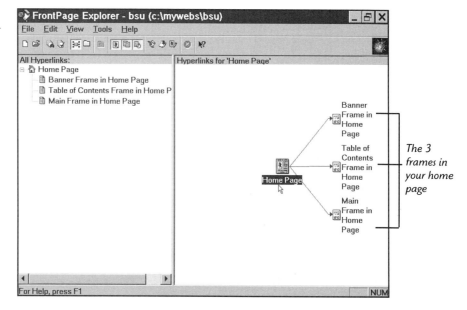

What are these pages for? Well, if you look at Figure 16.2, you'll see in the graphic that the page consists of three frames titled Banner, Contents, and Main. And if you look at Figure 16.4, you'll see three linked pages titled Banner Frame in Home Page, Table of Contents Frame in Home Page, and Main Frame in Home Page. In other words, each frame has its own web page ready for Editor.

Opening Your Framed Web Page

You're probably ready to open Index.htm in Editor and start working on your framed page. Nice idea, but grab a bat; FrontPage is about to throw you a curve ball. You can't open a framed page.

Remember that a framed page, such as Index.htm in our example, is a frame set. It's not an ordinary web page; it contains the codes that configure the frames in the user's browser. If you try to open the frame set (Index.htm here), Editor displays the Frames Wizard. As we'll see later, you'll use this wizard to modify your frames page, but that's not what you want to do right now.

So, you might be wondering, how do you actually view the framed page? You have to use your browser. Alas, this is more complicated than it should be. Since you can't open the page in Editor, you can't use Editor's File, Preview in <u>B</u>rowser command. Instead, you have to load your browser and use its Open command to find and open the page. Each browser does this a bit differently; refer to your browser's help files for specific instructions.

You should take a peek at your new framed page before you start editing the individual frames. Figure 16.5, for example, shows what the framed page looks like when you choose the Banner with Nested Table of Contents layout (refer to Figure 16.2). The Frames Wizard even provides descriptions of each frame.

 TIP **Keep your browser open to your framed page as you work on your** frames in editor. When you want to see how a change will affect the way your framed page looks, switch to the browser and click the Refresh or Reload button. To make the framed page more readily available from one computing session to another, add it to your browser's Bookmarks or Favorites list. This lets you load the page without using the browser's File, Open command.

http://www.quecorp.com

Fig. 16.5
If you preview your new framed page after you create it, you can see what the general layout looks like, as well as read the instructions the Frames Wizard added to each frame's associated web page.

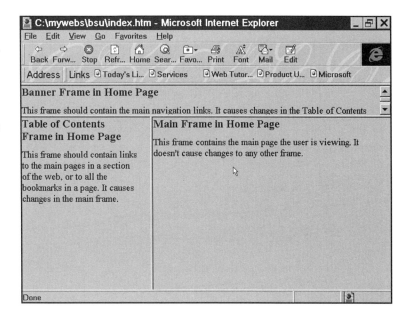

 CAUTION We mentioned earlier that some users have older browsers that can't display frames. If you're one of those users, you won't be able to view your frames as you create them. Go on the Web and download a browser that supports frames—Netscape 2.0 and Internet Explorer 3.0, for instance.

A different frame of mind

You can't easily change the frame of a house once you've put it up. Not so the frames of your new page. Want more or fewer frames? Is a row not high enough, or a column not wide enough? Do you want to change how the frames are linked to one another, or change the page to which a frame is linked? Return to the Frames Wizard and make the adjustments.

Starting the Frames Wizard again is a simple matter of opening the framed page (double-click it in Explorer or open it in Editor). FrontPage opens the wizard to the Edit Frame set Grid dialog box. Figure 16.6 displays the dialog box for a framed page created with the Banner with Nested Table of Contents layout.

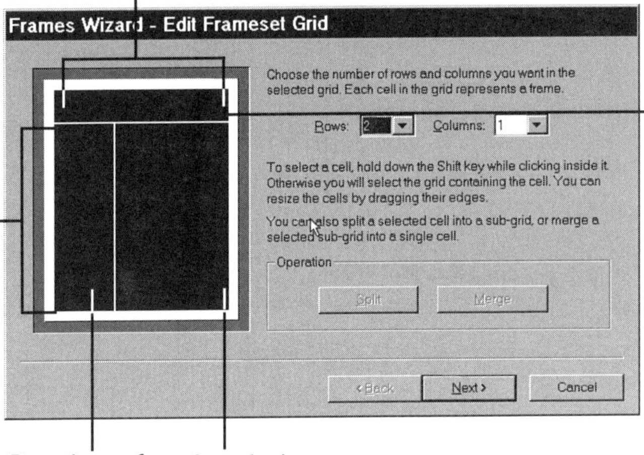

Fig. 16.6
Return to the Frames Wizard to add, delete, and resize frames.

Single column of main grid

First row of Main grid

Second row of main grid; single row of sub-grid

First column of sub-grid

Second column of sub-grid

Adding rows and columns

The framed page you see in the graphic isn't exactly what it seems to be. What appears as a single page actually is divided into grids and cells. Let's analyze the page a little more closely.

The entire page comprises one grid, consisting of two rows and one column. The second row actually is a second grid, or sub-grid, which itself has two columns. The grids are made up of cells, similar to those in a table. In Figure 16.6, for example, the entire grid contains three cells, while the sub-grid (the second row) consists of two cells.

You can change the number of rows and columns for any grid or sub-grid. You also can split and merge cells. You select a grid by clicking it; you select a cell by clicking it while holding down the Shift key.

More columns, please

Let's say, for example, that you want to divide the second row into three columns. Click either column in the second row; the page now looks like the one in Figure 16.7. Next, choose 3 in the Columns scroll box. The page now looks like the one in Figure 16.8.

http://www.quecorp.com

Fig. 16.7
Click your mouse to select a grid or sub-grid. Shift+click selects any cell in the page.

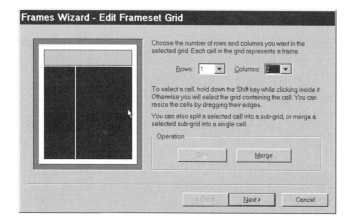

Fig. 16.8
The results of adding a column in this selected grid.

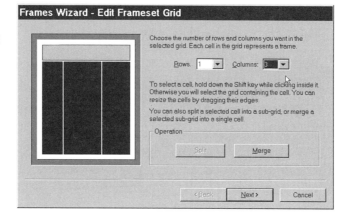

When you create a new frame, remember that it represents a new page, which you'll need to give a title and URL. You can take care of that in the wizard's next dialog box, which we'll talk about in a minute.

CAUTION **Changing the number of rows and columns in an existing framed page**, as well as merging and splitting cells, is not to be done capriciously. Remember, FrontPage has already established pages for each frame, as well as links connecting the frames. Changing the configuration not only means that you have to set up new pages and connections; it can also mean blowing away your old ones. Also, if you change a grid and then change it back to its original appearance, the cells might look like they're the same, but they might not have their attributes. You should spend time playing with this dialog box in an empty web before you try to use it on an existing web. Even better, plan your framed page carefully enough so that you don't need to mess with its configuration.

Merging and splitting

Do you have too many cells in a grid? In the Edit Frame set Grid window (see Figure 16.8), select the grid and click the Merge button. Merging a two-column grid, for example, turns it into a one-column grid; merging two rows of a three-grid turns it into a two-row grid.

You also can split a cell into several cells by selecting it and choosing the Split button. FrontPage always splits a cell into two rows and two columns; you can add or eliminate rows and columns by changing the values in the Rows and Columns selection boxes.

Changing attributes of a framed page, right?

When you're done scratching your head over the Edit Frame set Grid dialog box, click Next to move on to the Edit Frame Attributes dialog box. This one's a bit easier to understand, and it also has options that you're more likely to need. For our purposes, we'll stick with our original framed page (see Figure 16.7) and assume we haven't added any new frames.

The entire web page displayed on the left of the dialog box is grayed out at first. Kick-start the dialog box by clicking one of the frames; the fields on the right side display the frame's attributes (see Figure 16.9). (If you've clicked a new frame that you created in this editing session, all of the selection boxes will be empty.) Here's a brief description of each:

Fig. 16.9
You can specify a different page to load into your frame by entering the page's URL in the Edit Frame Attributes dialog box.

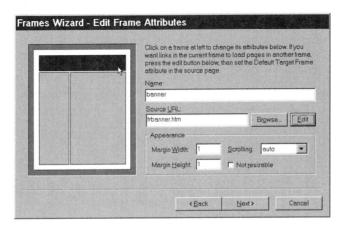

Name

The Name text box contains the name of your frame. This name is important; if the frame is a target frame, other pages look for this name. So the name of the frame should always stay the same.

Source URL

The Source URL text box provides the file name of the page that the browser initially loads into the frame; use it to replace an existing page with a new one. If you don't know the URL, click the Browse button to find it with the Choose Source URL dialog box.

The page must be a part of your web before you can use it. Refer to Chapter 12 for more information on adding web pages from outside your web.

Changing the target with Edit

Remember what a target frame is? It's the frame into which another frame loads pages when the user clicks a hyperlink. In the framed page in Figure 16.5, for example, the Main frame is the target frame for the Table of Contents frame.

You can change the target frame by clicking the Edit button. For example, say you want the Banner frame in Figure 16.5 (and selected in Figure 16.9) to target the Main frame instead of the Table of Contents frame. Follow these steps:

1 Click the Edit button. FrontPage switches you to Editor and opens the page.

2 Choose File, Page Properties from the menu bar. Editor displays the Page Properties dialog box. Choose the General panel.

3 Enter the name of your new target frame in the Default Target Frame text box and click OK.

4 Switch back to the Frames Wizard dialog box.

Appearance is everything

The Edit Frame Attributes dialog box also controls the appearance of your frames.

Enter new values, in pixels, in Margin Width and Margin Height to change the amount of space between the frame's border and its contents.

Click the Not Resizable check box if you want to prevent the user from being able to move the margins in her browser. If you don't click this box, the user can resize your frames by dragging and clicking the margins with his mouse.

Sizable frames have their advantages; they give the user more freedom to decide how she wants to view your information, such as widening a frame to make more text visible. And she can always restore the frames to their original state by clicking the browser's Refresh or Reload button.

Choose No in the Scrolling selection box if you don't want your user to be able to scroll a frame. The user won't be able to see any information on the page that's below the frame's margin.

CAUTION If you choose No in the Scrolling selection box, the information that is not visible is still accessible; a user can always download the page and see what's hidden.

Alternate currents

When you've finished editing your attributes, click the Next button to move to the Choose Alternate Content dialog box.

You might remember, way back at the beginning of this chapter, that the Frames Wizard template let you choose an alternate, frame-free page when you set up your frames. Here's where you get to change your mind.

If you initially decided to punish frameless users by not offering an alternate page, you can add one by typing its URL in the Alternate Page URL text box. Use the Browse button if you don't remember the name of the file.

On the other hand, if you have an alternate page that you're tired of maintaining, choose Clear.

Q&A *Can I get rid of the borders around my frames?*

You sure can, if you're willing to roll up your sleeves and hack some HTML code. (Yes, we promised that we wouldn't talk about HTML in this book, but this is such a common question that we're making an exception.)

Switch to Explorer and right-click the page that contains your frame set (index.htm in the examples in this chapter). From the quick menu, choose Open With (not Open). Windows opens an Open with Editor dialog box. Double-click Text Editor (notepad.exe). Windows runs NotePad and opens the file.

Next, peruse the document until you find a pair of angle brackets that contain the word "frameset" and a couple of numbers. The line might look like this:

<frameset rows="23%,77%">

Edit the line so that it looks like this:

<frameset rows="23%,77%" FRAMEBORDER="NO" BORDER="0" FRAMESPACING="0">

Save the file (choose File, Save) and exit NotePad to finish the job.

This method works for framed pages viewed with Microsoft's Internet Explorer browser but might not work for framed pages viewed with other browsers.

The end is near!

You're nearly at the end of the trail. Are you sure of all your selections? Click the Back button if you want to review the changes you've made with the wizard, or if you want to make additional changes. Otherwise, click the Next button to display the Save Page dialog box. If you're changing an existing frames page, simply click the Finish button. Answer Yes when the Frames Wizard asks you if you want to overwrite the existing URL. Otherwise, first enter a title and URL in the text boxes provided.

I'd rather do it myself

Once you've created a framed page with a template and modified it with the Frames Wizard, you have all the tools you need to create a framed page from scratch.

Start a new page in Editor with File, New and choose the Frames Wizard in the New Page dialog box. FrontPage opens the Choose Technique dialog box.

Instead of selecting the Pick a Template radio button, pick the Make a Custom Grid radio button and click Next. The wizard displays the Edit Frame set Grid dialog box.

If you get the uncanny feeling that you've been here before, you have—this is the dialog box that opens when you edit an existing frame set (refer to Figure 16.6). The steps you take to create a new framed page are nearly the same as editing an old one. For details, review the previous section, "A different frame of mind." Here's a summary:

1. Create your layout in the Edit Frameset Grid dialog box and choose Next.

2. Choose your attributes in the Edit Frame Attributes dialog box. Since you don't have a frame set yet, all of the boxes in this dialog box will be empty. Click the Next button when you're done.

3. Choose an alternate page in the Alternate Content dialog box and click Next.

4. Enter a title and URL in the Save Page dialog box and click the Finish button.

Connecting your frames

We've covered a lot of territory to get to this point, so let's review where we stand:

- We've got our frame set—index.htm in the examples—that defines what the page frames look like when displayed in a browser.

- Each frame is actually a regular web page; the browser loads the page into the frame when the user loads the framed page.

- You can set up a framed page so that clicking a hyperlink in one frame loads its linked page in another frame. The second frame is called the target frame.

The next step is to start creating new pages, as well as the hyperlinks that load the right pages into the right frames.

Opening a frame

You edit a page that goes into a frame like you do any other page—double-click it in FrontPage Explorer or use Editor's File, Open command. Consider editing your pages from the top of the link chain down. For example, the framed page that uses the Banner with Nested Table of Contents layout (refer to Figure 16.2) starts with the Banner frame at the top, which controls the Table of Contents frame to the left, which controls the Main frame to the right. The place to start, then, is the Banner Frame (refer to Figure 16.5).

The pages that the Frames Wizard sets up include short descriptions of the pages—what they contain and what other frames they target (see Figures 16.10 and 16.12 for examples). You'll replace these descriptions with your own graphics, links, text, or other content. The pages also include comments that will help you figure out what the pages do and how they're connected to the other pages in the web. These comments are invisible in a browser, so you don't have to delete them.

In our example, the Banner frame stays visible at all times; as the text in the page explains, it's where you put hyperlinks you want continuously available. It's also a good place to put a logo. The Banner frame might look something like the one in Figure 16.11; Figure 16.12 shows how the frame will appear in a browser. See Chapter 3, "Home, Sweet Home Page: Inside the Editor," for a refresher on editing web pages and Chapter 12, "Webward Ho! Adding Pages to Your Web," for details on creating hyperlinks.

Fig. 16.10
When you open a page the Frame Wizard created for a frame, you'll find instructions and comments that you can replace with your own material.

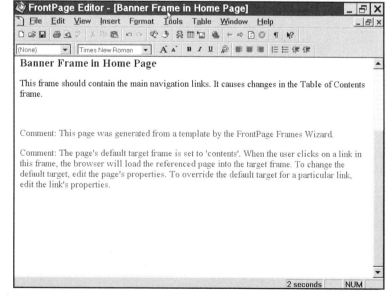

Fig. 16.11
The Banner page in Figure 16.10 after the instructions have been replaced with a logo and menu.

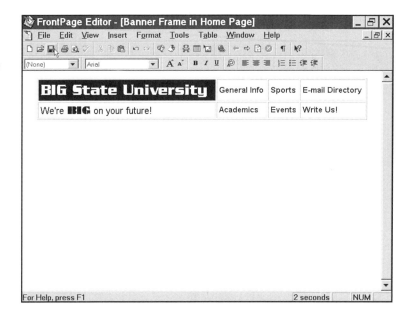

Fig. 16.12
Here's how the Banner page appears in a browser. The Table of Contents and Main frames still need to be edited.

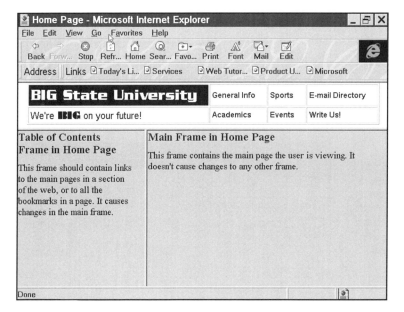

Another link in the chain

Move on to the next frame in the chain—in this example, the Table of Contents frame. The first step is to modify the page that appears in the browser when the user first loads the framed page. This can be a greeting or instructions. In Figure 16.13, for example, the original Table of Contents page now comprises a simple hello and directions on what the user should do next.

The next job is to create the pages that will appear in the Table of Contents frame when the user clicks a link in the Banner frame. (If you forgot how to build a page, you'll find details in Chapter 12.)

For example, General Info in Figure 16.13 becomes a link to a new table of contents page called General Information, shown in Figure 16.14. Thereafter, when a user clicks the General Info link, the General Information page appears in the Table of Contents frame, as in Figure 16.15.

Eventually, all of the links in the Banner frame open a table of contents page in the Table of Contents frame; likewise, all of the links in each table of contents page opens a page in the Main frame, until the framed page starts to look something like the one in Figure 16.16.

Fig. 16.13
A greeting has been added to the Table of Contents frame as the home page begins to take shape.

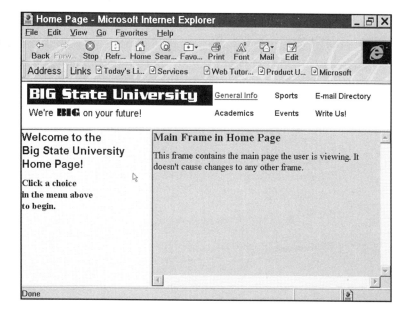

Fig. 16.14
This new General Information table of contents will appear in the Table of Contents frame when the General Info link in the Banner frame is clicked.

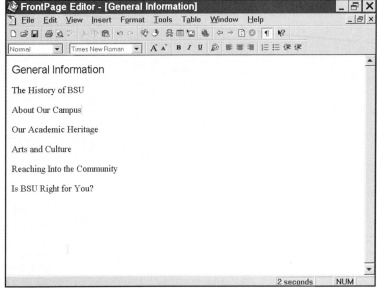

Fig. 16.15
This is how the General Information table of contents appears in the browser.

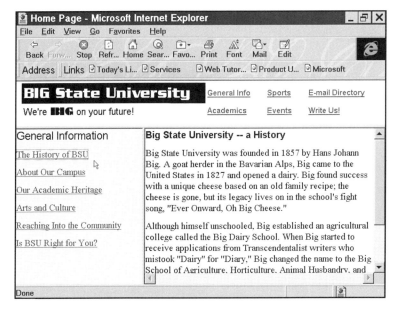

Fig. 16.16
All links are in place, and the framed page begins to look like a real home page. Add graphics and stir!

Table of contents frame

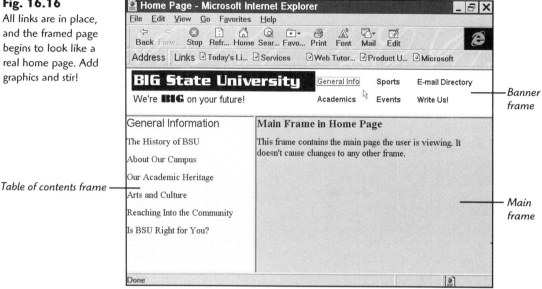

Banner frame

Main frame

TIP **As you develop the pages that will go into each frame, you will** probably need to tweak the margins and attributes. Now is the time to run the Frames Wizard again, as explained in the earlier section "A different frame of mind."

Changing default targets

When a frame targets another frame, all links in the frame load their pages into the targeted frame. But there are times when you'll want a specific link to load a page into a different frame.

For example, in Figure 16.16, clicking Write Us! In the Banner frame automatically displays the linked page in the Table of Contents frame. Imagine, though, that the link loads a feedback form that needs to appear in the Main frame. Here's how to do it:

1 Load the page that contains the link into Editor.

2 Right-click the link and choose Hyperlink Properties; Editor displays the Edit Hyperlink dialog box (see Figure 16.17).

Fig. 16.17
Change the default frame in the Edit Hyperlink dialog box if you'd like a link to load a page into a different frame.

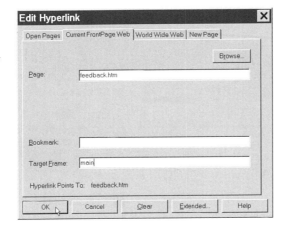

3. Enter the name of the new target frame in the Target Frame text box; Main in Figure 16.17.

4. Choose OK and save the page.

You also can change the default target for all of the links in any web page in the Page Properties dialog box. Right-click the page in Editor and choose Page Properties. Enter the new default in the Default Target Frame text box.

Converting your existing web

Maybe you already have a web up and running. How do you retrofit it to use frames?

Special targets

Whether you're changing the default target for a link or page, you also can use one of four special target names:

_blank This forces the browser to open a linked page in a new browser window.

_self This name sends the linked page to the same frame in which the link appears.

_top Use this name if you want the linked page to take the entire browser window; all frames disappear.

_parent This name tells the browser to display a linked page in a **parent frame**, which is a frame that has been split into smaller frames. For example, if at some point you divided a frame into three rows, the _parent name remerges the rows into a single frame.

Chapter 16 *Inducting Your Page into the Hall of Frames* **323**

Setting up a new framed home page to replace your old one is simple. You don't even have to scrap your old home page. Follow these steps:

Save your original home page to another file name. Open the page in editor, choose File, Save As, and fill out the Save As dialog box. For example, you might rename Index.htm to Oldindex.htm. If you're still going to use the page, give it a new title, too; for example, Home Page Without Frames.

Create your new framed page as explained in this chapter.

Save the new framed page with the file name of the old home page; in this example, Index.htm. FrontPage asks you if you want to replace the existing page; choose Yes (remember, you've saved the existing page to a new file name, so you won't lose it).

If you want to integrate your old home page into your web, simply create a link to it as you would any other web page.

A few tips on creating framed pages

Creating web pages for your frames is like building a boat with nothing but a saw and some nails; get ready to spend a lot of time planing and caulking until your craft is seaworthy. Here are a few tips to help you along:

Remember: the page that appears in a frame is identical to a page that doesn't; all of the tools available on the menu bar are at your disposal.

If you can't create your frames in exact order (and who among us is organized enough to do so?), use the To Do list to keep track of your work (see Chapter 20, "Maintaining Your Web," for more about the To Do list).

Keep logos, graphics, and type in proportion to the size of the frame. Your headings can't be as big in a skinny column as they can be in a full screen.

Make sure that you provide links that let the user get back to previous menus.

Less information is more information; users will be much happier if they don't have to constantly scroll the frames.

Use colors sparingly; you don't want your page to look like a Grateful Dead T-shirt (unless you're running a site for Deadheads). Light pastels are effective for creating contrast among your frames.

Use tables to arrange elements of a frame, but use table borders sparingly. Your frames already divide your page, and too many frames and tables will make your page look boxy.

17

Templates: Professional Pages, Painlessly

● **In this chapter:**

- **FrontPage has a web template for most occasions**

- **How do I modify this template?**

- **Guest Books and Search pages are templates I can really use**

- **I need a fancy page, not a whole web**

- **How do I create my own page template?**

Like a cookie cutter, templates can stamp out as many identical webs and pages as you need. There's no danger of dull uniformity though—these cookie cutters can be altered whenever you like . . . . ▶

Few objects are more familiar than the morning newspaper. Along with what greets us in the mirror, it's one of the first things we lay eyes on every day. Newspapers receive blizzards of mail when they make even minor changes to their layouts—which is why changes are seldom made. Compare today's *New York Times* front page with a picture of the newspaper's front page from fifty years ago, and they look remarkably alike.

Newspapers achieve their consistent look because they're laid out according to a strict pattern, or template. The news itself is often irritating, and always changing, but the mold in which it's presented is reassuringly familiar.

The Internet is as changeable as the daily news, and often just as irritating. As a web designer, you can balance that with web pages that look consistent and well thought-out. Templates are the easiest way to achieve such a look. With a template, the most dynamic content can be poured into a reassuringly stable mold.

FrontPage's templates may be all I need

Writing and assembling the content of a web is enough work for most of us. The way the web looks, while important, may take a back seat if we have to make every design decision on our own. Fortunately, we don't have to. FrontPage's collection of web templates gives us ready-to-wear webs that work perfectly well for most uses. Just add content, and you can go home for the day.

To view the FrontPage web templates, choose File, New, FrontPage Web in the FrontPage Explorer. In the New FrontPage Web dialog box that appears, click any of the templates on the list for a Description, as seen in Figure 17.1.

Fig. 17.1
Wizard or template, any of the choices listed here gives you the framework of a new web.

One ready-to-wear option: the Corporate Presence Web

The Wizards shown in Figure 17.1 are templates that offer custom choices and extra help as you set them up. The Corporate Presence Wizard, for example, lays out a kind of electronic corporate brochure for your company. As the Wizard creates the web, you choose what kinds of pages to include.

To see the kinds of pages the Wizard can set up for you, double-click Corporate Presence Wizard in the New FrontPage Web dialog box. In the Corporate Presence Wizard dialog box that appears, name the new web and click OK (if you're just experimenting, you can easily delete the web later).

Click Next in the Corporate Presence Web Wizard dialog box for the choices shown in Figure 17.2.

Fig. 17.2
Apart from the mandatory Home Page, the Wizard allows you to pick and choose your pages.

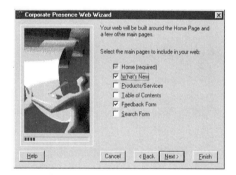

If this looks to be the type of web you want, work your way through the questions and options that appear on each of the Corporate Presence Wizard's screens. Click Finish on the last screen, and FrontPage creates the folder structure and sets up the pages of your new web.

All that remains for you to do (all!) is supply the content. Double-click any of the new web's pages in the FrontPage Explorer. The page opens in the FrontPage Editor; select the dummy text and type in your own, as shown in Figure 17.3.

There are a few interesting things going on in the page created by the Corporate Presence Wizard. The Wizard used the Include Bot to insert the Company Logo and navigation bar seen in Figure 17.3. Both items are stored in the web's _private folder, accessible to you for editing, but not accessible to web visitors (see Chapter 15, "WebBots and Other Web Bells and Whistles," for a complete description of the Include Bot and its use with the private folder).

Fig. 17.3
Selecting this dummy text and replacing it with your own is easy enough, but you still have to think up what you want to say.

The Company Logo and Navigation Bar have been inserted with the Include WebBot, hence the robot-pointer.

Comments don't display in the browser—they're strictly for internal consumption in the FrontPage Editor.

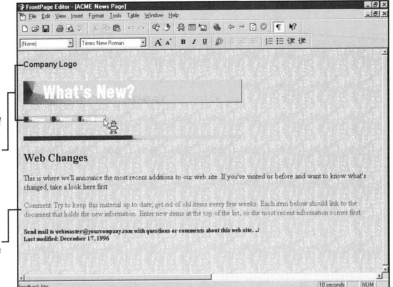

> **66** *Plain English, please!*
>
> A **navigation bar** is like the image maps we looked at in Chapter 13, "Lights, Action, Click! Hotspots, Video, and Sound;" two or more images with hotspots, grouped together. Sometimes they're mere formatted hyperlinks. The navigation bar in Figure 17.3 is actually three GIF images containing hotspots with links to pages in the web. **99**

What's a Comment

Comments, which display in a different colored font and offer editing tips throughout the Corporate Presence web, can be deleted, or replaced with Comments of your own. Comments don't appear in a browser (your own or anyone else's). They're simply annotations, internal notes to help you keep track of web chores.

To edit an existing Comment like the one shown in Figure 17.3, just double-click it. The Comment dialog box appears; type new text and click OK to insert the Comment at the cursor (see Figure 17.4).

Fig. 17.4
If you're in the habit of writing post-it notes to yourself or to others, you'll find Comments a handy feature.

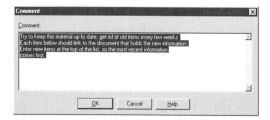

To create a new Comment, click Insert, Comment. Type your text in the Comment dialog box, and click OK. And to get rid of a Comment, click it and press Delete.

I need a page template, not a whole new web

FrontPage's collection of web templates offers many shortcuts and design ideas—the navigation bar in the Corporate Presence Wizard web for example. They're worth exploring, and it's very likely that you'll find most of what you need in one or the other. And of course you don't have to use the templates strictly as they were intended. Even if you have no interest in a Corporate Presence Web, there's nothing to stop you from grabbing some of the template's elements and using them in a web devoted to something entirely different. You can also customize the existing web templates as much as you want, deleting and adding pages, changing the formatting, and rearranging them in any way that's of use.

But what if you've got a web already under construction, and you're after a specialized page or two, not an entire new web? Lurking in the FrontPage Editor is a collection of **page templates**.

To view the page templates, click File, New on the FrontPage Editor menu bar. The New Page dialog box pops up, as seen in Figure 17.5.

Add a guest book to your web

The page templates let you add specialized pages with built-in functions. Open any of the page templates in an existing web, add your own text and graphics, and you've got an instant search page, or FAQ (Frequently Asked Questions) page, or any of the other purpose-built pages.

Fig. 17.5
Page templates give you the structure of different specialized pages. As with the web templates, just add your own content.

The Guest Book page template makes a good addition to any web. The very name sounds a lot more inviting, not to say civilized, than, say, "feedback page." (I don't know about you, but to me "feedback" suggests regurgitation rather than response, and I invariably refuse to provide it.) A Guest Book makes a visitor feel mildly uncivil for ignoring it.

Responses are what you're after when you add a Guest Book page to your web. It's a place where visitors can leave their comments on your site. You'll benefit from the sometimes helpful critiques, while your visitors, having contributed to the web, might be encouraged to return.

To give your web a guest book, choose File, New in the FrontPage Editor. In the New Page dialog box that appears, double-click Guest Book. An untitled Guest Book page pops into your web, as seen in Figure 17.6.

Fig. 17.6
Although you can make any modifications you like, the Guest Book page is practically ready for use right out of the box.

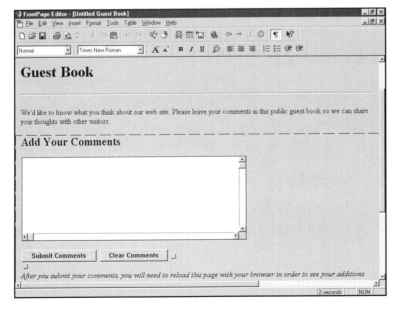

http://www.quecorp.com

The Guest Book template stores visitor comments in a GUESTLOG.HTM page, and has an Include Bot installed to display the contents of GUESTLOG.HTM right on the Guest Book page. To test the Guest Book, first save the page, then click the Preview in Browser button on the Editor toolbar. Type a sample comment in the browser, and click Submit Comments. Click the browser's Refresh or Reload button, and you'll see your sample comment appear on the Guest Book page (you might have to scroll down a little way to see it).

Q&A *I've saved my Guest Book page, but I don't see a GUESTLOG.HTM page in the FrontPage Explorer.*

Save all your work, then close the web. Now open the web again, and you'll see the GUESTLOG.HTM page listed with the other pages in the Explorer.

TIP **If you don't want visitors to access the GUESTLOG.HTM page,** where visitor comments are stored, drag the page into the _private folder in the FrontPage Explorer's folder view. Visitors will still be able to read prior comments on display in the Guest Book page, but they won't be able to alter those comments.

Getting lost visitors? Add a search page

In Chapter 15, we looked at the Search WebBot, which adds a search feature to any page. The Search Bot allows visitors to search all the pages in the web for text that they enter in the form. With the Search Page template, you get the Search Bot, together with a page full of search tips that visitors might find handy.

To add a search page to your web, choose File, New in the FrontPage Editor. In the New Page dialog box that appears, double-click Search Page. You get an untitled search page like the one seen in Figure 17.7.

The search page is fully functional as is, but you might want to rewrite some of the jargon-laden text. One suggestion: change the title "Query Language" to Search Tips or something similar. And while there are those who delight in the sound of phrases like "text search engine" and "arbitrary Boolean expressions," visitors will thank you for an English translation.

Once you've made your changes, save the page to add it to your web.

Fig. 17.7
This search page is ready to use, but you may want to revise some of the text.

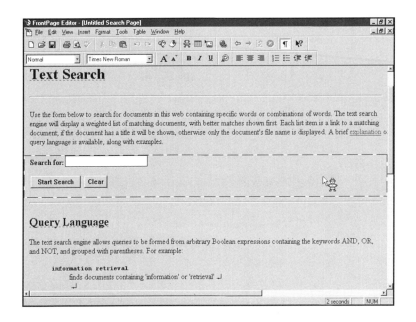

How to say "Boo" to Booleans

Boolean expressions, Boolean operators—since we encounter these terms all the time, perhaps we can spare a thought for their creator. George Boole was a self-taught nineteenth century English mathematician who invented Boolean algebra. His book, *An Investigation of the Laws of Thought*, proposed a system of symbols to substitute for the words used in formal logic. Using symbols instead of words, problems in logic could then be solved algebraically, an idea that laid the foundations for computer science.

In Boole's system, operators like AND, OR, and NOT take the place of mathematical operators like plus and minus. Search engines like the one supplied by FrontPage carry out their searches based on these operators. Searching for "George AND Boole", for example, would turn up all the instances in which the two words appeared together.

I want my own template

For web designers intent on a consistent look, taking a well-crafted page and turning it into a template is a good idea. You at once set the standard for your other pages, and also make it easy for those pages to live up to your standard.

To create a template out of any web page:

1. In the FrontPage Editor, open the page you want to turn into a template. It can be any sort of page, including pages with graphics, hyperlinks, and WebBots.

2. Click File, Save As. In the Save As dialog box that pops up, click the As Template button.

3. Type a Title, Name, and Description in the Save As Template dialog box that appears next (see Figure 17.8).

The Title identifies your template in the New Page dialog box.

Fig. 17.8
Creating a template is as easy as naming a web page.

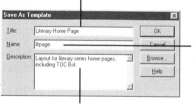

The name is the file name of your template—make it memorable in case you ever want to track down the file.

The Description appears in the New Page dialog box along with the title.

4. Click OK in the Save As Template dialog box. The page is saved as a template in its own folder in the \PROGRAM FILES\MICROSOFT FRONTPAGE\PAGES folder, as shown in Figure 17.9.

Once you've created your template, use it just as you would use any of the other page templates. Your creation appears with the other templates in the New Page dialog box—just click File, New to view it.

To apply the template to a page, double-click it in the New Page dialog box. Select any text you want to replace, type the new text, then save the page as a regular .HTM file.

Fig. 17.9
Page templates can include graphics and WebBots as well as formatted text.

Each page template is stored in its own folder within the Pages folder.

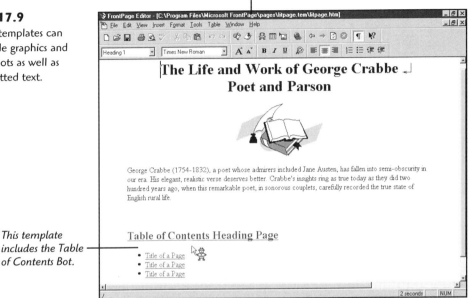

This template includes the Table of Contents Bot.

TIP If your template is for a home page, save the new page to which you've applied the template with the name INDEX.HTM. That makes it the current home page in your web.

Editing custom templates

To make changes in your new template, you'll have to dig it out of FrontPage's filing system first:

1. Click the Open button on the Editor toolbar. In the Open File dialog box, click the Other Location tab.

2. On the Other Location tab of the Open File dialog box, click From File, then click the Browse button.

3. In the Open File dialog box that appears, make your way to the \PROGRAM FILES\MICROSOFT FRONTPAGE\PAGES folder.

4. Double-click the folder with the file name you gave your template. It'll have the .tem extension, as shown in Figure 17.10.

http://www.quecorp.com

Fig. 17.10
Getting there is a bit of a chore, but editing templates is just like editing regular pages.

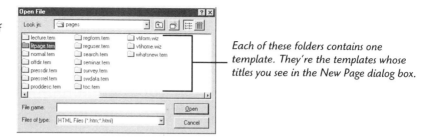

Each of these folders contains one template. They're the templates whose titles you see in the New Page dialog box.

 5 Now double-click your template file to open it. Make any changes you wish, and click the Save button on the toolbar to save the template.

To delete a custom template, just right-click the template folder in the Open File dialog box (see Figure 17.10) and choose <u>D</u>elete on the context menu.

18

Let's Talk! The Fine Art of Web Conversation

● **In this chapter:**

- What's a discussion group?
- Inside the Discussion Web Wizard
- I want to register my users!
- What are all these new pages for?
- How your web saves and displays messages
- Decorating the chat room: How to edit web pages
- Keep it up! How to be a responsible moderator

A discussion group gives your web its own virtual water cooler. All you have to do is provide the topic.............. ▶

A hardy group of bookworms meets at the library to talk about the Zoroastrian influences in Moby Dick. Meanwhile, in a church basement across town, local environmentalists exchange ideas on how to make compost bins out of old Chevy Vegas. And at Sid's Sports Bar, patrons argue vigorously over whether the 1996 Chicago Bulls could have beaten the 1986 Boston Celtics (they decide not).

Name a subject, and the chances are somebody's talking about it. So it's only natural that computer users would bring the fine art of conversation to the Internet.

Most of the talk goes on in Usenet newsgroups, areas on the Internet in which users can post messages and respond to other people's postings. Deja News, a Web repository for newsgroup information, estimates conservatively that about 15,000 newsgroups are active on the net, producing 500 megabytes of material a day. That's enough to fill more than 150,000 copies of this book every year. And it doesn't include the many forums and chat groups sponsored by bulletin board systems and services such as America Online and CompuServe.

Apparently, people can't get enough conversation. So why not start your own electronic discussion group? FrontPage provides tools that let you set up a group in your own web. Discussion group members can post messages and

Discussion group terminology

Discussion groups have a glossary of terms all to themselves. Many of the words are borrowed from similar types of services, such as Usenet newsgroups and discussion groups on information systems, such as CompuServe and America Online.

A **discussion group web** is the web in which you create and maintain your discussion group. Other generic terms for discussion groups are **forum** and **special interest group** (SIG).

A **restricted** or **protected** web requires users to register and use a password to gain entry.

An **article** is netspeak for **message.** The act of publishing a new message is called **submitting** or **posting**.

A **topic** is the subject of a message. When you post a new message, give it a title called a **topic heading** (also called a **header**).

A **thread** is a series of messages and responses under a single topic heading.

A **moderator** is the person who manages the newsgroup.

http://www.quecorp.com

reply to other members' messages. Your group can be public, available to anyone with a browser, or private, accessible only to employees of your company, members of your club, or patrons of Sid's Sports Bar.

> **TIP** **Before you go to the trouble of setting up a discussion group,** make sure you have a topic that will attract users. With 15,000 Usenet groups in existence, just about every general topic imaginable has been covered. You probably won't have much success if, for example, you start a discussion group for music lovers. The best discussion groups focus on a narrow topic that appeals to a small but highly interested group. So while general music might not fly, a discussion group devoted to your favorite band might have appeal (unless your favorite already has a newsgroup, such as Abba, The Beatles, America, the Beach Boys, the Beastie Boys, the Bee Gees, Black Sabbath, the Dead Kennedys, Indigo Girls, The Monkees...). Discussion groups are most useful for organizations such as businesses, clubs, and schools that have specific subjects to discuss.

Let's talk about discussion groups

You create a discussion group in a separate web. You can add a discussion group web as a sub-web to an existing web, or the discussion group web can stand on its own. When the discussion web is part of a larger web, it creates its own pages and folders as needed.

In most cases, a discussion group is made up of three components: a table of contents page that lists the posted messages; a submission form, which lets users compose and post messages; and an optional search form, which lets users search for messages by keywords. If your discussion group is restricted, then the web also includes a registration form.

Figure 18.1 shows a typical contents page. The top half of the window includes a welcome and links to the contents, search, and post pages; the bottom half displays the subject headings for the first four messages.

Fig. 18.1

Pull up a chair and chat a while: A simple opening page for a discussion group, with a greeting and a list of messages.

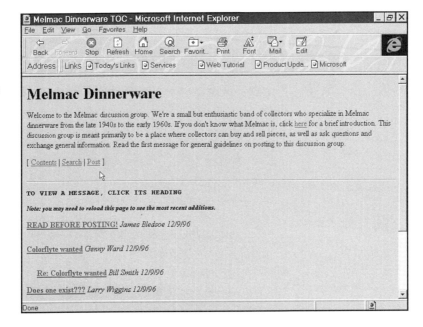

A discussion group lets users respond to messages, thus creating message threads. In Figure 18.1, for example, the message titled "Colorflyte Wanted" garnered one reply, which is indented beneath it.

Users read messages by clicking a heading in the contents. For example, clicking "Colorflyte Wanted" in Figure 18.1 displays the message in Figure 18.2. When the user wants to reply to a message or post a new one, he uses a form such as the one in Figure 18.3.

Discussion group messages are stored on the server by a special piece of software called a **form handler**. You can't set up a discussion group without one of these handlers. See Chapter 14, "It's Good Form: Letting Your Readers Write Back," for more information about forms.

Chapter 18 *Let's Talk! The Fine Art of Web Conversation* **341**

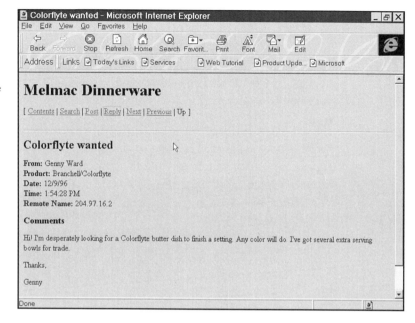

Fig. 18.2
Clicking a message on the contents page (Figure 18.1) displays the message. The user can add to the message thread by clicking the Reply link.

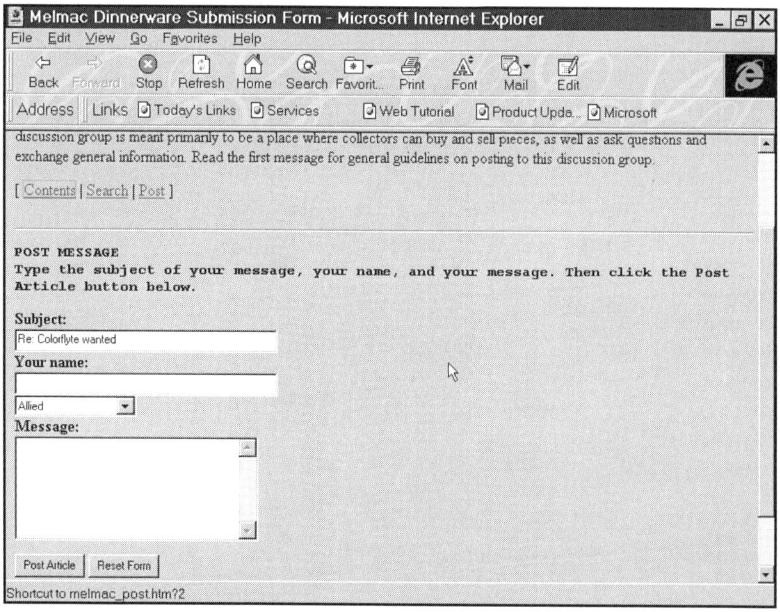

Fig. 18.3
Answering a message or posting a new topic is as simple as filling out a form.

More wizardry

While you should have some basic understanding of how forms work, you don't need an advanced degree in Discussiongroupology to set up a discussion group web. FrontPage has a wizard that handles a lot of the drudgery for you. Just choose the options and headings you want, and the wizard does the rest.

So what do you say we get started? Open Explorer. If you're going to add the Discussion Group web to an established web, open that web. Whether your discussion web is part of a larger web or a stand-alone, follow these steps:

1 Start a new web (press Ctrl+N or choose File, New, FrontPage Web). FrontPage displays the New FrontPage Web dialog box.

2 If you're adding to a web, check the Add to Current Web checkbox. If you're building an independent discussion web, leave this box unchecked.

3 Select the Discussion Web Wizard in the Template or Wizard selection box and choose OK, or double-click the Wizard. FrontPage opens the first Wizard dialog box; read the instructions and click Next. FrontPage displays the dialog box in Figure 18.4, which is where the real labor begins.

Fig. 18.4
The wizard lets you choose the components you want your discussion web to include. A table of contents is necessary if you want users to have easy access to messages.

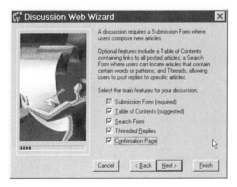

What will my discussion web include?

Here's where you choose various options that members of your discussion group will have. The first item, Submission Form, is the form in which users compose messages. A discussion group without messages has a certain absurdist appeal but isn't terribly functional, so FrontPage requires you to include a submission form.

The remaining four options control various features available to members of the discussion group:

- Put a check in the Table of Contents checkbox if you want a list of hyperlinks to messages. While this feature is optional, it's a practical necessity; without it, users have no easy access to the discussion web's messages.

- Choose Search Form if you'd like your readers to be able to find messages based on words and phrases in topic heads. A search feature probably isn't needed for a discussion web that contains only a handful of messages, but it becomes a valuable tool for active discussion groups whose messages number in the hundreds. Off-hand, we can't think of any reason why you wouldn't want a search form.

- Choose Threaded Replies if you want your readers to be able to respond to messages. Otherwise, users can only post original messages.

- Choose Confirmation Page to give your reader a message that an article has been posted successfully.

Done with this page? Check the Next box to move on.

What shall we talk about?

In the next dialog box, enter a discussion group title in the first text box. This title will appear on all discussion group pages, so make it descriptive.

Next, enter a new name for the folder that will hold all the messages. A descriptive name might be helpful down the road if you're working with lots of webs and folders, or if someone else might also be responsible for maintaining the discussion web. Whatever you choose, the name must begin with an underscore (_).

When you're done, click the Next button again.

Q&A ***What's all that stuff at the bottom of the dialog box about hidden files?***

FrontPage sets up some web folders as hidden; that is, you can't normally see their contents in Explorer. One of these folders contains your discussion group messages. To make the contents of a hidden folder visible, choose Tools, Web Settings from Explorer's menu bar. Click the advanced tab in the FrontPage Web Settings dialog box. Under Options, put a check next to Show Documents in Hidden Directories.

Setting up the submission form

The next dialog box lets you determine the types of input fields your submission form will include. The Subject field contains the subject of the message, while the Comments field is the message itself. You can also let the user choose from a drop-down menu of categories or products. For example, a music discussion group might include categories such as Heavy Metal, Punk, Grunge, Industrial, and Show Tunes. You might use a products menu for a customer support web.

Choose your weapons and click Next to continue.

For your eyes only

Is this some highfalutin discussion group reserved for you and your fellow illuminati? If so, click the first radio button, Yes, Only Registered Users Can Post Articles, in the next dialog box. Users will need to fill out a registration form before they can join the discussion group. If you don't care who tosses in their two cents, click the No, Anyone Can Post Articles radio button.

Now for a word on registering your users. If you're going to restrict access to your discussion group, the discussion web must be a separate web. That is, it can't be a sub-web of a main web. However, if the main web already is restricted, so is the discussion web.

Made your selections? Then click Next to proceed.

The Table of Contents

The next two dialog boxes set preferences for the table of contents. (If you didn't put a check next to Table of Contents way back in the first dialog box, these two dialog boxes won't appear.)

The first dialog box lets you decide if you want oldest or newest messages to appear at the top of the table of contents. Most discussion groups list messages from oldest to newest. But listing newest messages first has its advantages; frequent visitors don't have to scroll to the bottom of the page to find out what messages have been posted since their last visit. Make a choice and click the Next button.

In the next dialog box, choose whether you want the table of contents to be the home page of the discussion web. You don't want to do this if you're adding the discussion web to an existing web, since the wizard will replace your current home page with the new one. Click the Next button when you're done.

Search

If you decided to include a Search form in your discussion group web, FrontPage lets you choose what information to display after the user conducts a search. All searches report the subject, but you can also set up your web to report the message size, in kilobytes; the date when the message was submitted; and the score, which is a number that tells you how closely a message matches the search criteria.

A score of 1000 means a perfect match, while lower scores indicate partial matches. By themselves, scores usually are meaningless; if a user's search yields one match, the user is probably going to read the message whether its score is 957 or 432. But scores can help the user decide what messages to read first when a search produces a long list of message headings.

When you're done, click the Next button.

Color coordination

The next dialog box lets you pick colors. As is the case with a regular web, you can choose the colors for your text, links, and background. Choose the Default button if you want to use the standard colors that FrontPage provides; choose Custom if you want to set your own colors.

If you decide to pick your own colors, you can select a new color for any element by clicking its button; the wizard opens the Color dialog box (see Figure 18.5). For example, if you want a white background instead of the default gray, click the button next to Solid under the Background heading, click the white button in the Color dialog box's palette, and choose OK. The wizard shows you what the new color will look like in the example under Heading.

Fig. 18.5
Give your discussion web some pizzazz by adding color. You can change your colors later if you don't like what you selected.

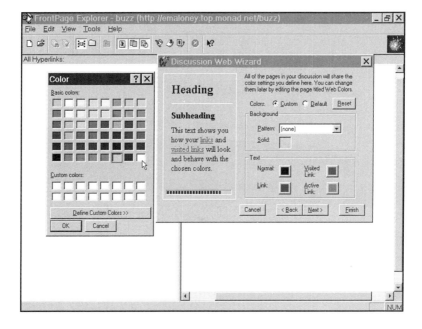

The Color dialog box also lets you define a custom color; click the Define Custom Color button in the Color dialog box to expand the dialog box.

You'll find more information on defining custom colors, and on changing colors in general, in Chapter 8, "Color Me Fun!"

Choose Next when you're done.

How shall we frame our discussion?

The next dialog box lets you decide if you want to use frames—that is, if you want to put your table of contents in one mini-window and your messages in another. Keep in mind that older browsers can't display frames. Here are your choices:

- **N**o Frames displays the table of contents and messages on separate pages. The user must use hyperlinks or his browser's Back and Forward buttons to switch between the two.

- **D**ual Interface displays frames only if the user's browser supports frames; otherwise, the browser displays a frameless page.

- Contents **A**bove Current Article continuously displays a banner at the top of the browser window, the table of contents beneath the banner, and messages at the bottom.

- Contents Be**s**ide Current Article displays the banner at the top and splits the remainder of the page vertically; the table of contents appears on the left side of the browser window and the messages on the right side.

When you click an option, the wizard previews the page on the right side of the screen.

Done? Click the Next button to display the last page of the wizard, and click the Finish button. If your discussion group web is open to everyone, the wizard takes you back to Explorer.

May I see your passport, please?

If you chose to restrict the web with the registration option (see the previous section "For your eyes only"), you still have some setup chores to take care of.

The wizard opens the Web Self-Registration Form in Editor, which is the form users must fill out to register for the discussion group. The forms page also includes instructions on what you need to do to restrict your web. Here's the plain-English version:

1 Switch to Explorer and choose **T**ools, **P**ermissions from the menu bar. Explorer opens the Permissions dialog box.

2 In the Settings panel, choose Use Same Permissions as Root Web if your discussion group web is part of a main web that is restricted. Should your discussion group be a stand-alone web, choose Use Unique Permissions for This Web.

3 If you're using the permissions of the root web, choose OK; you're done. If you're using unique permissions, choose **A**pply and keep reading.

4. Click the Users tab and select Only Registered Users Have Browse Access.

5. Click the OK button.

6. Return to the registration form in Editor and save it into your web.

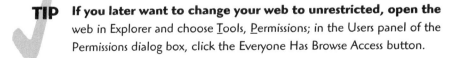

TIP If you later want to change your web to unrestricted, open the web in Explorer and choose Tools, Permissions; in the Users panel of the Permissions dialog box, click the Everyone Has Browse Access button.

So what's my discussion web look like?

When you're done setting up your discussion group web, look at your handiwork in FrontPage Explorer to get a sense of what files the wizard created and where the data is going. Figure 18.6 displays a web called Melmac in folder and hyperlink views. Your files will be somewhat different depending on what options you chose in the wizard. Here's a rundown of the files in the figure.

The table of contents page

Melmac Dinnerware TOC, or Index.htm, is the table of contents page. If the discussion web were part of a larger web, the page would be called melmac_toc.htm. Unedited, your contents page will look something like the one in Figure 18.7.

The index.htm file itself contains only the Contents heading and the note directly beneath it. It pulls the rest of the page's pieces from WebBot components in other files.

At the top is a header, which contains links to the main pages of the discussion web. FrontPage keeps the header in the _private folder; in this case, it's called melmac_head.htm.

The message headings, beneath the Contents heading in Figure 18.7, are in the file tocproto.htm, which is in the _melmac folder. This file is updated whenever a user posts a new message.

The Last Changed message at the bottom of the page is in a footer, which is stored in a file called melmac_foot.htm in the _private folder.

Fig. 18.6
User folder view (top) to see the files in your discussion group, and use hyperlink view (bottom) to get a sense of how the pages are linked.

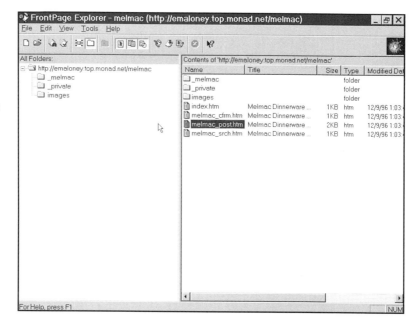

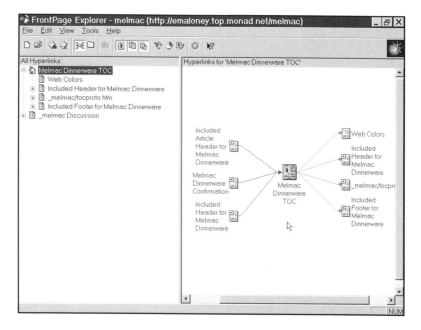

Fig. 18.7
The table of contents page lets users read a message by clicking its heading.

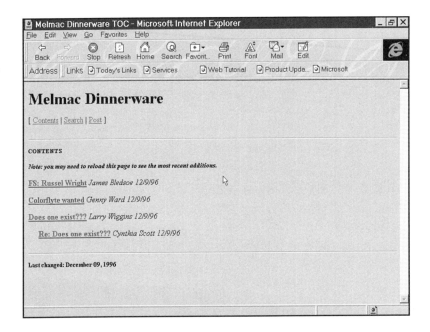

 TIP If your discussion web is part of a larger web, the Discussion Web Wizard automatically adds a Home hyperlink to the header. This link takes the user to the main web's Index.htm page. You'll need to change this link if you want users to return to a different page in your web. Also, you'll need to create a link from another page in your web to the table of contents page.

I submit to you...

The submission form, Melmac_post.htm, gives the user a place to fill out and post a message. This is the page the user sees when he clicks the Post hyperlink (see Figure 18.8).

The chances are you'll want to edit this page to make it more descriptive. Note, for example, that the wizard places dummy text in the Product field, which is the drop-down menu between the From and Comments text boxes. We'll look at how to edit your discussion web pages in a minute.

Fig. 18.8
The submission form is where users add messages to the discussion group or reply to messages that have been posted.

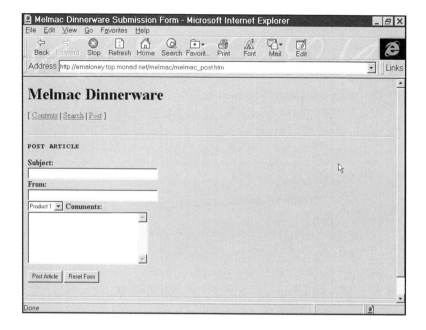

 TIP If your web is restricted, the From text box does not appear; the user's name is automatically added to the posted message.

Search me!

Melmac_srch.htm contains the search form with which the user finds messages (see Figure 18.9). The actual search component—the text box and the buttons beneath it—is a WebBot.

You can't edit your WebBot directly; you have to do it in the WebBot's properties dialog box, which you display by right-clicking the WebBot and choosing WebBot Component Properties from the quick menu. We'll look at this dialog box in a moment.

We got your message

Melmac_cfrm.htm contains a simple, one-line confirmation message, which a user gets when he or she creates and posts a message. FrontPage sets up this file if you choose the confirmation page option when you run the Discussion Group Wizard. You can open this page in Editor and change the message if you don't like the one FrontPage provides.

Fig. 18.9
The search page includes a search WebBot that does the actual grunt work. You can change the look and feel of the search page with the WebBot's Properties dialog box.

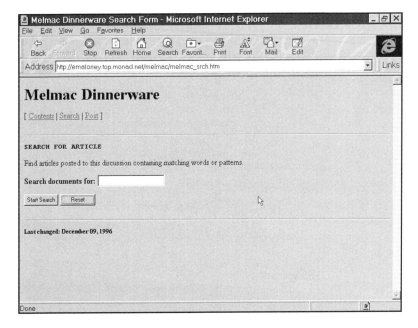

Where are my messages?

Where and how does the server save the messages? In its own folder; _melmac in Figure 18.6, for example. In folder view, click the folder in the left panel to see its contents in the right panel. Each message is stored in its own file, which are named 00000001.htm, 00000002.htm, and so forth. Figure 18.10, for example, shows the files that contain the four messages listed on the contents page in Figure 18.4.

As the discussion group moderator, you can view and modify these files individually, as we'll see a bit later.

When users post messages, the web updates a WebBot component in _melmac, tocproto.htm, with the heading, author, and date. This is the file that the table of contents uses to display message topics.

 Q&A *My data folder is empty. What's wrong?*

Do you have your web set up to view hidden files? Choose Tools, Web Settings from Explorer's menu bar to open the FrontPage Web Settings dialog box. Click the Advanced tab and make sure you've got a check next to Show Documents in Hidden Directories.

Fig. 18.10
The web saves messages as separate files and numbers them sequentially. You can quickly review message titles in Explorer using folder view.

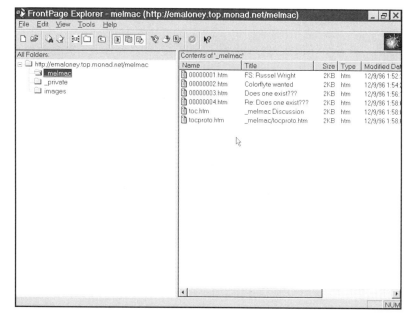

_private—Keep out!

The Discussion Web Wizard puts several files in the _private directory, including your headers and footers and a page containing your web's colors. You can open any of these files directly in Editor to edit them.

Modifying your discussion web pages

The discussion web wizard creates bare-bones pages that include basic links and instructions, but not much else. Edit your pages as you do any other; open the web in Explorer, and open your web pages in Editor.

We've already covered the necessary editing tools in other chapters. Chapters 6, "Editing Tools You'll Learn to Love," and 7, "Form and Function: Formatting Text," discuss editing and formatting, Chapter 8 shows you how to use colors, and Chapter 14, "It's Good Form: Letting Your Readers Write Back," provides important information on how to change form fields. But here are a few tips that relate directly to discussion groups.

Change the banner

Change your banner to include a welcome message. The banner is in a separate header file; to open it, right-click the banner and choose Open from the quick menu. Make your changes and save the file. Figure 18.11 shows the contents page from Figure 18.7 with an introduction added.

Fig. 18.11
Change your banner to include a welcome message or information on how to use the web.

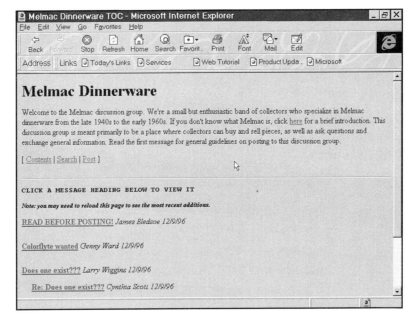

Have pages, will link

Remember, these are just plain old web pages, so you can create hyperlinks to other pages that might contain important news and information. In Figure 18.11, for example, the welcome includes a link to a page that gives the uninitiated visitor more information on the discussion group and its goals.

READ THIS FIRST!

If your discussion group has guidelines, put them in the first message and keep them posted, as in Figure 18.11.

Showing good forms

If you created a product drop-down menu with the wizard, you'll need to change its contents in the submission form. Chapter 14 gives you complete information on field options, but here's a short review of the steps:

1. Right-click the drop-down menu field and choose Form Field Properties from the quick menu. Editor opens the Drop-Down Menu Properties dialog box.

2. The Choice box will include dummy names, such as Product1, Product2, and Product3. Delete them with the Remove button.

3. To enter your own product names, choose the Add button. The Add Choice dialog box opens.

4. Type the name of your choice in the Choice text box and choose OK. Editor returns you to the properties dialog box.

5. Follow the previous two steps as many times as you need to, until all of your choices are entered. Choose OK in the properties dialog box when you're done.

TIP Your submission form is like any other form, so feel free to add, delete, and modify fields. You can even add radio buttons and checkboxes. For more information, turn to Chapter 14. Pay particular attention to how you name new fields, since the user sees these names when he reads a message.

Changing your search form

Would you like to change the information the user gets when he conducts a search of the discussion group? Or change the appearance of the search page itself?

Open the search page in Editor (it's the one with _srch in the file name). Right-click the search WebBot and choose WebBot Component Properties from the quick menu. Editor displays the WebBot Search Component Properties dialog box shown in Figure 18.12.

Fig. 18.12
You can add or drop the information a user sees after a search by clicking the appropriate checkboxes at the bottom of the WebBot's properties dialog box.

The top part of the dialog box, under the Search Input Form heading, lets you change the labels in the WebBot and the length of the search field. At the bottom of the page, you can add or remove the score, file date, and file size from the user's search results display.

A web of a different color

Unhappy with the color scheme you chose when you ran the Discussion Web Wizard? The web maintains a reference page from which your other web pages get their colors. Change the colors in the reference page, and you change the colors in all your pages. You can specify new colors for your background, text, and hyperlinks; you also can use a background image.

The page is in the _private directory, and its file name includes the string _styl (for example, melmac_styl.htm). In Explorer, you can identify the page by its title, Web Colors.

Changing your color settings is simple. Open the file in Editor and choose File, Page Properties from the main menu. Editor displays the Page Properties dialog box. Click the Background tab and make your changes.

Refer to Chapter 8 to learn more about how to use this dialog box.

Moderating your discussion group

Now that you're the Big Moderator on Campus, you have a responsibility to keep your discussion group organized and on target. Your most important jobs are to ensure that posted messages are appropriate and legal and take the right action when they're not. Also, you need to keep track of the discussion group's size to make sure you don't suck up all of your drive space.

You don't say...

What's appropriate depends on the nature of your web. A message that's perfect for the Strange Things Found in People's Stomachs discussion group probably doesn't belong in the Sino-Soviet Relations discussion group. Your web should include a statement describing the group's mission.

What's legal is a bit trickier. Your biggest danger is running afoul of libel laws. We don't have time to go into a detailed explanation of libel, but it's basically a false, malicious statement about another person that causes the person damage.

How libel laws apply to the sponsor of a discussion group is still unclear; U.S. courts have yet to make a definitive ruling. But the chance exists that you could be held responsible for libelous messages that you've read and allowed to be published, much as a newspaper is responsible when it prints a libelous letter to the editor.

So what do you do when you see a message that doesn't belong in the discussion group? Unfortunately, FrontPage doesn't include many tools for managing messages, so your options are limited: you either can edit the offending message or, with some trouble, delete it.

Editing messages

You edit a message the same way you edit any web page. Open the message in Editor (remember: your messages are in a subfolder), delete or replace the offensive material, and re-save the message.

In fairness to the poster and other group members, you should indicate that the message has been deleted by replacing it with something like, "This message deleted by moderator because of inappropriate material."

Deleting messages

Deleting messages is an important part of discussion group maintenance. Unfortunately, while you can do it, FrontPage doesn't offer any tools that make the job simple.

As we discussed above, you delete messages to get rid of offensive and potentially illegal material. But you should also delete messages to avoid hard drive cram and tidy up your table of contents.

You have to delete not only the file containing the message, but the entry in the page that holds the table of contents. Here's how:

1. Open the web in Explorer and find the message you want to delete.

2. Right-click the file name and choose Delete from the quick menu.

3. In Editor, open the tocproto.htm file; you'll find it in the same folder that contains your messages.

4. Find the line that contains the heading for the message you just deleted and delete it. Also delete the line "Form Results Inserted Here" that appears below the heading.

5. Save the file.

TIP **Here's an alternative way to delete a message. Delete the** message header in the tocproto.htm first and save the file. Return to Explorer. In Hyperlink View, the file containing the message you deleted from tocproto.htm appears at the bottom of the left panel. Right-click the file and choose delete from the quick menu.

TIP **It's a good idea to store deleted messages, at least for a month or** two. The easiest way to do this is to create a new folder for your old messages. Call it something like archive or oldmess. Then drag the messages you're deleting into the folder. Once they're there, you can use Windows Explorer to perform additional file management tasks, such as moving the messages to a floppy disk for long-term storage. See Chapter 20, "Maintaining Your Web," for information on how to create and manage folders in your web.

Read this before you delete

When you're deleting messages, delete entire threads or single, stand-alone messages (that is, messages that have no replies). If you delete messages within a thread, you'll introduce breaks in the continuity of the thread, and navigating the thread might become confusing to the user.

Do not delete the top message in a thread without deleting its responses as well.

Put a lid on it!

FrontPage gives you one other tool for trimming your discussion group: you can limit the size of the individual messages.

For technical reasons, this probably won't have a major impact on the amount of space your discussion web takes (your server sets aside a minimum amount of storage space for every message, even if the message is only a few words). However, a limit can prevent users from rambling on endlessly and make messages easier to read.

Open the submission form page in Editor and follow these steps:

1 Right-click the comments field in the submission form and choose Form Field Validation from the quick menu. Editor opens the Text Box Validation dialog box.

2 Under the Data Length heading, enter a maximum number of characters in the Max Length text box.

3 Choose OK and save the file.

Part VI: Publishing and Maintaining Your Web

Chapter 19: **This Web Is Suitable for Publication**

Chapter 20: **Maintaining Your Web**

19
This Web Is Suitable for Publication

● In this chapter:

- I'm ready to publish my web!
- What should I know about networks and the Internet?
- What are FrontPage server extensions?
- I need a good server for my web
- Can my PC serve as a server?

The ultimate freedom for authors of any stripe: publishing their work whenever they wish. Authors looking to do just that need look no further than FrontPage . . . . ●>

Writing is the easy part of the job. Getting published is another story, and the early travails of some authors are legendary. Although hundreds of millions of his books have been sold, Theodore "Dr. Seuss" Geisel's first effort was rejected 27 times. A chance meeting with a college-chum-turned-publisher finally led to the publication of *To Think That I Saw it On Mulberry Street*.

Geisel's persistence, though admirable, isn't unusual among writers. Most keep hammering away at publishers' doors, despite mountains of rejection letters. Writers who want readers don't have much choice.

Until now, that is. Armed with FrontPage and connected to a network, any author becomes his or her own publisher. Web publishing is a revolution of sorts, in which the barriers between writer and publisher have been knocked down. Anarchy? Maybe, but it's the kind of anarchy that free spirits like the Cat in the Hat and his creator would have welcomed.

How do I publish my web?

Publishing on the Internet, or any network, is simple in theory. A **server** is a powerful computer with plenty of storage space and memory. A **client** is any computer that connects to the server over the network. To publish on the network, the author sends his material (a FrontPage Web, for example!) to the server. There, the material is available to any client who taps into the server. The author's work, in other words, is published on the network.

There's no mystery to this process. Whenever you view a World Wide Web page in your browser, your computer is a client tapping into a server. The page you view was previously sent to the server by its author, where it's accessible to the multitude of clients who dial into the Internet (see Figure 19.1).

Fig. 19.1
The relationship between clients and servers is easy to grasp; it's what happens between them that can boggle the mind.

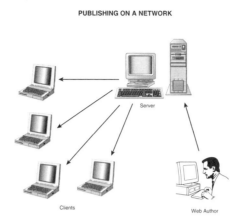

PUBLISHING ON A NETWORK

What should I know about web publishing?

If network publishing were as straightforward as Figure 19.1 suggests, you wouldn't need to read this chapter. Unfortunately, life is not so simple. For one thing, you, the web author, are also a client when you visit your web. If you store your web on your own computer and install the required software, you can also be a server. Wearing all those hats can tax your ingenuity, not to mention your patience.

Furthermore, getting computers to communicate with each other is like negotiating an uneasy peace between warring states; it's a delicate job that requires strict rules and constant monitoring. Even the language of networks sounds like diplomacy. Computers on the Internet obey a common set of **protocols**, called **TCP/IP**: Transmission Control Protocol/Internet Protocol, which are rules that govern the way data is sent back and forth. File locations on the Internet also adhere to strict conventions. Page **URLs**, or Uniform Resource Locators, allow for no flights of naming fancy; each one, down to the last forward slash, is as carefully wrought as a Manhattan Zip Code.

Why this obsessive concern with conventions and standards and protocols? Like the real world, the computer world is a fragmented place. PCs and Macintoshes, Windows and Unix, these and many other hardware and software types speak different languages. They have different, usually incompatible designs. But remarkably, these diverse technologies do manage to coexist, if uneasily, on the Internet, the United Nations of computers. Like Dr. Johnson's dog walking on its hind legs, "it is not done well, but then, one is surprised to see it done at all."

What do network complications mean for my web?

The web that you've carefully crafted in FrontPage follows the various Internet conventions. The formatting codes are in HTML, the World Wide Web's universal word processing language. The images you've inserted are in the standard GIF or JPEG formats, easily read by most browsers. So it seems reasonable to assume that you can just pack off your web to the server of your choice and settle right down to a little publishing party.

Unfortunately, not. In order to give us all those fancy formatting effects, clever WebBots, and other luxuries, FrontPage takes a few liberties with the general Internet standards. Servers, running software to manage the webs they store and clients they serve, must either account for FrontPage's eccentricities, or ignore them. Furthermore, there are different server platforms (Windows NT and Unix are the two most common ones), and different server software programs.

FrontPage's Server Extensions

Those servers that can accommodate FrontPage webs' special features have the FrontPage Server Extensions installed. FrontPage Server Extensions are programs and scripts that make different brands of server software compatible with FrontPage. Webs published to a server with the FrontPage Extensions will look and act the way you designed them, complete with operational WebBots and fancy formatting.

If you publish your web to a server lacking the FrontPage Server Extensions, you'll lose some FrontPage features. Your text, graphics, and hyperlinks should work just fine. WebBots and most formatting effects will be lost. Hotspots may or may not operate they way you intended, depending on the server software in use.

That doesn't mean you should avoid careful formatting, WebBots, and Hotspots. Even if your server doesn't have the FrontPage Server Extensions now, it may install them eventually. In the meantime, they'll do no harm on a server without FrontPage Extensions because they'll simply be ignored.

Microsoft is waging a campaign to persuade Internet Service Providers to make their servers FrontPage-friendly by including the FrontPage Server Extensions. Given Microsoft's track record and position in the marketplace, who can doubt that their campaign will succeed? In the meantime, check to see if a prospective server has the FrontPage Extensions installed before posting your web.

If you're running your own server, you can install the extensions yourself. There are different extensions for different brands of server software, and Microsoft makes the extensions available to developers at the FrontPage web site, **http://www.microsoft.com/frontpage/**.

Publishing a web: ways and means

There are three sorts of venues for published FrontPage webs:

- Many ISPs (Internet Service Providers) provide storage space for their subscribers' webs. Some ISPs charge for the service, others do not. As of this writing, CompuServe, one of the biggest ISPs, provides each subscriber with two megabytes of free web storage space.

- Organizations that maintain World Wide Web servers sometimes provide storage space for employees' webs. And **intranets**, networks of computers within an organization that use the protocols and standards of the Internet, can accommodate FrontPage webs. If the network's servers have the FrontPage extensions installed, publishing your web on the intranet should be easy to do.

- With the right software, you can turn your own machine into a server and publish your web there. The FrontPage Personal Web Server bundled with FrontPage, and the Microsoft Personal Web Server included in the bonus pack, are two such software packages.

Publishing on an ISP

Posting your web on an Internet Service Provider's server is a lot like subscribing to the phone service. The phone company provides a telephone number, phone lines, and the network that allows calls in and out. An ISP similarly supplies you with an URL, storage space on their server, and the hookup to the Internet that allows millions of browsers to view your pages.

There are obvious advantages to housing your web on an ISP's server, not the least of which is that you won't have to leave your computer on all the time and permanently tie up a phone line!

If your existing ISP is also a **presence provider** and offers web hosting services, your best bet is to contact them directly for instructions on uploading your FrontPage web. The procedure will vary from service to service, and you'll save yourself a lot of trouble if you go to the source for details.

Shopping around for a presence provider whose servers use the FrontPage extensions? Microsoft maintains a list of providers compatible with FrontPage webs. You'll find the list of registered providers at **http://microsoft.saltmine.com/frontpage/wpp/list/** (see Figure 19.2).

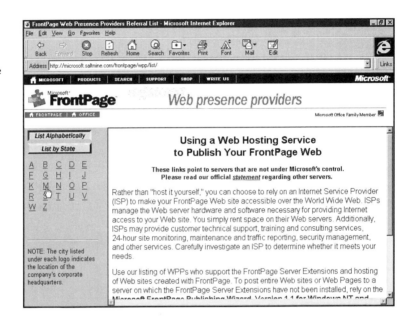

Fig. 19.2
The services on Microsoft's list all support the FrontPage extensions.

Whether you choose a local provider, or one of the giant services like CompuServe or AT&T, compare prices and ask questions before signing up. Some services charge a flat rate, others charge on a sliding scale determined by the number of visitors to your web. You'll also want to make sure that you have full access to your web in order to make changes and update content.

Publishing on an intranet

Intranets, those local computer networks that look, and behave, like the World Wide Web, are a natural place to publish FrontPage webs. A web so published, available to everyone on the network, could be a combination electronic notice board and company newsletter. Group projects can also take the form of webs, which make them a handy organizational tool.

To post a web on an intranet server, you'll need to contact the network administrator for the server's network address. Most likely you'll need the administrator's permission to upload material as well. With those items in hand, you're ready to publish your web on the intranet:

1 Connect to the network, and open your web in the FrontPage Explorer. Choose File, Publish FrontPage Web to pop up the Publish FrontPage Web dialog box shown in Figure 19.3.

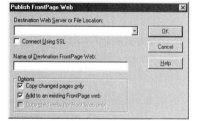

Fig. 19.3
Although the options in this dialog box aren't exactly self-explanatory, the web publishing operation is pretty simple.

> **TIP** The Explorer File menu displays the last four webs that have been opened. To open any of them, just click the web name.

2 In the Destination Web Server or File Location text box, type the URL or network address of the server to which you're posting the web.

3 SSL stands for Secure Socket Layer, which enables secure data transfers between web, clients, and server. It's used for things like sending credit card numbers over the network. If your server supports SSL, click the Connect Using SSL checkbox should you need secure data transfers. Otherwise, leave it deselected.

4 In publishing your web on the server, all you're doing is copying the web, pages, folders, links, and all, to the server. In the Name of Destination FrontPage Web text box, type a name for the copy of the web that you are creating on the server. If you want your published web to have the same name as your original web, just leave the default entry in this field.

Plain English, please!

FrontPage is not alone in this, because any program that has anything to do with networks seems to become madly jargon-happy. The Publish FrontPage Web dialog box contains some fine examples of the genre. The **Destination Web Server** is the server to which you're copying the web. The **Destination FrontPage Web** is the copy of the current web that you're about to make for posting on the server. Simple ideas, confusing lingo—if you've had anything to do with networks before, you'll recognize the pattern.

5. If this is the first time you've published the web to the server, the Options in the Publish FrontPage Web dialog box won't apply, so you can ignore them whether they're selected or not.

 Q&A *How come the Copy child webs option in the Publish FrontPage Web dialog box is grayed-out (and what's a child web anyway)?*

The Copy child webs option is only activated if the root web is the open web. The root web is a blank web created by default when you install FrontPage. All the other webs you create on the same server (in this case, the server is probably your PC), are **child webs**. If you open the root web, selecting the Copy child webs option would copy all the webs on the current server to a new server or new file location.

6. Click OK in the Publish FrontPage Web dialog box to copy the current web to the server you've named in the Destination Web Server or File Location dialog box.

If the destination server supports the FrontPage server extensions, your publishing job is done.

If the destination server doesn't support the FrontPage extensions, FrontPage takes note of the fact. At that point, the FrontPage Web Publishing Wizard starts up automatically, and you're guided through the process of copying your web to the server.

TIP **If you need the Web Publishing Wizard, and it hasn't appeared** automatically, you can run it manually. Click Start, Programs, Accessories, Internet Tools, Web Publishing Wizard to run the Web Publishing Wizard.

Can I be my own server?

Some writers, fed up with the myopia of the publishing industry, publish their own work. But even the most determined do-it-yourselfer goes to a professional printer to handle the actual printing of the book. No matter how well-equipped one's home office, trying to mass-produce books with a laser printer and hobbyist's bindery wouldn't be very efficient.

Just about as efficient, in fact, as trying to turn an ordinary PC into a network server. Actual servers are equipped with the hardware and software to serve many client computers at the same time; PCs are not. For the FrontPage web publisher, the realistic publishing choice is a server, not the trusty PC on your desk.

What about FrontPage's own server software?

If you chose not to install the Microsoft Personal Web Server included with the FrontPage 97 Bonus Pack, the FrontPage Personal Web Server runs automatically whenever you run FrontPage. The FrontPage Personal Web Server *is* server software, and a cousin of the software that powerful servers use to juggle thousands of web sites and clients. The FrontPage Personal Web server is a bit of a poor relation, however. Although capable within the limits of its intended uses, it doesn't have the horsepower to serve the traffic that your web will deserve to get.

> *Plain English, please!*
>
> The **Microsoft Personal Web Server** is part of the FrontPage 97 Bonus Pack, and if you didn't already have server software installed, it's the server recommended by the FrontPage installation program. The **FrontPage Personal Web Server** is built into FrontPage, but it's only used if the Microsoft Personal Web Server hasn't been installed. Why do two different programs have such confusingly similar names? Probably for the same reason that there's a FrontPage Explorer, a Windows Explorer, and an Internet Explorer (and yes, I don't know what the reason is either).

The FrontPage Personal Web Server's job is to help you create and test your web, including your links and other web gadgetry. As a personal server, it works as the host for your web, with you as the sole client. It loads automatically when you run FrontPage, and works in the background as you build your web, appearing only as a button on the taskbar. You don't need to do anything with it; you can't, in fact, do much with it, as you can see in Figure 19.4.

Fig. 19.4
The FrontPage Personal Web Server has no toolbars, and a very limited menu!

The FrontPage Personal Web Server is configured for you when you install FrontPage, and it comes with the FrontPage extensions pre-installed.

The Microsoft Personal Web Server can serve a client or three...

The FrontPage Personal Web Server isn't really designed to handle a lot of network traffic, but the Microsoft Personal Web Server included with the bonus pack is a more potent package. Most who install the Microsoft Personal Web server will use it for running and testing their webs on their own PCs, though that doesn't mean it can't serve a few clients. Indeed, if you're on a network it might be convenient to let a browser or two into your web, especially if you're working with colleagues on a joint web project.

As long as both FrontPage and the Microsoft Personal Web Server are up and running, your system can serve any client computers on the network who have, and use, your IP (Internet Protocol) address. Your IP address is like a telephone number, and it'll have been assigned by the network administrator.

To view your IP address and other network settings from the FrontPage Explorer, click Help, About Microsoft FrontPage Explorer. In the About Microsoft FrontPage dialog box that appears, click Network Test.

The FrontPage TCP/IP Test dialog box appears, as seen in Figure 19.5.

Click Start Test, and your network settings will appear in a moment or two.

Fig. 19.5
The TCP/IP test checks your network settings and displays your IP address.

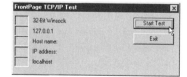

How do I turn the Microsoft Personal Web Server off?

The Microsoft Personal Web Server, once installed, runs whenever you turn your computer on. That's very convenient if you're working on your web, or operating your computer as a small-time server. If you're doing neither of those things, you can shut down the Microsoft Personal Web Server and stop it from gobbling up some of your system's memory.

To turn off the Microsoft Personal Web Server, double-click the Personal Web Server icon, which you'll see at the right of the taskbar, near the clock (see Figure 19.6). What's in an IP address?

What's in an IP Address

Internet Protocol (IP) addresses conform to a standard, like your own ten digit area code and telephone number. IP addresses consist of four numbers separated by periods. Each number is less than 256; 200.45.123.10. is an example of an IP address.

Why should you care about IP addresses at all? If you're setting yourself up as a small-time server, you might want to restrict access to your web to a particular group of users—colleagues working on a project with you, for example. With the use of an **IP address mask,** you can allow access to only those computers with a specific set of IP addresses (see the discussion of permissions the following section).

An IP address mask is an IP address with some of the numbers replaced by asterisks. The asterisks function as wildcards—they represent any and all numbers. So if you wanted to allow access to your web only to those computers with IP addresses beginning with 200.45, you'd enter the following IP address mask: 200.45.*.*.

Fig. 19.6
The Microsoft Personal Web Server occupies a tiny chunk of your taskbar when it's up and running.

 TIP **If you don't see the Microsoft Personal Web Server icon on your** taskbar, click Start, Settings, Control Panel. In the Control Panel window, double-click the Personal Web Server icon.

The Personal Web Server Properties dialog box appears. Click the Startup tab, and choose Stop to turn off the Microsoft Personal Web Server. If you don't want the Microsoft Personal Web Server to run whenever you run windows, clear the Run the Web server automatically at startup checkbox, as shown in Figure 19.7.

If you do choose not to run the Microsoft Personal Web Server at startup, you'll have to start it manually whenever you run FrontPage. To start the Microsoft Personal Web Server manually, click Start, Settings, Control Panel. In the Control Panel window, double-click the Personal Web Server icon.

Click the Startup tab in the Personal Web Server properties dialog box that appears, and click Start to run the Personal Web Server.

Fig. 19.7
Unlike those two-way televisions in Orwell's 1984, you can shutdown the Microsoft Personal Web Server whenever you want to.

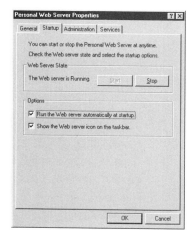

Who's in, and who's out: setting Permissions for the FrontPage Personal Web Server

Vandals are far from unknown in the computer world. Some write viruses that infect files and hard drives. Others enjoy busting into web sites with the sole aim of defacing pages. FrontPage has a fence you can erect to keep vandals, and anyone else, out of your web.

If you are running the FrontPage Personal Web Server, and you want to restrict access to your web, or permit others to act as authors or administrators:

1 Open your web in the FrontPage Explorer.

2 Click Tools, Permissions for the Permissions dialog box shown in Figure 19.8.

3 In the Settings tab of the Permissions dialog box, choose Use unique permissions for this web and click Apply.

4 To set the access level of individual users, click the Users tab and choose Add. The Add Users dialog box pops up (see Figure 19.9).

Fig. 19.8
If you're planning to be your own server, you'll want to restrict access to authoring and administering your webs.

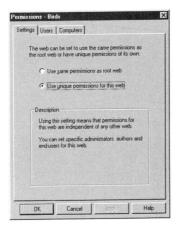

Fig. 19.9
By giving users a password, you restrict or enable their access to your web.

Set the access level with one of these options.

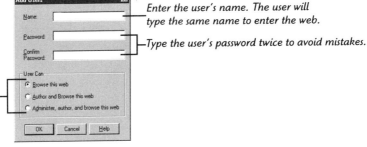

Enter the user's name. The user will type the same name to enter the web.

Type the user's password twice to avoid mistakes.

Q&A *The Add button on the Permissions dialog box Users tab is grayed out!*

Click the Settings tab and choose Use u̱nique permissions for this web, then click A̱pply. The Add and Edit buttons are only activated when you set unique permissions for a specific web.

   5 Click OK in the Add Users dialog box when you've finished adding the new user.

   6 If you need to set permissions for one or a group of computers, click the Computers tab and choose A̱dd. The Add Computers dialog box seen in Figure 19.10 appears.

   7 In the Add Computers dialog box, enter the IP address or IP address mask of the computer(s) whose access you're controlling (see the sidebar *What's in an IP Address?* for an explanation of IP masks). Set the permission level, and click OK.

Fig. 19.10
Here's where you choose to let in, or keep out, computers by their IP addresses.

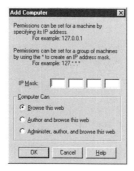

8 Click OK in the Permissions dialog box when you're finished setting your web's security.

If you prefer to set access levels for your entire site, not just individual webs, open your Root Web in the FrontPage Explorer and go through the steps previously outlined to grant or deny access.

Who's in, and who's out, Part II: administering webs with the Microsoft Personal Web Server

If you're running the Microsoft Personal Web Server, web administration works a little differently. To get at the Microsoft Personal Web Server administration tools, double-click the Personal Web Server icon on the Taskbar. In the Personal Web Server dialog box that appears, click the Administration tab and choose Administration.

That runs your browser, which loads the Internet Services Administrator page shown in Figure 19.11.

To grant and deny access to your web, click the Local User Administration link. That takes you to the Internet Local User Administrator page; to add new users and their passwords, click the New User button. Fill in the new user fields and choose Add to save the entry. When you've finished your web administration chores, click the browser's Close button.

Fig. 19.11
The Internet Services Administrator page is like a web site for controlling access to your server.

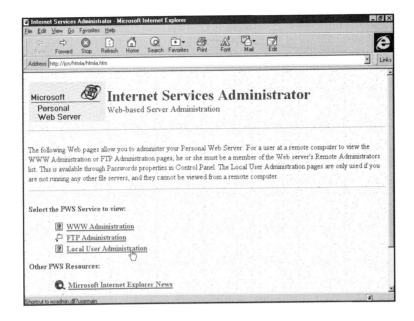

TIP The list of authorized users or groups of users that you build in the Internet Services Administrator pages will apply to all your webs. To control access to individual webs, choose Tools, Permissions in the FrontPage Explorer and follow the steps outlined in the previous section, "Who's in, and who's out: setting Permissions for the FrontPage Personal Web Server."

I've got server software other than the Personal Web Server

If you've installed a server software package other than the Personal Web Server program bundled with FrontPage, you'll need to configure it.

Buried away in the FrontPage program folders is a utility designed to configure just such software. The FrontPage Server Administrator is the program, and you'll find it in the Program Files\Microsoft FrontPage folder. To run the program, use the Windows Explorer or My Computer to navigate to the Program Files\Microsoft FrontPage folder and double-click the FrontPage Server Administrator icon. If you don't see the icon, open the Program Files\Microsoft FrontPage\bin folder and double-click FPSRVWIN.EXE to run the FrontPage Server Administrator. Figure 19.12 shows the FrontPage Server Administrator window.

Fig. 19.12
You might have to install the appropriate FrontPage extensions for your particular server software, which you can do in the Server Administrator.

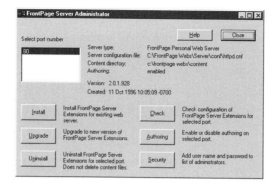

Check your server package's documentation for the correct settings to apply in the FrontPage Server Administrator. If you need to download specific FrontPage server extensions for your package, you'll find them at the FrontPage World Wide Web site, at **http://www.microsoft.com/frontpage**.

20
Maintaining Your Web

● **In this chapter:**

- **How to find and fix bad hyperlinks**

- **Danger! Links to the World Wide Web can be bad for your health!**

- **Add, delete, and move pages the *right* way**

- **Much ado about To Do Lists**

Done with your web? That's what you think. Now you've got to keep the darned thing up and running! . . . . ▶

Maintaining a web is like managing corporate office space. The original floor plan looks great until someone complains that his cubicle is too small, you need to find room for three new copiers, and two full-time employees are replaced by six temps. Suddenly, you've got blocked doorways, desks in the hall, and employees climbing over each other to get to the bathrooms.

Of course, if your web stays the same forever, you'll never have to look at it again. But most of us add, update, and remove pages and hyperlinks as our web changes to meet new needs. If you don't plan carefully, you'll soon get e-mail from bewildered users wondering why the New Products link takes them to a photo of the company softball team.

Maintaining your web requires that you know the correct way to make a change and that you make your changes with patience. FrontPage offers a few tools to help you out, but you have to do some of the work manually. This chapter teaches you the tools; the patience will have to come from your own personal toolkit.

When links go bad

Like a chain, a web is only as strong as its weakest link. Users who click hyperlinks only to get the dreaded "File Not Found" message will quickly grab their rucksacks and head for a more friendly campground. With about 15,000,000 web sites to visit, who needs the aggravation?

The best way to fix bad links is to avoid creating them in the first place. So what makes a link go bad? Some links are just born that way, but most of them were good links that went astray:

- You created a link but didn't create a page to go with it, as detailed in Chapter 12, "Webward Ho! Adding Pages to Your Web."

- You linked to a page on the World Wide Web that no longer exists, or you entered an incorrect URL for the page.

- You changed the names or locations of web pages to which you've created links.

- You changed the name of a link but forgot to either create a new page or change the name of the existing target page.
- You deleted a page but not the links to that page.

You can avoid all of these problems by taking care to verify links and create target pages as you build your web.

Still, problems will crop up as you refine your site. And if you've got links to sites on the World Wide Web, you're subject to the whims and fancies of other webmasters as they modify their pages.

The only solution is to make link verification a part of your regular routine. Luckily, you don't have to check your links by hand; Explorer provides a verification tool that does the job for you.

Verily, verify

Verification takes only a few moments of your time. Open the web in Explorer and choose Tools, Verify Hyperlinks from the menu bar. Explorer tests all of the internal links—that is, links to pages in your web—and then displays the Verify Hyperlinks dialog box in Figure 20.1.

Fig. 20.1
This web has one bad internal link and six external links that still need to be checked.

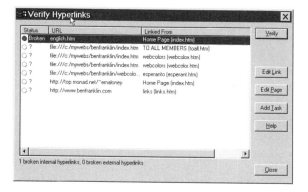

The dialog box lists two kinds of links. Bad internal links are preceded by a red dot and the word "Broken." External links are preceded by a yellow dot and a question mark, meaning that you still need to test them. In Figure 20.1, for example, Explorer has found one bad internal link and six untested external links.

What about my external links?

You still need to verify your external links—the ones that target pages outside of your web. If these pages are on your local drive or on a local network to which you're connected, then click the Verify button.

If the target pages are on the World Wide Web, then you need to be on the Web. Open your browser and connect to the Web. You don't need to go to any specific web site; you just need to be online. When you're connected, click the Verify button.

Verification can take a split second or a few minutes, depending on how many links you're testing and if they're internal or external. Don't be impatient if you've got a lot of links to the World Wide Web; FrontPage has to find each site, which can take a while. A meter at the bottom of the dialog box reports FrontPage's progress.

When FrontPage finishes testing the external links, it turns the bad links into red dots and the good links into green dots. In Figure 20.2, for example, five of the external links are OK; the last one is not.

Fig. 20.2
Click the Verify button to test external links; in this case, FrontPage turns up a second bad link. Also the dots in front of the good links turn green.

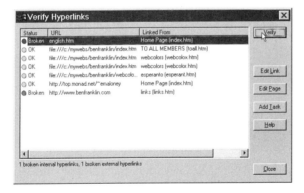

 Q&A *FrontPage tells me I've got a bad link to the World Wide Web that I know for a fact is good. How can it be so stupid?*

You might not be connected to the Web. The Verify Hyperlinks dialog box won't tell you that you're not connected; it simply reports a bad link. Make sure you're connected and try again. The other possible cause of an inaccurate report is that the server you're trying to reach is unavailable; it's either shut down or busy with too much traffic. You can get more information on what the problem is by trying to connect to the site with your browser.

A link is just a link

Did all of your external links check out OK? Wait—don't start doing cartwheels just yet. Explorer has verified only that, in fact, a page exists at the other end of your link. Whether it's the *right* page is another matter.

A page could have the same URL but no longer have the same content. Or it might exist for the sole purpose of telling you that it's empty. Or it might be there to inform people that the site has been moved to another URL.

There's only one way to verify the content of a linked page, and that's to visit it with your browser. This is inconvenient, especially if you've got links to dozens of external sites, but it's the only way. (We warned you that web management required some patience!)

If it's broke, fix it

Once you've tracked down a bad link, the next task is to fix it. You can start your repairs from within the comfy confines of the Verify Hyperlinks dialog box, but you'll have to do the repair itself manually. Select the link you want to fix and choose the Edit Page button. FrontPage opens the page in Editor with the link selected.

If a page doesn't exist for the link and you don't plan to create one, remove the link by placing your insertion point in the linked text and choosing Edit, Unlink.

Otherwise, edit the link by choosing Edit, Hyperlink or pressing Ctrl+K. Editor opens the Edit Hyperlink dialog box. Here, you have several options:

- If you want to link to a page that's open in Editor, choose the Open Pages tab and create the new link.

- If you want to link to a page that isn't open but is in your web, choose the Current FrontPage tab and create the link.

- If the page you're linking to is on the World Wide Web, choose the World Wide Web tab and change the URL.

- If you haven't created the linked page yet, choose the New Page tab. You can give the page the default URL—that is, the URL of the bad link—or you can use a new URL. Click the Edit New Page Immediately radio button to work on the page right away, or click the Add New Page to To Do List to create the page and work on it later.

You'll find complete instructions on how to use the Edit Hyperlink dialog box in Chapter 12.

Don't forget to save any pages that you've worked on. Then, switch back to the Verify Hyperlinks dialog box in Explorer. You'll find that the dot next to the bad link is now dark yellow, and FrontPage has changed its status to Edited. This doesn't mean that the link has been fixed—only that you've changed it. To confirm that you indeed repaired the link, click the Verify button again.

What's this Edit Link button?

Do you have a number of pages that contain the same bad link? If you've got an existing page you want to point them to, you can fix them all at once.

Select any of the bad links and click the Edit Link button. FrontPage opens the Edit Link dialog box in Figure 20.3. You'll see a list of all pages with the bad link near the bottom of the dialog box. Type the name of the new linked page in the With text box.

Fig. 20.3
You can change several bad links at once in the Edit Link dialog box.

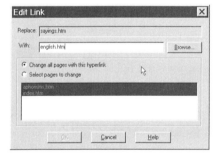

If you want to change all links, click the Change All Pages with This Hyperlink radio button. To change selected links, click the Select Pages to Change radio button and select the pages individually in the selection box below. To select more than one page, hold down the Ctrl key while you click each page.

Click OK when you're done, and click Verify in the Verify Hyperlinks dialog box to check your work.

Browsing for a page

The Edit Link dialog box works best if you know the page you're linking to and can type in the name. Otherwise, you'll have to find the page with the Browse button. This gets a little tricky, but here's the idea:

1 When you click the Browse button, FrontPage switches you to your browser (which means, of course, that you have to have a browser installed).

2 If the page is on the World Wide Web, connect to the Web and open the page.

3 If the page is on a local drive, use the browser's open file command to find and open it. Different browsers have different ways of opening files from your hard drive; refer to your browser's help files for instructions.

4 Whether you follow Step 2 or 3, when you've found the page, switch back to the Edit Link dialog box. The URL of the page appears in the With text box.

5 Choose OK.

TIP The Edit Link dialog box lets you enter the name of a page that doesn't exist. While this might seem silly at first, you can change a number of links at the same time, then switch to Editor and create the page.

TIP If you find a bad link but don't want to fix it right away, add it to the To Do list by clicking the Add Task button in the Verify Hyperlinks dialog box. The To Do List shows the task as Fix Broken Hyperlink. When you're ready to make the repair, open the To Do list and click the Do Task button; FrontPage opens the page in Editor, ready for repair.

Recalculating Links

As you add and delete pages and links to your site, it's a good idea to recalculate the web regularly. Recalculation is especially important if several people are making changes to the web or you've made changes from outside FrontPage (deleting files with Windows Explorer, for example). To recalculate, choose Tools, Recalculate Links from the menu bar.

When you recalculate, the server updates the Explorer display and regenerates pages that are dependent upon other pages. For example, some WebBots automatically generate text indices that become outdated if a page in the index is deleted; recalculation updates the index.

If you've got a big web, be prepared to wait a few minutes while the server recalculates.

Getting rid of loose changes

Boston is a notoriously difficult city in which to find your way around. Some streets that are on maps don't exist or have been renamed, others that should go one place actually go somewhere else, and still others don't seem to go anywhere at all. To make matters worse, the city's streets do not seem to be laid out with any logic; you can't make a right-hand turn without the possibility that you'll actually end up driving in a circle.

Boston is so confusing because it wasn't built according to a plan. It evolved from one year to the next, with streets added, changed, or removed according to a need or fancy.

The last thing you want your web site to turn into is a cyberspace version of Boston. So how do you add, delete, and move pages without throwing your whole web into chaos?

Maintaining some semblance of control over your web requires that you conscientiously follow proper procedures. Each type of change you want to make has specific rules that you must follow.

Adding pages

Chapter 12 details the steps you take to add and import pages. Follow them. Experienced users might be tempted to add pages with Windows Explorer, from the DOS prompt, or via other software such as Microsoft Word. In fact, you might even get away with such ad hoc web-spinning. But if you don't know exactly what you're doing, what seems like a shortcut now will create problems that you'll have to fix later.

Creating folders and moving pages

One common problem you'll face as your web grows is an overwhelming number of files in your main web folder. You can waste a lot of time in folder view scrolling through hundreds of files looking for a specific page or graphic.

The solution is to group your files into folders. FrontPage already provides you with a folder called Images in which you can put your graphics. You can do the same for any category of file that you want to name. For example, if you're running a corporate site that includes dozens of pages devoted to product information, why not toss them all into a folder called Products? You can even put folders in your folders; for instance, your Products folder might include subfolders called Old, New, and Recalled.

Creating a folder is easy. Here's how:

1. Open Explorer. If you're not already in Folder View, choose View, Folder View.

2. If you're creating a folder within a folder, click the folder in the left panel.

3. Choose File, New, Folder from the menu bar. Explorer creates a folder icon called New_Folder.

4. Rename the folder. When you create a folder, Explorer automatically selects the New_Folder name and puts you in edit mode; simply type the new folder name. Otherwise, you can put Explorer in edit mode by selecting the folder and pressing F2.

A moving experience

You move files by dragging them into their new folders. Click the file you're moving and, pressing the mouse button, drag it into the target folder.

As you drag the file through the Explorer window, your mouse pointer turns into a circle with a line through it, the international symbol for "forget it, pal." But when you touch the folder, you'll get your pointer back, with a little box attached to its tail, as in Figure 20.4. Release the mouse button and let Explorer do the rest.

To move several files at once, press the Ctrl key as you click each file. Then, click any of the selected files and drag them to their new location.

Fig. 20.4
You move a file by dragging and dropping it into the target folder.

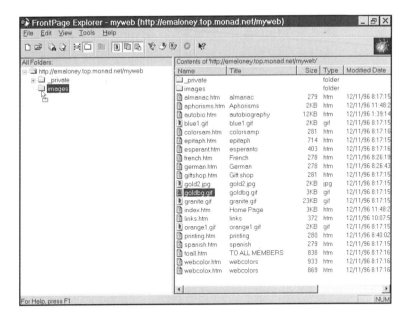

 Q&A *How will moving my files affect my links?*

It won't; Explorer automatically renames links to the file so that they stay intact.

 TIP If you're moving files into a subfolder, display the subfolder in the left panel by clicking the plus sign next to the parent folder.

CAUTION Pages that contain links cannot be dragged into your _private folder.

Out of sight, out of site

You might have noticed that your web includes a folder called _private. This folder is special—anything it contains can't be viewed in a browser without special authorization. This is great for hiding files, as we'll see in a minute, but you can't put files here to which you've created links.

Deleting pages

Deleting web pages is easy—maybe too easy. Select the page in Explorer and press the Delete key. Explorer asks you if you really, really want to go through with this; select Yes and the page is gone.

But there's a catch—in fact, a couple of them. Explorer does not fix links to a deleted file, and there's no way to revive the file once you kill it.

Methinks my links have kinks

When you delete a file, Explorer makes no effort to fix broken links. In fact, it won't even warn you if links are about to be broken. The responsibility for fixing them lies entirely on your shoulders.

Deleting a page is like removing a toilet. Just as a plumber disconnects the pipes before he yanks the commode, so you should fix your hyperlinks before you kill the page.

Start by putting Explorer in Hyperlink View (View, Hyperlink View from the menu bar). Also make sure that Hyperlinks to Images on the View menu is checked. Click the page you're going to delete, so that the links to and from the page appear in the right panel.

In Figure 20.5, for example, Autobiography is the page to be deleted. To the left are two pages that link to Autobiography - Home Page and Autobiography itself. Since the second link is contained within Autobiography, it'll disappear when Autobiography is deleted, so the only link to worry about is the one from Home Page.

It would be nice if Explorer included a command that said, "Unlink the link to Autobiography in Home Page." No such luck; you have to do it by hand. Double-click the page that contains the link (Home Page in this example) to open it in Editor. Here, you have three options:

- Select the linked text and delete it.
- Unlink the link with Edit, Unlink.
- Choose Edit, Hyperlink from the menu bar and change the link so that it points somewhere else.

Fig. 20.5
If Autobiography is to be deleted, then the link to it from Home Page has to be fixed.

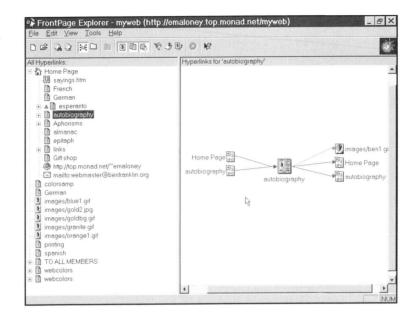

When you return to Explorer, the page with the link will have disappeared from the right panel.

Sheltering your orphans

You still have one other housekeeping chore. If the page you're deleting has links to other pages, then you have to make sure those other pages still have links to them. These files are to the right of the page you're deleting; in Figure 20.5, ben1.gif, Home Page, and autobiography.

To find out if you're about to orphan any of these files, right-click each file, choose Move to Center from the main menu, and check the other links to that file. If a file that's important to your web suddenly becomes unattached, you'll need to create a link to it from some other page.

The example in Figure 20.5 doesn't seem to present any problems. The image file will continue to be available to other pages that need it; the Home Page is index.htm and therefore remains available; and Autobiography is a link within the page that is to be deleted. So, with the only link to Autobiography fixed, it's now safe to delete Autobiography.

> **TIP** Whenever you delete pages, always verify your links with Tools, Verify Hyperlinks.

Cleaning up the mess

After you've eaten your Thanksgiving turkey, do you still need the leftover gravy? Maybe yes, maybe no—but in any case, you don't want to leave it in the refrigerator. The same goes for leftover files that used to belong to now-deleted pages. These might include graphics, audio clips, forms, headers, footers, and WebBots.

Decide what you want to do with these files right away. Move them into an oldfile folder or delete them. If you put off this task, you'll forget what the file is for. Eventually, you'll succumb to the First Law of Neglected Files, which says that the perceived value of a useless file increases with its age, and the file will sit there until the Armageddon.

Gone, but not forgotten

Before you go on a deletion binge, keep this in mind: Explorer does not have an Undo command. And if your web is on your hard drive, Explorer doesn't send deleted pages to Windows 95's Recycle Bin. In other words, when a page is gone, it's really, really, gone; you can't get it back.

To save yourself a lot of headaches and gnashing of teeth, consider copying files to another folder before you delete them. For example, you can create a folder called oldfiles and put your deleted files there. To make sure your old files can't be viewed from a browser, put the folder in your _private folder.

Create your oldfiles folder as explained earlier in this chapter. Next, copy the file you're going to delete into the folder. You can do this in one of two ways:

> Hold down the Ctrl key and drag the file into the folder as you would if you were moving it. When you touch the folder with your mouse pointer, the little box on the pointer's tail will contain a plus sign.

> Right-click the file and choose Cut from the quick menu. Open the target folder and paste the file by choosing E̲dit, P̲aste from the main menu or pressing Ctrl+V.

Then delete the original file.

 TIP **You also can move the orphan files to your oldfile folder by** dragging them into the folder. This is quicker than copying, pasting, and cutting. However, you must be absolutely sure that no other pages in your web point to the orphan file. If you overlook a link, FrontPage simply redefines that link so that it points to the new location.

How to rename a file

You can rename any file in FrontPage Explorer by following these steps:

1. Switch to folder view (choose View, Folder View from the menu bar).
2. Select the file in the right panel.
3. Press F2. FrontPage puts you in edit mode.
4. Type the new file name. Remember to give it a proper extension.
5. Press Enter.
6. If other pages in the web refer to the file, FrontPage will ask you if you want to update these pages to prevent broken links. Choose Yes.

The To Do List: keeping track of loose ends

So much to do, so little time. FrontPage can't help you find any more time, but it can help you keep track of what you have to do.

FrontPage's To Do List is a mini-project manager that lets you maintain an inventory of unfinished jobs. You can see at a glance what still needs to be done, launch tasks from the list, and mark finished tasks as complete.

You open the To Do List from Explorer or Editor by clicking the To Do Button (it's on the Standard toolbar in Editor) or choosing Tools, Show To Do List from either menu bar. Figure 20.6 shows an example of a short To Do List. The list includes the name of the task; who has been assigned to do it; whether the task is a high, medium, or low priority; the page that must be opened to finish the task; and a description.

Fig. 20.6
The To Do List lets you keep track of unfinished tasks. You can finish any task by selecting it and choosing the Do Task button.

As you'll see in a minute, some of this information is added automatically when you create an entry.

Before we go any further with our explanation of the To Do List dialog box, let's see how you add jobs to the list.

TIP You can sort the To Do List by any column; simply click the column's heading.

Lest I forget...

Most entries in the average To Do List are reminders to finish a page in Editor. Perhaps you've created a page but don't have time to finish it, or you've cleared a spot for an image that you haven't gotten from the graphics department yet, or you need to update the information on a page. Whatever the task, add it to the list by choosing Edit, Add To Do Task from Editor's menu bar. FrontPage opens the Add To Do Task dialog box in Figure 20.7.

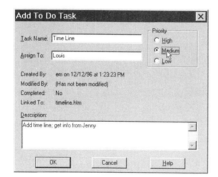

Fig. 20.7
Adding a task to the list is as simple as choosing Edit, Add To Do Task from the menu bar and filling in the blanks.

This dialog box is pretty self-explanatory. Enter a name for your task in the Task Name text box and the person who will do the task in the Assign To text box. Keep the names in the Assign To text box consistent so you can sort the To Do List dialog box by the Assigned To heading; if you assign a task to Robert, don't assign his next task to Bob.

Next, enter a description of the task in the Description text box. A short description will be easier to read in the To Do List dialog box, but also make sure that it's clear and precise.

Finally, choose a priority for the task by clicking the High, Medium, or Low radio button.

While you're in the Add To Do Task dialog box, notice that FrontPage adds some information automatically: when the task was created, who created it, and in what web page the task must be done.

When you're finished, click the OK button.

TIP Do you need to add a task but don't have the page open? No problem; you can add it from Explorer. Open the web that contains the page and select the page. Choose Edit, Add To Do Task from Explorer's menu bar. FrontPage opens the Add To Do Task dialog box. Fill it out as explained above and click the OK button.

Adding other tasks

Tasks aren't always related to a specific page. For example, you might want to add a reminder to import a web or add a discussion group to the existing web. To add such a task, open the To Do List dialog box and click the Add button (refer to Figure 20.6). You'll get the same Add To Do Task dialog box you see in Figure 20.7, only the Linked To heading won't have a page listed after it.

You can easily identify a task added this way; when you return to the To Do List dialog box, the entry's Linked To column will be empty. The Verify Links entry in Figure 20.6 is an example.

When a task has no page listed in the Linked To column, the Do Task button is grayed out; you'll have to perform the task manually. Remember to return to the To Do List to mark the task as complete (more on completing tasks in a moment).

Automatic list-building

Occasionally, FrontPage will offer you the option of adding a task from a dialog box. Here are two examples:

- When you verify hyperlinks in Explorer and FrontPage finds broken links, you can add the task of fixing the links to your To Do List. Click the Add Task button in the Verify Hyperlinks dialog box. You'll find more on verifying links earlier in this chapter.

- When you create a hyperlink and then create a new page in the Create Hyperlink dialog box, FrontPage lets you edit the new page immediately or add it to the To Do List. See Chapter 12 for more information.

TIP **If the To Do List includes a task that you don't want to complete,** you can delete it from the list. Click the Complete button to open the Complete Task dialog box, choose the Delete This Task radio button, and click OK.

To Doing it

One of the To Do List's best features is that you can launch a task from the To Do List dialog box.

Let's say, for example, that you want to fix a broken link, such as the Fix Broken Hyperlink task in Figure 20.6. Open the To Do List dialog box, select the task, and click the Do Task button. FrontPage opens the page (in this example, Home Page) in Editor and, just to make your life a little easier, selects the link to be fixed.

TIP **By default, FrontPage closes the To Do List dialog box when you** choose to do a task. To keep it open, put a check next to Keep Window Open at the top of the dialog box.

To Done!

When you've finished making your changes, save the page. FrontPage displays a dialog box asking you if you want to mark the task as completed. If your work is done, choose Yes; the next time you open the To Do List dialog box, the task will no longer be listed.

If you still have more work to do, choose No. The task remains on the To Do List. FrontPage does, however, note that you've made changes and when you made them. You can get this information by selecting the task in the To Do List dialog box and choosing the Details button; FrontPage opens the Task Details dialog box, which includes a Modify By heading that records the most recent changes to the page.

Q&A **How do I mark a task as completed if the task isn't linked to a page?**

Open the To Do List dialog box, select the task, and click the Complete button. FrontPage opens the Complete Task dialog box. Choose the Mark the Task as Completed radio button and click OK.

History lessons

Although a completed task disappears from your To Do List dialog box, FrontPage still keeps track of it. You can view a history of your tasks by putting a check next to Show History in the To Do List dialog box. The dialog box displays your completed tasks along with your unfinished ones, as well as a new Completed column that lists the dates on which completed tasks were done.

Index

A

ActiveX controls
  adding, 297-299
  downloading, 297-299
Add Choice dialog box, 273
Add Computers dialog box, 376
Add File to Import List dialog box, 220
Add Task button (Verify Hyperlinks dialog box), 387
Add to Custom Colors button, 134
Add To Do Task commands (Edit menu), 395
Add To Do Task dialog box, 395-396
Add Users dialog box, 375
adding
  ActiveX controls to Web pages, 297-299
  automatic table of contents in Web pages, 295-297
  bulleted lists, 20
  comments to Help screens, 72-73
  Corporate Presence Wizard, content, 327-328
  custom colors, 134-135
  entries to drop-down menus, 273-274
  feedback pages to Web pages, 329-331
  frames to discussion group webs, 346-347
  Java applets, 297-299
  new background colors, 191
  plug-ins to Web pages, 297-299
  Search Bots, 289-291, 331-332
  sounds to Web pages, 252-253
  tables, cells, 184
  tasks to the To Do List, 395-397
  video to Web pages, 253
  Web Pages to Web sites, 208-209
  see also inserting

Administration tab, setting (Microsoft Personal Web Server), 377-378
Advanced tab, forms configuration, 284
Align Left button, 119
Align Right button, 119
aligning
  paragraphs, 119-120
  text
    with images, 159
  Web pages, 119-120
alignment (cell property), 181-182
alignment (Insert Table dialog box), 171
Alt+F, Edit menu (FrontPage Explorer), 38
Alt+N, new Web page creation, 38
Alta Vista search engine, 289-290
animated graphics, 151
Annotate command (Edit menu), 72-73
Annotate dialog box, 72-73

Appearance tab (Image Properties dialog box), 159
applying
   default colors to text, 141-142
   font effects, 113-114
   FrontPage Editor, heading styles, 116
   templates to Web pages, 333-334
   text, marquee effects, 117-118
   text styles, 19
Arial font, 110-111
articles (discussion groups), 339
asterisks, password appearance, 264
automatic table of contents, adding, 295-297
.AVI (Video for Windows) format, 253

B

Back button, 71
background colors
   design guidelines, selecting, 146-147
   dithering, 133
   modifying, 144-145
   reference pages, modifying, 144-145
   selecting, 130-131
   text, displaying, 139-140
   troubleshooting reference pages, 146

Background command (Format menu), 130, 139
background images
   GIF files, 137
   JPEG files, 137
   textured colors, 136-137
   Web
      Mosaic Web site, 138-139
      Netscape Web site, 138-139
      obtaining, 138-139
      Thalia's Guide Web site, 139
      Yahoo! Web site, 138-139
Background Sound command (Insert menu), 252
Background Sound dialog box, 252
bad hyperlinks, 382-388
   fixing, 385-386
      Edit Link dialog box, 386-387
      recalculating hyperlinks, 387-388
   preventing through verification, 383-385
   see also hyperlinks
banners, discussion group webs, 354
blank lines, spacing in bulleted lists, 122
blinking text, special effects, 114-115
Bold button, 118

bolding text, 118-119
Bookmark command (Edit menu), 226
Bookmark Define dialog box, 72
Bookmark dialog box, 86
bookmarks, 72, 86-87
   creating, 86
   deleting, 87
   hyperlinking, 226-228
   linking, 225-226
   visiting, 87
Boolean operators, 332
borders, 160
   frames, deleting, 314-315
   inner, hiding, 191
   inside, coloring, 190
   tables, coloring, 189-190
broken hyperlinks
   fixing, 391-392
   repairing, 43
Browse button (Edit Link dialog box), 229, 387
building discussion group webs, 342
   color settings, 345-346
   confirmation page, 343
   restricting access, 344
   search forms, 343-345
   submission forms, 342-344

table of contents, 343-345
threaded replies, 343
titles, 343
see also creating
Bulleted List button, 121
bulleted lists
  blank lines, spacing, 121-122
  customizing bullets, 121-122
  Web pages
    adding, 20
    creating, 121-122
bullets
  bulleted lists, customizing, 122
  properties, selecting, 122
buttons
  Add Task (Verify Hyperlinks dialog box), 387
  Add to Custom Colors, 134
  Align Left, 119
  Align Right, 119
  Back, 71
  Bold, 118
  Browse, 229
  Browse (Edit Link dialog box), 387
  Bulleted List, 121
  Center Align, 119
  Check Spelling, 100
  Clear, 216
  Complete (To Do List dialog box), 397
  Contents (Topic screens), 71

Create or Edit Hyperlink, 24, 212, 217
Decrease Indent, 120
Decrease Text Size, 55, 115
Define Custom Colors, 141
Details (To Do List dialog box), 397
Do Task, 387, 394-396
Do Task (To Do List dialog box), 397
Edit Link, 386
Edit Page (Verify Hyperlinks dialog box), 385
Find (Topic screens), 71-72
Folder View, 34, 46, 152
Glossary, 73
Help, 63-64
Hyperlink View, 25, 34, 205
Increase Indent, 120
Increase Text Size, 55, 115
Index (Topic screens), 71-72
Insert Image, 151
Insert Table, 169, 171
Insert WebBot Component, 290
Italics, 118
Make Transparent, 160
Maximize, 59
Merge, 312
New FrontPage Web, 16

Open FrontPage Web, 27
Open Recent FrontPage Web, 48
Paste, 230
Show FrontPage Explorer, 25, 152, 216
Show/Hide, 87, 173
Split, 312
Text Color, 140
To Do, 394
Underline, 118
View FrontPage Editor (Explorer toolbar), 80

C

capitalization in replacement strings, 107-108
Caption Properties (Table menu command), 176
Caption Properties dialog box, 176
captions, creating in tables, 176
cell padding, 173
cell properties
  alignment, 181-182
  modifying, 180-181
Cell Properties dialog box, 181-183
cells
  adding, 184
  copying and pasting, 189
  deleting, 187

moving, 187
selecting, 177-178
single cell insertion, 185
spacing, 173
splitting, 312
text, selecting, 178-179

Center Align button, 119

changing fonts, 111-112

characters, text boxes, constraining, 266-267

check boxes, 260
form fields
properties, 269-270
selecting, 269-270

Check Spelling button, 100

Check Spelling dialog box, 102-103
bulleted status indicators, 102-103
spellchecking options, 102-103

child webs
defined, 370
troubleshooting, 370

Choose Alternate Content dialog box, 314

Choose Technique dialog box, 315

choosing, *see* **selecting**

circular hotspots, 243-246

Clear button, 216

clearing text, 95-96

clicking, plus sign icons, 43-44
clients, defined, 14
Clip Art tab, 151
Clipboard
copying and pasting, 239
inserting files, 239
text
copying, 98-99
cutting, 97-98
pasting, 97-98
URLs, copying, 230

Close FrontPage Web command (File menu), 48

closing
Microsoft Personal Web Server, 373-375
Web pages, 26-27, 48, 210-211

Color dialog box, 132, 346
basic colors heading, 132-133

color matrix box, selecting, 133-134

coloring
discussion web elements, 345-346
inside borders, 190
tables, borders, 190

colors
background, creating, 191
color adjustments, 162-164
color matrix box, selecting, 133-134
design guidelines, selecting, 146-147
discussion group webs, modifying, 356

displaying text, 139-140
dithering, 133
ease of reading, designing, 129-130
hue, 135
luminosity, 135
mixing, 131-132
modifying text blocks, 140-141
reference pages, 144
RGB values, 135
saturation, 135
textured, 136-137
Web pages, selecting, 129-130

columns
adding to frames, 310-312
Contents Of... Panel, 47
deleting, 187
inserting, 184
moving, 187
multiple, 183
selecting, 176
widths, modifying, 182-183

commands
Bookmark menu, Define, 72
Edit menu
Add To Do Task, 395
Annotate, 72-73
Bookmark, 226
Hyperlink, 385
Replace, 105
Undo Clear, 99
Undo Drag, 99
Unlink, 214, 391
File menu
Close FrontPage Web, 48

Delete FrontPage
Web, 27, 50
Import, 41, 153
New, 315
Open Editor, 211
Preview in
Browser,
21, 261
Publish FrontPage
Web, 369
Font menu, Special
Styles, 114
Format menu
Background,
130, 139
Font, 112, 141
Help menu
Microsoft
FrontPage
Help, 65
Microsoft on the
Web, 75
Insert menu
Background
Sound, 252
Comment, 329
From File, 248
Horizontal Line,
20, 142, 161
Marquee, 117
Other Components, 297
Video, 253
Insert Table menu,
Insert Cell, 184
New menu,
FrontPage Web,
33
online help, 56
Options menu
Display History
Window, 71
Keep Help On
Top, 73

Programs menu,
Microsoft FrontPage, 16
Table menu
Caption Properties, 176
Insert Caption, 176
Table Properties,
180, 189
Tools menu
Permissions, 375
Recalculate
Hyperlinks, 41
Recalculate
Links, 387
Show To Do
List, 394
Thesaurus, 103
Verify Hyperlinks,
43, 383
Web Settings,
344, 352
View menu
Folder View,
46, 101, 389
Forms Toolbar, 260
Hyperlink View,
41, 391
Hyperlinks to
Images, 45
**Comment command
(Insert menu), 329
Comment dialog
box, 329
comments (Corporate Presence
Wizard)**
adding to Help
screens, 72-73
creating, 328-329
editing, 328-329
GUESTLOG.HTM
page, 331

**Complete button (To
Do List dialog
box), 397
Complete Task dialog
box, 397
configuring**
forms (Advanced
tab), 284
Microsoft Personal
Web Server,
374-375
see also setting
**Confirm Delete
dialog box, 27
Confirm tab**
forms, implementing, 283-284
submission forms,
283-284
**confirmation page
(discussion
webs), 343**
messages, 351-352
**connecting frames,
316-322**
default target
frames, changing,
321-322
links, creating,
319-321
**constraining characters in text boxes,
266-267**
content
adding viaCorporate
Presence Wizard,
327-328
inserting via
FrontPage Editor,
19-21
**Contents button
(Topic screens), 71
Contents Of...Panel,
modifying tables,
47-48**

Contents panel (Help
  Topics dialog
  box), 65
context-sensitive
  help, 62-64
  help on menu
    commands, 64
  obtaining, 39-41
  question mark
    (toolbar), 63
Control bars, sizing
  program win-
  dows, 59
converting
  files to HTML, 238
  images into GIF,
    155-156
copying
  tables, cells, 189
  text, 98-99
  URLs with Clip-
    board, 230
  using clipboard, 239
corporate logos on
  Web pages (Include
  Bot), 327-328
Corporate Presence
  Web Wizard dialog
  box, 327
Corporate Presence
  Wizard, 327-329
  comments
    creating, 328-329
    editing, 328-329
  content, adding,
    327-328
  corporate logos,
    327-328
Create Hyperlink
  dialog box,
  213, 217,
  225-229, 245
Create or Edit
  Hyperlink button,
  24, 212, 217

creating
  bookmarks, 86
  bulleted lists,
    121-122
  Corporate Presence
    Wizard, comments,
    328-329
  custom colors,
    131-132
  drop-down menus in
    form fields,
    272-273
  folders, 389
  frames, 304-309,
    315-316
    alternate
      pages, 306
    custom grids,
      305-306
    file names,
      306-307
    templates,
      305-306
  hidden fields in
    forms, 284-285
  hyperlinks, 212-216,
    228-232
    discussion group
      webs, 354
    Web pages, 22-27
  Image Composer,
    textured color,
    136-137
  image maps,
    248-250
  images, hotspot
    links, 243-246
  indents in para-
    graphs, 120
  marquees on Web
    pages, 117-118
  new background
    colors, 191

  numbered lists on
    Web pages, 123
  reference
    pages, 144
  table captions, 176
  tables, 169
  templates, 333-334
  text
    subscript,
      114-115
    superscript,
      114-115
  web frameworks,
    16-18
  Web pages
    polygonal hot-
      spots, 246
    rectangular
      hotspots, 246
    see also building
      duscussion group
      webs
Cross File Spelling
  command, 101-102
Ctrl+B
  boldface text, 55
  text indentation, 55
Ctrl+Down Arrow,
  down one para-
  graph, 59
Ctrl+End, end of
  line, 58
Ctrl+Home, top of
  page, 58
Ctrl+I, italics
  text, 55
Ctrl+Left Arrow, left
  one word, 58
Ctrl+Right Arrow,
  right one word, 59
Ctrl+U, underline
  text, 55
Ctrl+Up Arrow, up
  one paragraph, 59

Current FrontPage tab (Edit Hyperlink dialog box), 385
custom colors
  adding, 134-135
  background limitations, 134-135
  creating, 131-132
  low-resolution monitors, displaying, 132
  removing, 134-135
  Web page limitations, 134-135
custom grids (frames), 305-306
custom templates
  deleting, 334-335
  editing, 334-335
customizing
  bullets, 122
  colors for discussion group webs, 356
  FrontPage Editor, 55
  submission forms in discussion group webs, 355
  submit button for forms, 275-276
  see also modifying
cutting text, 97-98

D

data types
  form fields
    decimals, 268-269
    digits checkbox, 268
    letters checkbox, 268
    limiting, 265-266
    selecting, 268-269
    whitespace checkbox, 268
    integer, 265-266
    no constraints, 265-266
    number, 265-266
    text, 265-266
    value limits in form fields, 267
decimals, form fields, 268-271
Decrease Indent button, 120
Decrease Text Size button, 55, 115
default colors, applying to text, 141-142
Define command (Bookmark menu), 72
Define Custom Colors button, 141
Delete FrontPage Web command (File menu), 27, 50
deleted messages, storing, 357-358
deleting
  bookmarks, 87
  borders on frames, 314-315
  graphics, 156
  hotspots, 248
  marquees, 118
  messages
    discussion group webs, 357-358
    threads, 358-359
  sounds from Web pages, 252-253

  tables
    cells, 187
    columns, 187
    rows, 187
  templates on Web pages, 334-335
  text, 90-91, 95-96
    Replace command, 107-108
  Web pages, 27, 50, 391-393
    fixing broken hyperlinks, 391-392
    linking orphan files, 392
    managing leftover files, 393
    old file folders, 393
  see also removing
design guidelines, selecting
  background colors, 146-147
  colors, 146-147
designing
  colors, ease of reading, 129-130
  fonts for Web pages, 112-113
  forms, 277-278
Details button (To Do List dialog box), 397
dialog boxes
  Add Choice, 273
  Add Computers, 376
  Add File to Import List, 220
  Add To Do Task, 395-396
  Add Users, 375
  Annotate, 72-73

Background Sound, 252
Bookmark, 86
Bookmark Define, 72
Caption Properties, 176
Cell Properties, 181-183
Check Spelling, 102-103
Choose Alternate Content, 314
Choose Technique, 315
Color, 132, 346
Comment, 329
Complete Task, 397
Confirm Delete, 27
Corporate Presence Web Wizard, 327
Create Hyperlink, 23, 213, 217, 225-229
Drop-Down Menu Properties, 274
Edit Frame Attributes, 312-314
Edit Frame set Grid, 309-310
Edit Frameset Grid, 316
Edit Hyperlink, 247, 321-322, 385-386
Edit Link, 386-387
File Location, 34
Find, 68
Find Occurrence, 105
Font, 112
FrontPage TCP/IP Test, 373
FrontPage Web Settings, 344, 352
Getting Started with Microsoft FrontPage, 16
Help Topics, 65-68
  Contents panel, 65
  Find panel, 67-68
  Index panel, 67
Horizontal Line Properties, 20, 143, 161
Image, 151
Image Properties, 159
Import File, 220
Import Files to FrontPage Web, 154, 219
  managing files, 220
Insert From File, 248
Insert Rows or Columns, 184
Insert Table, 170-171
  alignment, 171
  borders, 172
Insert WebBot Component, 290
List Properties, 123
Marquee Properties, 117
Name and Password Required, 17
Name/Value Pair, 284
New FrontPage Web, 16-17, 31-33, 342
New Page, 144, 208, 217, 305
Normal Web Template, 17
Open File, 211, 221
Page Properties, 130, 200, 322
Permissions, 375
Preview in Browser, 21
Radio Button Properties, 271
Radio Button Validation, 271
Replace, 105
Replace in FrontPage Web, 106
Sample Sprites Catalog, 164
Save As, 211
Save as File, 218
Save As Template, 333
Save Image to FrontPage Web, 155-156
Save Page, 315
Scheduled Image WebBot Component Properties, 294
Select a File, 233-235
Select Background Image, 136
Spelling, 100
Symbol, 85
Table, 180
Table Properties, 171, 189-191
Task Details, 397
Text Box Properties, 264
Text Box Validation, 265
Thesaurus, 103-104

Verify Hyperlinks, 383-384
Video, 253
Web Template, 34
WebBot Include Component Properties, 293
WebBot Search Component Properties, 290, 355
WebBot Table of Contents Properties, 296
WebBot Timestamp Component Properties, 297
Windows Connect To, 20
discussion group webs, 338-339
  adding frames, 346-347
  building, 342
    color settings, 345-346
    confirmation page, 343
    restricting access, 344-345
    search forms, 343-345
    submission forms, 342-344
    table of contents, 343-345
    threaded replies, 343
    titles, 343
  creating hyperlinks, 354
  customizing submission forms, 355
  deleting messages, 357-358
  editing messages, 357
  libel laws, 357
  limiting messages, 359
  message storage, troubleshooting, 352-353
  messages
    confirmation page option, 351-352
    search forms, 351
    submission forms, 350-351
  moderating, 356-359
  modifying
    banners, 354
    colors, 356
    search forms, 355-356
  saving messages, 352-353
  setting registration options, 347-348
  storing messages, 352-353
  table of contents page, 348-350
Discussion Web Wizard, 342-353
  Color dialog box, 345-346
  Search Form dialog box, 345
  Submission Form dialog box, 344
  Table of Contents dialog boxes, 345
Display History Window command (Options menu), 71-72

displaying
  custom colors on low-resolution monitors, 132
  Link View, Web page structure, 25-26
  text colors, 139-140
  see also viewing
dithering
  colors, 133
  defined, 133
Do Task button, 387, 394-397
docking floating toolbars, 56
documents
  replacing words, 104-105
  returning to (from Help window), 71
  searching text strings, 108-109
downloading
  ActiveX controls, 297-299
  Java applets, 297-299
  plug-ins, 297-299
drag-and-drop method, 96-97
drop-down menus, 260
  entries
    adding, 273-274
    modifying, 274
  form fields, creating, 272-273
  resizing, 272-273
Drop-Down Menu Properties dialog box, 274

E

Edit Frame Attributes dialog box, 312-314
Edit Frameset Grid dialog box, 309-310, 316-317
Edit Hyperlink dialog box, 247, 321-322, 385-386
Edit Link button, 386
Edit Link dialog box, 386-387
Edit menu commands
 Add To Do Task, 395
 Annotate, 72-73
 Bookmark, 226
 Hyperlink, 385
 Replace, 105
 Undo Clear, 99
 Undo Drag, 99
 Unlink, 214, 391
Edit Page button (Verify Hyperlinks dialog box), 385
editing
 Corporate Presence Wizard, comments, 328-329
 frames, 309-315
  alternate pages, 314-315
  attributes, 312-314
  row and column additions, 310-312
  Web pages, 317-318
 hotspot properties, 247-248

 messages, discussion group webs, 357
 templates for Web pages, 334-335
 see also modifying
effects, applying to fonts, 113-114
electronic bookmarks, 72, 86-87
 creating, 86
 deleting, 87
 visiting, 87
entering passwords, 17-18
entries
 adding to drop down menus, 273-274
 modifying drop down menus, 274
establishing permissions (Web Self-Registration Form), 347-348
Excel, form handlers, 280-283
Excite Web search engine, 289-290
exiting, *see* closing
expanding Hyperlink View (FrontPage Explorer), 43-44
external links, testing, 383-385

F

feedback pages, adding, 329-331
File Location dialog box, 34
File menu commands
 Close FrontPage Web, 48

 Delete FrontPage Web, 27, 50
 Import, 41, 153
 New, 315
 Open Editor, 211
 Preview in Browser, 21, 261
 Publish FrontPage Web, 369
files
 ASCII, inserting, 233-234
 converting to HTML, 238
 GIF, 150
  converting files into GIF, 155-156
 hidden, 344
 HTML, inserting, 233
 importing, 220-221
 inserting with Clipboard, 239
 JPEG, 150
 moving, 389-390
 non-HTML
  inserting, 234-239
  linking, 223
 old file folders, 393
 orphans, linking, 392
 renaming, 394-395
 RTF (Rich Text Format), converting to HTML, 238
 unrecognized, saving, 238-239
 Web, importing, 221
 Web pages, deleting, 391-393
Find button (Topic screens), 71

Find dialog box, 68
Find Occurrence
   dialog box, 105
Find panel (Help
   Topics dialog box),
   67-68
fixing
   bad hyperlinks,
      385-386
      Edit Link dialog
         box, 386-387
      recalculating
         hyperlinks,
         387-388
   broken hyperlinks,
      391-392
   see also repairing
Folder View
   (FrontPage Ex-
   plorer), 34-38
      Contents Of...Panel,
         column widths, 47
      launching, 46
      Modified By
         column, 47
      Modified Date
         column, 47
      Name column, 46
      Size column, 46
      Title column, 46
      Type column, 47
Folder View button,
   34, 46, 152
Folder View com-
   mand (View menu),
   46, 101, 389
folders
   creating, 389
   files, moving,
      389-390
   hidden, 344
   Images
      importing images,
         153-155

storing images,
   152-153
into Web pages,
   152-153
old file folders, 393
_private folder, 390
Font command
   (Format menu),
   112, 141
Font dialog box, 112
   Effects option,
      113-114
   preview option, 112
Font menu com-
   mands, Special
   Styles, 114
fonts
   Arial, 110-111
   changing, 111-112
   defined, 110-111
   designing Web
      pages, 112-113
   effects, applying,
      113-114
   Sans Serif, 112-113
   selecting, 110-111
   Serif, 112-113
   Times New Roman,
      110-111
form fields
   creating drop-down
      menus, 272-273
   data types
      decimals,
         268-271
      digits check-
         box, 268
      Letters check-
         box, 268
      whitespace
         checkbox, 268
   hidden fields,
      284-285

limiting
   data types,
      265-266
   integers, 268-269
   text, 268
naming, 265
properties, view-
   ing, 261
selecting
   check boxes,
      269-270
   data types,
      268-269
   setting radio but-
      tons, 270-271
   sizing text boxes,
      262-263
text boxes
   asterisks, 264
   starter text,
      263-264
types
   check box,
      260-261
   drop-down menu,
      260-261
   one-line text box,
      260-261
   push button,
      260-261
   radio button,
      260-261
   scrolling text box,
      260-261
   selecting, 262
   value added, 267
form handlers, 340
   data options (Results
      tab), 279-283
   selecting, 278-279
   servers, 278
Format menu
   commands
      Background,
         130, 139

Font, 112, 141
Formatting Toolbar (FrontPage Editor), 19-25
forms, 340-341
  brevity, 277-278
  clarity, 277-278
  configuring with Advanced tab, 284
  creating hidden fields, 284-285
  defined, 258-260
  designing, 277-278
  fields
    naming, 265
    selecting, 262
    types, 260-261
  handlers, selecting, 278-279
  implementing, 283-284
  normal button, 275-276
  reset button, 275-276
  selecting reset button, 275-276
  simplicity, 277-278
  sizing text boxes, 262-263
  submit button, 275-276
  value added form fields, 267
forms handlers, spreadsheets, 282-283
Forms Toolbar command (View menu), 260
forums, *see* discussion group webs
frames, 302-309
  changing attributes, 312-314
  connecting, 316-322
  default target frames, changing, 321-322
  links, creating, 319-321
  creating, 304-309, 315-316
    alternate pages, 306
    custom grids, 305-306
    file names, 306-307
    templates, 305-306
  deleting borders, 314-315
  discussion group webs, adding, 346-347
  editing, 309-315
    adding rows and columns, 310-312
    alternate pages, 314-315
  opening, 308-309
  options, 346-347
  replacing home pages, 322-323
  sizable, 314
  target, changing, 313
  Web pages, editing, 317-318
Frames Wizard, 304-315
  Choose Alternate Content dialog box, 314-315
  Choose Alternate Content window, 306
  Choose Technique window, 305
  Edit Frame Attributes dialog box, 312-314
  Edit Frameset Grid dialog box, 309-310
  Pick Template Layout window, 305
  Save Page dialog box, 315-316
  Save Page window, 306-307
frequencies, marquee intervals, 117-118
From File command (Insert menu), 248
FrontPage
  components
    Bonus Pack, 13-14
    Editor, 13-14
    Explorer, 13-14
    Personal Web Server, 13-14
  home page, 366-367
  launching, 16-18
  Private folders, 291-293
  Root Web, 50
  Web development, planning, 15
  Web pages
    closing, 26-27
    opening, 26-27
FrontPage Editor
  as compared to word processors, 54-55
  background colors, selecting, 130-131
  features, 54-55
  floating toolbars, 56

graphics **411**

font sizes, 115
form field types, 260-261
heading styles, applying, 116
Insert command, 232
launching, 53-54
locating destination sites, 229
saving unrecognized files, 238
Server Administrator, installing non-FrontPage server software, 378-379
server extensions, installing, 366-367
starting, 80
status bars, display options, 55
tables
  border, 189
  cell properties, 180-181
  creating, 169
  creating captions, 176
  entering text, 175
  modifying, 179
  selecting elements, 176-177
text
  formatting, 19
  inserting, 19-21
toolbar display options, 55
typing text, 80-87
  double-spacing, 84-85
  line breaks, 83-84
  spacing limitations, 82
  special characters, 85

FrontPage Explorer
context-sensitive help, obtaining, 39-41
Folder View, 34-38
Hyperlink View, 34-38
launching, 31
menu bar, 38
quick menus, implementing, 38
status bar functions, 41
templates
  defined, 33
  Personal Web, 33-36
  selecting, 31-33
toolbar, utilizing, 38-39
FrontPage Personal Web Server
capacities, 371-372
executing, 371-372
functions, 371-372
permissions, setting, 375-377
FrontPage TCP/IP Test dialog box, 373
FrontPage Web command (New menu), 33
FrontPage Web Settings dialog box, 344, 352

G

Getting Started dialog box
troubleshooting, 49-50

Web pages
  opening, 48-49
  selecting, 50
Getting Started with Microsoft FrontPage dialog box, 16
GIF (Graphics Interchange Format), 150
background images, 137
converting files into GIF, 155-156
importing GIF files, 152-155
making images transparent, 160-161
Glossary button, 73
graphics
animated, 151
borders, creating, 160
color adjustments, 162-164
deleting, 156
eliminating excess white space, 164
Image Composer, 162-166
image formats, 150
  converting graphics into GIF, 155-156
inserting into pages, 151
lines, inserting, 20
loading Web pages, 198-199
making transparent, 160-161
moving, 157-158
resizing, 156-158

selection handles, 156
sprites, 164-166
wrapping text, 158-160
see also images
Graphics Interchange Format, *see* **GIF**
grids
  cells, splitting, 312
  editing, 310-312
  merging, 312
grouping image maps, 249-250
Guest Book template
  GUESTLOG.HTM page, 331
  troubleshooting, 331
  Web page feedback, 329-331
GUESTLOG.HTM page, troubleshooting, 331

H

hard drives, Web site storage, 34-36
headers
  Include Bot, inserting, 291-293
  Web pages, inserting, 291-293
heading styles, applying, 116
Help button, 63-64
Help History window, 71
Help menu commands
  Microsoft FrontPage Help, 65
  Microsoft on the Web, 75
help system
  context-sensitive help, 62-64
  help on menu commands, 64
  question mark (toolbar), 63
  Help screens, 69-74
    adding comments, 72-73
    bookmarks, 72
    Glossary button, 73
    icons, 69
    Instruction screens, 73-74
    keeping visible, 73
    printing, 72
    Topic screens, 71-73
  Internet help resources, 74-75
  Microsoft FrontPage Support Online, 74-75
  search features, 65-68
    Contents panel (Help Topics dialog box), 65
    Find panel (Help Topics dialog box), 67-68
    Index panel (Help Topics dialog box), 67
Help Topics dialog box, 65-68
  Contents panel, 65
  Find panel, 67-68
  Index panel, 67
Help window
  moving, 63
  resizing, 63
hidden fields, creating, 284-285
hidden folders, 344
hiding inner borders, 191
home pages, replacing with frames, 322-323
Horizontal Line command (Insert menu), 20, 142, 161
Horizontal Line Properties dialog box, 20, 143, 161
horizontal lines, 161
  Web pages, inserting, 142-143
hotspots
  circular, 243-246
  creating from images, 243-246
  defined, 243
  deleting, 248
  moving, 247
  polygonal, 246
  properties, editing, 247-248
  rectangular, 246
  viewing, 250-251
HTML (HyperText Markup Language), 14-15
  files, inserting, 233
HTTP (Hypertext Transfer Protocol), 14-15

hue, 135
Hyperlink command (Edit menu), 385
Hyperlink View (FrontPage Explorer), 34-38
expanding, 43-44
hyperlinks, viewing, 41-43
simplifying, 45
Hyperlink View button, 25, 34, 205
Hyperlink View command (View menu), 41, 391
hyperlinks, 211
bad links, 382-388
fixing, 385-387
preventing through verification, 383-385
bookmarks, 225-226
broken links, fixing, 391-392
creating, 212-216, 228-232
creating for bookmarks, 226-228
defined, 13
discussion group webs, creating, 354
in-coming, 41-43
out-going, 41-43
recalculating, 387-388
removing, 214
repairing, 43
viewing, 242-243

Hyperlink View (FrontPage Explorer), 41-43
Web pages, creating, 22-27
see also links
Hyperlinks to Images command (View menu), 45
HyperText Markup Language, *see* **HTML**
Hypertext Transfer Protocol, *see* **HTTP**

I

Image Composer, 162-166
color adjustments, 162-164
sprites, 164-166
textured color, 136-137
Image dialog box, 151
image maps
defined, 248
placing, 249-250
Web pages, creating, 248-250
Image Properties dialog box, 159
images
background textures, 136-137
borders, creating, 160
color adjustments, 162-164

eliminating excess white space, 164
formats, 150
converting images into GIF, 155-156
hotspot links, creating, 243-246
Image Composer, 162-166
inserting into pages, 151
loading Web pages, 198-199
making transparent, 160-161
moving, 157-158
resizing, 156-158
Scheduled Image Bot, 294-295
Scheduled Include Bot, 295-299
selection handles, 156
sizing, 160
sprites, 164-166
storing in Images folder, 152-153
wrapping text, 158-160
see also graphics
Images folder
importing, 152-155
storing, 152-153
images maps
grouping, 249-250
see also hotspots
implementing
Confirm tab for forms, 283-284
FrontPage Explorer quick menus, 38
toolbar, 38-39

replacement strings, cautions, 107
Import command (File menu), 41, 153
Import File dialog box, 220
Import File to FrontPage Web dialog box, 154, 219
  managing files, 220
importing
  from Web, 221
  image files
    into Images folder, 153-155
    into Web pages, 152-153
  pages, 219-220
  text, 91-92
in-coming hyperlinks, 41-43
Include Bot, header insertion, 291-293
Increase Indent button, 120
Increase Text Size button, 55, 115
indents, creating, 120
Index button (Topic screens), 71
Index panel (Help Topics dialog box), 67
inner borders, hiding, 191
Insert Caption (Table menu command), 176
Insert Cell command (Insert Table menu), 184

Insert From File dialog box, 248
Insert Image button, 151
Insert menu commands
  Background Sound, 252
  Comment, 329
  From File, 248
  Horizontal Line, 20, 142, 161
  Marquee, 117
  Other Components, 297
  Video, 253
Insert Rows or Columns dialog box, 184
Insert Table button, 169-171
Insert Table dialog box, 170-171
  alignment, 171
  borders, 172
  cell padding, modifying, 173
  cell spacing, adjusting, 173
  table width, specifying, 174
Insert WebBot Component button, 290
Insert WebBot Component dialog box, 290
inserting
  files
    ASCII, 233-234
    non-HTML, 234-239
    files with Clipboard, 239

graphic lines into Web pages, 20
headers (Include Bot), 291-293
horizontal lines in Web pages, 142-143
HTML files, 233
images into pages, 151
Scheduled Image Bot, 294-295
Scheduled Include Bot, 295-299
Search Bot, 290-291
single cells, 185
Table of Contents Bot, 295-297
tables
  columns, 184
  rows, 184
text in Web pages, 19-21
Timestamp Bot, 297
see also adding
installing
  FrontPage Server Extensions, 366-367
  non-FrontPage server software, 378-379
Instruction screens, 73-74
integers, form fields, limiting, 268-269
internal links, testing, 383-385
Internet
  help resources, 74-75
  Microsoft FrontPage Support Online, 74-75

see also Web
Internet Service Providers
  obtaining, 367-368
  publishing Web pages, 367-368
  selecting, 367-368
Internet Services Administrator (Microsoft Personal Web Server), 377-378
intranets
  network administrators, publishing role, 369-370
  publishing Web pages, 368-370
  Secure Socket Layer, 369-370
IP (Internet Protocol) addresses
  components, 373-374
  defined, 373-374
  masks, 373-374
  wildcards, 373-374
italicizing text, 118-119
Italics button, 118

J - K

Java applets
  downloading, 297-299
  Web pages, adding, 297-299
Joint Photographic Experts Group, *see* **JPEG**
JPEG (Joint Photographic Experts Group), 150
  importing JPEG files, 152-155
  Web page background images, 137-138
Keep Help On Top command (Options menu), 73
keyboard shortcuts
  Alt+F, Edit menu (FrontPage Explorer), 38
  Alt+N, new Web page creation, 38
  Alt+Tab (minimizing/maximizing Help window), 71
  Ctrl+B (boldface text), 55
  Ctrl+Down Arrow, down one paragraph, 59
  Ctrl+End, end of line, 58
  Ctrl+F (Find command), 64
  Ctrl+Home, top of page, 58
  Ctrl+I (italics text), 55
  Ctrl+K, 385
  Ctrl+Left Arrow, left one word, 58
  Ctrl+M (text indentation), 55
  Ctrl+N (New FrontPage Web dialog box), 342
  Ctrl+N (New Page dialog box), 305
  Ctrl+Right Arrow, right one word, 59
  Ctrl+U (underline text), 55
  Ctrl+Up Arrow, up one paragraph, 59
  Ctrl+V, 393
  F1 (help on menu commands), 64
  Page Down, down one screen, 58
  Page Up, up one screen, 58
  Shift+Enter (line breaks), 84
  Shift+F1 (Help button), 63
keyboards
  selecting
    lines of text, 93-94
    paragraphs, 94-95
    text, 90-95
    text blocks, 92
    words, 92-93
  text
    bolding, 118-119
    copying, 98-99
    deleting, 95-96
    italicizing, 118-119
    underlining, 118-119

L

launching
  Folder View (FrontPage Explorer), 46
  FrontPage, 16-18

FrontPage Editor, 53-54
FrontPage Explorer, 31
FrontPage Personal Web Server, 371-372
spell checker, 100
Thesaurus, 103
letters checkbox, form fields, 268
libel laws and discussion group webs, 357
limiting
  data types in form fields, 265-266
  integers in form fields, 268-269
  messages in discussion group webs, 359
  text in form fields, 268
line breaks, 83-84
Link View, displaying, 25-26
linking
  hyperlinks
    bookmarks, 225-226
    creating, 212-216
    images in hotspots, 243-246
    non-HTML files, 223
    Web pages, 22-23, 211-216
links
  creating for bookmarks, 226-228
  endless loops, 200
  planning (Web site design), 204-206

Web TOCs, 204-205
  removing, 214
  see also hyperlinks
List Properties dialog box, 123
loading Web pages, 198-199
locating destination sites, 229
low-resolution monitors, custom color display, 132
luminosity, 135

M

Make Transparent button, 160
Marquee command (Insert menu), 117
Marquee Properties dialog box, 117
marquees
  creating, 117-118
  deleting, 118
  intervals, setting, 117-118
masks, IP addresses, 373-374
Maximize button, 59
Merge button, 312
merging grids, 312
messages
  confirmation page option for discussion group webs, 351-352
  deleted, storing, 357-358
  deletion criteria, 357

discussion group webs
  deleting, 357-358
  editing, 357
  libel laws, 357
  limiting, 359
  saving, 352-353
  search forms, 351
  storing, 352-353
  troubleshooting, 352-353
submission forms
  customizing, 355
  discussion groups webs, 350-351
  threads, 340-341
  deleting, 358-359
see also discussion group webs
Microsoft FrontPage command (Programs menu), 16
Microsoft FrontPage Help command (Help menu), 65
Microsoft FrontPage Support Online, 74-75
Microsoft Gallery Web site, 151
Microsoft Image Composer, 162-166
  color adjustments, 162-164
  sprites, 164-166
Microsoft on the Web command (Help menu), 75
Microsoft Personal Web Server
  Administration tab, setting, 377-378
  capacities, 372-373

configuring, 374-375
functions, 372-373
Internet Services
 Administrator,
 377-378
IP addresses,
 372-373
permissions, setting,
 377-378
taskbar icon,
 374-375
turning off, 373-375
**Microsoft Web
 Gallery, 298**
**Microsoft Web site,
 FrontPage home
 page, 366-367**
.MID files, 252-253
**mixing colors,
 131-132**
**modems, download
 speed (FrontPage
 Editor), 57**
**moderating discus-
 sion group webs,
 339, 356-359**
**Modified By column
 (Folder View), 47**
**Modified Date col-
 umn (Folder
 View), 47**
modifying
 background colors,
  144-145
   reference pages,
    144-145
 banners in discus-
  sion group
  webs, 354
 colors for discussion
  group webs, 356
 Contents Of...Panel,

column widths, 47
drop-down menu
 entries, 274
replacement
 strings, 108
RGB values, 135
Search Bot proper-
 ties, 291
search forms in
 discussion group
 webs, 355-356
tables, 179
 column width,
  182-183
 text size, 115
 text blocks, colors,
  140-141
see also customizing;
 editing
**Mosaic Web site,
 138-139**
mouse
 drag-and-drop
  method for text,
  96-97
 navigating Web
  pages, 57-59
 selecting
  lines of text,
   93-94
  paragraphs, 94-95
  text, 90-95
  text blocks, 92
  words, 92-93
moving
 files, 389-390
 Help window, 63
 hotspots, 247
 images, 157-158
 tables
  cells, 187
  columns, 187
  rows, 187

text via drag-and-
 drop method,
 96-97
multiple pages
 replacing text,
  105-106
 spellchecking,
  101-102

N

**Name and Password
 Required dialog
 box, 17**
**Name column (Folder
 View), 46**
**Name/Value Pair
 dialog box, 284**
**naming form
 fields, 265**
**narrowing Hyperlink
 View (FrontPage
 Explorer), 45**
navigating Web pages
 keyboards, 57-59
 mouse, 57-59
navigation bars, 328
**Netscape Web site,
 138-139**
**network administra-
 tors, intranet
 publishing role,
 369-370**
networks
 clients, defined, 14
 overview, 14
 protocols, de-
  fined, 14
 servers, defined, 14
 Web publishing
  concerns, 366-367

New command (File menu), 315
New FrontPage Web button, 16
New FrontPage Web dialog box, 16-17, 31-33, 342
New Page dialog box, 144, 208, 217, 305
New Page tab (Edit Hyperlink dialog box), 385
newsgroups, 338-339
non-FrontPage server software, installing, 378-379
non-HTML files, linking, 223
Normal Web Template dialog box, 17
Notepad, form handlers, 280-283
numbered lists, creating, 123

O

obtaining
   background images, 138-139
   context-sensitive help, 39-41
   Internet Service Providers, 367-368
   see also downloading
one-line text box, 260
online help
   commands, 56
   obtaining, 39-41
   toolbars, 56
Open Editor command (File menu), 211
Open File dialog box, 211, 221
Open FrontPage Web button, 27
Open Pages tab (Edit Hyperlink dialog box), 385
Open Recent FrontPage Web button, 48
opening
   blank Web pages, 80
   frames, 308-309
   Web pages, 26-27, 211
      Getting Started dialog box, 48-49
   Web sites, 49-50
Options menu commands
   Display History Window, 71
   Keep Help On Top, 73
orphan files, linking, 392
Other Components command (Insert menu), 297
out-going hyperlinks, 41-43

P

padding cells, 173
Page Down, down one screen, 58
Page Properties dialog box, 130, 200, 322
Page Up, up one screen, 58
pages
   HTML, inserting, 233
   ranges, spellchecking, 101-102
   Web
      adding, 22, 208-209
      closing, 210-211
      deleting, 391-393
      hyperlinks, 211
      importing, 218-220
      inserting ASCII files, 233-234
      inserting non-HTML files, 234-239
      linking, 211-216
      opening, 211
      saving, 210
      see also Web pages
palettes, custom colors, removing, 134-135
paper clip (Help screens), 73
paragraphs
   aligning, 119-120
   creating indents, 120
   selecting, 94-95
passwords
   asterisks in text boxes, 264
   entering, 17-18
   permissions, 376
Paste button, 230
pasting text, 97-98

permissions
  discussion group webs, setting, 347-348
  passwords, 376
  setting
    FrontPage Personal Web Server, 375-377
    Microsoft Personal Web Server, 377-378
    Web Self-Registration Form, establishing, 347-348
Permissions command (Tools menu), 375
Permissions dialog box, 375
placing image maps, 249-250
planning Web sites, 15, 203-206
  links, 204-206
  testing sites, 206
  Web table of contents, 204-205
plug-ins
  downloading, 297-299
  Web pages, adding, 297-299
polygonal hotspots, 246
Preview in Browser command (File menu), 21, 261
Preview in Browser dialog box, 21
printing Help screens, 72

Private folders, 291-293, 390
program windows, sizing, 59
Programs menu commands, Microsoft FrontPage, 16
properties
  bullets, 122
  editing hotspots, 247-248
  modifying, Search Bot, 291
  viewing, form fields, 261
protected web, 339
protocols
  defined, 14
  HTTP functions, 14-15
  TCP/IP, 365
Publish FrontPage Web command (File menu), 369
publishing Web pages
  Internet Service Providers, 367-368
  intranets, 368-370
  overview, 364-365
push buttons, 260

Q - R

question mark (toolbar), 63
quick menus, implementing, 38
Radio Button Properties dialog box, 271
Radio Button Validation dialog box, 271

radio buttons, 260
  form fields, setting, 270-271
  versus check boxes, 270-271
Recalculate Hyperlinks command (Tools menu), 41
Recalculate Links command (Tools menu), 387
recalculating hyperlinks, 387-388
rectangular hotspots, 246
red, green, blue values, *see* **RGB values**
reference pages
  background colors
    modifying, 144-145
    troubleshooting, 146
  Web pages, creating, 144
registration options
  discussion group webs, setting, 347-348
  Web Self-Registration Form, 347-348
removing
  custom colors, 134-135
  hyperlinks, 214
  links, 214
  see also deleting
renaming files, 394-395

repairing
  hyperlinks, 43
  see also fixing
Replace command (Edit menu), 105
Replace dialog box, 105
Replace in FrontPage Web dialog box, 106
replacement strings
  capitalization, 107-108
  Find Occurrences dialog box, 105-106
  implementing, cautions, 107
  modifying, 108
replacing
  home pages with frames, 322-323
  text in multiple pages, 105-106
  words in documents, 104-105
resizing
  drop-down menus, 272-273
  Help window, 63
  images, 156-158
restricted web, 339
restricting
  Hyperlinks View (FrontPage Explorer), 45
Results tab (form handlers)
  bulleted list, 279-283
  database option, 279-283
  definition list, 279-283
  HTML, 279-283

RGB (red, green, blue) values, 135
  dithering, 133
  modifying, 135
Root Web functions, 50
rows
  adding to frames, 310-312
  deleting, 187
  inserting, 184
  moving, 187
  see also tables
RTF (rich text format) files, converting to HTML, 238

S

Sample Sprites Catalog dialog box, 164
Sans Serif fonts, 112-113
saturation, 135
Save As dialog box, 211
Save as File dialog box, 218
Save As Template dialog box, 333
Save Image to FrontPage Web dialog box, 155-156
Save Page dialog box, 315
saving
  messages in discussion group webs, 352-353

  unrecognized files, 238
  Web pages, 210
Scheduled Image Bot
  functions, 294-295
  Web pages, inserting, 294-295
Scheduled Include Bot
  functions, 295-299
  Web pages, inserting, 295-299
scientific styles, text special effects, 114-115
scroll bars, navigating, 57-59
scrolling text box, 260
Search Bot
  functions, 289-291
  properties, modifying, 291
  Web pages
    adding, 289-291, 331-332
    inserting, 290-291
search engines (Web)
  Alta Vista, 289-290
  Boolean operators, 332
  Excite, 289-290
  spiders, 289-290
  text strings, 289-290
search features, 65-68
  Contents panel (Help Topics dialog box), 65
  Find panel (Help Topics dialog box), 67-68

Index panel (Help Topics dialog box), 67
search forms, 343-345
   discussion group webs
      messages, 351
      modifying, 355-356
searching
   synonyms (Thesaurus dialog box), 104
   text strings, 108
   Web pages, 289-291
Secure Socket Layer, 369-370
security, passwords, 17-18
Select a File dialog box, 233-235
Select Background Image dialog box, 136
selecting
   background colors, 130-131
      design guidelines, 146-147
   bullet properties, 122
   check boxes in form fields, 269-270
   colors
      color matrix box, 133-134
      design guidelines, 146-147
      Web pages, 129-130
   data types for form fields, 268-269

   fonts, 110-111
   form field types, 262
   form handlers, 278-279
   FrontPage Explorer templates, 31-33
   Internet Service Providers, 367-368
   lines of text, 93-94
   paragraphs, 94-95
   reset button in forms, 275-276
   tables, 176-177
      cell text, 178-179
      cells, 177-178
      columns, 176
   text, 90-95
      blocks, 92
      color in Web pages, 139-140
      words, 92-93
selection handles, 156
Serif fonts, 112-113
servers
   defined, 14
   form handlers, 278
   FrontPage Server Extensions, 366-367
   non-FrontPage software, installing, 378-379
   recalculation, 387-388
setting
   colors for discussion group webs, 356
   FrontPage Personal Web Server permissions, 375-377
   marquee intervals, 117-118

   Microsoft Personal Web Server Administration tab, 377-378
   permissions, 377-378
   radio buttons in form fields, 270-271
   registration options for discussion group webs, 347-348
   starter text for text boxes, 263-264
   see also configuring
Show FrontPage Explorer button, 25, 152, 216
Show To Do List command (Tools menu), 394
Show/Hide button, 173
simplifying Hyperlink View (FrontPage Explorer), 45
single cell insertion, 185
sites (Web)
   Netscape, 138
   Yahoo, 138
sizable frames, 314
Size column (Folder View), 46
size handles, text boxes, 262-263
sizing
   images, 160
   program windows, 59
   text, modifying, 115
   text boxes, 262-263

sounds
.MID files, 252-253
.WAV files, 252-253
Web pages
adding, 252-253
deleting, 252-253
spacing bulleted lists, 122
special characters, 85
special effects
applying fonts, 113-114
blinking text, 114-115
scientific styles in text, 114-115
special interest groups (SIG), *see* **discussion group webs**
Special Styles command (Font menu), 114
spellchecking
launching, 100
text, 100
Web pages, 101-102
Spelling dialog box, 100-101
Split button, 312
splitting cells, 312
spreadsheets, forms handlers, viewing, 282-283
sprites, 164-166
starter text, setting in text boxes, 263-264
starting, *see* **launching**
Status bar
display options, 55
modem download speeds, 57

storing
deleted messages, 357-358
images in Images folder, 152-153
messages
deleted, 357-358
discussion group webs, 352-353
Web sites on hard drive, 34-36
styles, 82
submission forms, 342-344
Confirm tab, 283-284
discussion group webs
customizing, 355
messages, 350-351
subscripts, creating, 114-115
superscripts, creating, 114-115
Symbol dialog box, 85
synonyms (Thesaurus dialog box)
replacing, 103-104
searching, 104

T

Table dialog box, 180
Table menu commands
Caption Properties, 176
Insert Caption, 176
Table Properties, 180, 189

Table of Contents Bot
functions, 295-297
table formats, troubleshooting, 297
Web pages, inserting, 295-297
Table of Contents page, 348-350
Table Properties command (Table menu), 180, 189
Table Properties dialog box, 171, 180, 189-191
tables
background colors, adding, 191
borders, 189-190
captions, creating, 176
cell properties
alignment, 181-182
modifying, 180-181
cell text, selecting, 178-179
cells
adding, 184
copying and pasting, 189
deleting, 187
moving, 187
padding, 173
selecting, 177-178
spacing, 173
columns
deleting, 187
inserting, 184
modifying, 182-183

moving, 187
selecting, 176
copying and pasting, 189
creating, 169
deleting, 187
elements, 171
entering text, 175
modifying, 179
moving, 187
rows
   deleting, 187
   inserting, 184
   moving, 187
selecting, 176-177
troubleshooting with Table of Contents Bot, 297
widths, 174

tabs
Appearance (Image Properties dialog box), 159
Clip Art, 151
Current FrontPage (Edit Hyperlink dialog box), 385
New Page (Edit Hyperlink dialog box), 385
Open Pages (Edit Hyperlink dialog box), 385
World Wide Web (Edit Hyperlink dialog box), 385

target frames, changing, 313

Task Details dialog box, 397

tasks
adding to the To Do List, 395-396
from dialog boxes, 396-397
launching, 397
marking as complete (To Do List), 397-398

TCP/IP (Transmission Control Protocol/Internet Protocol), 365

templates
Corporate Presence Wizard, 327-329
defined, 33
frames, 305-306
Personal Web, 33-36
selecting 31-33
viewing, 326
Web pages
   applying, 333-334
   creating, 333-334
   deleting, 334-335
   editing, 334-335

testing
hyperlinks, 383-385
Web sites, 206

text
applying default colors, 141-142
blocks
   colors, modifying, 140-141
   selecting, 92
bolding, 118-119
bookmarks, 86-87
   creating, 86
   deleting, 87
   visiting, 87
capitalization, replacement strings, 107-108
clearing, 95-96
colors, displaying, 139-140
copying, 98-99
cutting, 97-98
deleting, 90-91
   Replace command, 107-108
   undoing, 99
documents, replacing, 104-105
drag-and-drop method, moving, 96-97
entering into tables, 175
form fields, limiting, 268
formatting (FrontPage Editor), 19
heading styles, applying, 116
importing, 91-92
indents, 120
italicizing, 118-119
marquee effects, applying, 117-118
multiple pages, replacing, 105-106
pasting, 97-98
replacement strings, 105-106
replacing synonyms, 103-104
searching synonyms, 104
selecting, 90-95
size, modifying, 115
special effects
   blinking, 114-115
   scientific styles, 114-115
spellchecking, 100

strings, searching, 108
styles, 19, 82
subscript, creating, 114-115
superscript, creating, 114-115
typing, 80-87
   double-spacing, 84-85
   line breaks, 83-84
   spacing limitations, 82
   special characters, 85
   word wrap feature, 80-81
underlining, 118-119
unreadable, 202
Web pages
   aligning, 119-120
   inserting, 19-21
   readability, 202
wrapping around images, 158-160
Text Box Properties dialog box, 264
Text Box Validation dialog box, 265
text boxes
   characters, limiting, 265-266
   constraining characters, 266-267
   forms, sizing, 262-263
   passwords as astericks, 264
   setting starter text, 263-264
   size handles, 262-263
Text Color button, 140

textured color, creating, 136-137
Thalia's Guide Web site, 139
Thesaurus command (Tools menu), 103
Thesaurus dialog box, 103-104
   meanings, 103-104
   searching synonyms, 104
   synonym replacement, 103-104
threads, 339
   deleting messages, 358-359
   replies, 343
Times New Roman font, 110-111
Timestamp Bot
   functions, 297
   Web pages, inserting, 297
Title column (Folder View), 46
To Do button, 394
To Do List (mini-project manager), 394-398
   adding tasks, 395-396
      from dialog boxes, 396-397
   completed tasks, 397-398
   launching tasks, 397
toolbars
   display options, 55
   online help, 56
Tools menu commands
   Permissions, 375

   Recalculate Hyperlinks, 41
   Recalculate Links, 387
   Show To Do List, 394
   Thesaurus, 103
   Verify Hyperlinks, 43
   Web Settings, 352
Tools menu commands (Explorer)
   Verify Hyperlinks, 383
   Web Settings, 344
Topic screens, 71-73
   adding comments to Help screens, 72-73
   bookmarks, 72
   Glossary button, 73
   Help History window, 71
   printing Help screens, 72
   returning to main Help Topics dialog box, 71
topics (discussion groups), 339
Transmission Control Protocol/ Internet Protocol, *see* **TCP/IP**
transparent images, 160-161
troubleshooting
   child webs, 370
   discussion groups webs, message storage, 352-353
   Getting Started dialog box, 49-50

Guest Book template, 331
GUESTLOG.HTM page, 331
reference pages, background colors, 146
Table of Contents Bot, table formats, 297
turning off Microsoft Personal Web Server, 373-375
Type column (Folder View), 47
typing text, 80-87
double-spacing, 84-85
line breaks, 83-84
spacing limitations, 82
special characters, 85
word wrap feature, 80-81

U - V

Underline button, 118
underlining text, 118-119
Undo Clear command (Edit menu), 99
Undo Drag command (Edit menu), 99
undoing text deletions, 99
Uniform Resource Locators, *see* **URLs**
Unlink command (Edit menu), 214, 391

URLs (Uniform Resource Locators)
components, 24
copying with Clipboard, 230
defined, 24
UseNet newsgroups, 338
users
discussion group webs, limiting messages, 359
Web page permissions, 375-377
value-added form fields, 267
verification (hyperlinks), 383-385
Verify button (Verify Hyperlinks dialog box), 384
Verify Hyperlinks command (Explorer Tools menu), 43, 383
Verify Hyperlinks dialog box, 383-386
vertical alignment (cell property), 182
video
.AVI format, 253
Web pages, adding, 253
Video command (Insert menu), 253
Video dialog box, 253
View FrontPage Editor button (Explorer toolbar), 80

View menu commands
Folder View, 46, 101, 389
Forms Toolbar, 260
Hyperlink View, 41, 391
Hyperlinks to Images, 45
viewing
form field properties, 261
frames, 308-309
hotspots, 250-251
hyperlinks, 242-243
spreadsheets, forms handlers, 282-283
templates, 326
see also displaying
visiting bookmarks, 87

W

.WAV files, 252-253
Web (World Wide Web)
bookmarks
hyperlinking, 226-228
linking, 225-226
defined, 30
destination sites, locating, 229
files
inserting ASCII, 233-234
inserting nonHTML, 234-239
hyperlinks
creating, 212-216, 228-232

functions, 13
removing, 214
importing, 218-221
links, removing, 214
Mosaic Web site,
background
images, 138-139
Netscape Web site,
background
images, 138-139
obtaining background images,
138-139
pages
inserting ASCII
files, 233-234
inserting non-HTML files,
234-239
search engines
Alta Vista,
289-290
Excite, 289-290
Thalia's Guide Web
site, background
images, 139
URLs, defined, 24
Yahoo Web site,
background
images, 138-139
Web browsers
form fields, 258-260
frames, opening,
308-309
Web pages
adding
ActiveX controls,
297-299
automatic table of
contents,
295-297
bulleted lists, 20
feedback pages,
329-331

Java applets,
297-299
plug-ins, 297-299
Search Bot,
289-291, 331-332
sounds, 252-253
video, 253
aligning text,
119-120
applying
templates,
333-334
text styles, 19
background colors,
design guidelines,
146-147
background images
GIF files, 137
JPEG files, 137
child webs, troubleshooting, 370
closing, 26-27,
48, 210-211
colors, design
guidelines,
146-147
comments
adding, 328-329
editing, 328-329
GUESTLOG.HTM
page, 331
creating
bulleted lists,
121-122
image maps,
248-250
marquees,
117-118
numbered lists,
123
reference pages,
144
templates,
333-334

defined, 30
deleting, 27, 50,
391-393
borders, 314-315
fixing broken
hyperlinks,
391-392
linking orphan
files, 392
managing leftover
files, 393
old file folders,
393
sounds, 252-253
templates,
334-335
downloading
ActiveX controls,
297-299
editing
frames, 317-318
templates,
334-335
fonts, designing,
112-113
frames, 302-309
alternate pages,
306, 314-315
changing attributes,
312-314
connecting,
316-322
creating, 304-309,
315-316
editing, 309-315
FrontPage Editor,
heading styles, 116
FrontPage Server
Extensions,
366-367
hotspots, 243-246
HTML, defined,
14-15

Web sites

hyperlinks, 211
image maps
   defined, 248
   placing, 249-250
Include Bot
   corporate logos, 327-328
   headers, 291-293
inserting
   graphic lines, 20
   horizontal lines, 142-143
   Scheduled Image Bot, 294-295
   Scheduled Include Bot, 295-299
   Search Bot, 290-291
   Table of Contents Bot, 295-297
   text, 19-21
   Timestamp Bot, 297
Internet Service Providers, publishing, 367-368
intranet publishing, 368-370
keyboards, navigating, 57-59
linking, 211-216
Microsoft Personal Web Server, 372-373
modem download speeds, 57
modifying background colors, 144-145
mouse, navigating, 57-59
moving hotspots, 247
opening, 211

Getting Started dialog box, 48-49
opening blank pages, 80
password permissions, 376
permissions, setting, 375-377
polygonal hotspots, creating, 246
Private folders, 291-293
publishing overview, 364-365
rectangular hotspots, creating, 246
saving, 210
searching, 289-291
   text strings, 108
Secure Socket Layer, 369-370
selecting
   background colors, 130-131
   colors, 129-130
   Getting Started dialog box, 50
   text color, 139-140
spellchecking, 101-102
submission forms, 283-284
templates (Corporate Presence Wizard), 326-329
viewing hotspots, 250-251
Web publishing
FrontPage Server Extensions, installing, 366-367

Internet Service Providers, 367-368
intranets, 368-370
network concerns, 366-367
planning, 15
TCP/IP, 365
URLs, 365
Web Self-Registration Form (Editor), 347-348
Web Settings command (Tools menu), 344, 352-353
Web sites
adding pages, 22
bad hyperlinks, 382-388
   fixing, 385-387
   preventing through verification, 383-385
   recalculating hyperlinks, 387-388
common design problems, 198-203
   bad writing, 199
   endless loop of links, 200
   inconsistent formatting, 203
   main headings, 201-202
   poor page design, 200-201
   slow loading pages, 198-199
   unreadable text, 202
defined, 30

displaying structure (Link View), 25-26
frameworks, creating, 16-18
Guest Book template, 329-331
hard drive, storing, 34-36
hyperlinks, viewing, 41-43
linking, 22-27
measures of successful site, 196-198
Microsoft Gallery, 151
Netscape, 138
opening, 26-27, 49-50
planning, 203-206
 links, 204-206
 testing sites, 206
selecting colors, 129-130
Yahoo, 138
Web Template dialog box, 34
WebBot Search Component Properties dialog box, 290, 355
WebBot Table of Contents Properties dialog box, 296
WebBot Timestamp Component Properties dialog box, 297
WebBots
 defined, 288-289
 functions, 288-289
 Search Bot, 289-291
wildcards, IP addresses, 373-374

windows
 Control bars, sizing, 59
 Help
  moving, 63
  resizing, 63
 Help History, 71
Windows Connect To dialog box, 20
word wrap feature, 80
World Wide Web, *see* Web
wrapping text around images, 158-160

X - Y - Z

Yahoo Web site, 138-139

Check out Que® Books on the World Wide Web
http://www.quecorp.com

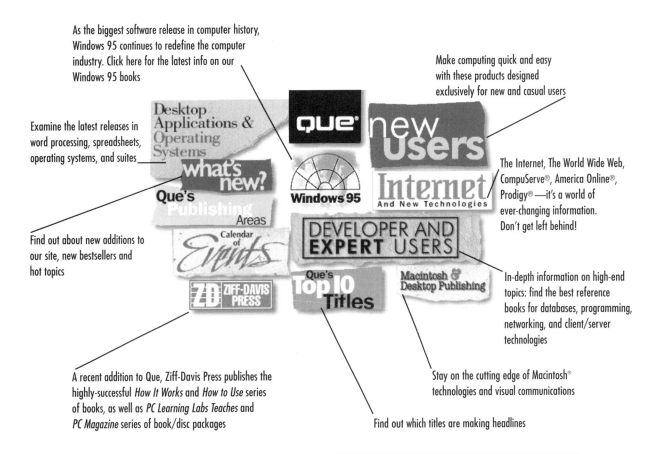

As the biggest software release in computer history, Windows 95 continues to redefine the computer industry. Click here for the latest info on our Windows 95 books

Make computing quick and easy with these products designed exclusively for new and casual users

Examine the latest releases in word processing, spreadsheets, operating systems, and suites

The Internet, The World Wide Web, CompuServe®, America Online®, Prodigy® —it's a world of ever-changing information. Don't get left behind!

Find out about new additions to our site, new bestsellers and hot topics

In-depth information on high-end topics: find the best reference books for databases, programming, networking, and client/server technologies

A recent addition to Que, Ziff-Davis Press publishes the highly-successful *How It Works* and *How to Use* series of books, as well as *PC Learning Labs Teaches* and *PC Magazine* series of book/disc packages

Stay on the cutting edge of Macintosh® technologies and visual communications

Find out which titles are making headlines

With 6 separate publishing groups, Que develops products for many specific market segments and areas of computer technology. Explore our Web Site and you'll find information on best-selling titles, newly published titles, upcoming products, authors, and much more.

- Stay informed on the latest industry trends and products available
- Visit our online bookstore for the latest information and editions
- Download software from Que's library of the best shareware and freeware

Copyright © 1997, Macmillan Computer Publishing-USA, A Viacom Company

Technical Support:

If you need assistance with the information in this book or with a CD/Disk accompanying the book, please access the Knowledge Base on our Web site at **http://www.superlibrary.com/general/support**. Our most Frequently Asked Questions are answered there. If you do not find the answer to your questions on our Web site, you may contact Macmillan Technical Support **(317) 581-3833** or e-mail us at **support@mcp.com**.

Complete and Return this Card for a *FREE* Computer Book Catalog

Thank you for purchasing this book! You have purchased a superior computer book written expressly for your needs. To continue to provide the kind of up-to-date, pertinent coverage you've come to expect from us, we need to hear from you. Please take a minute to complete and return this self-addressed, postage-paid form. In return, we'll send you a free catalog of all our computer books on topics ranging from word processing to programming and the internet.

Mr. ☐ Mrs. ☐ Ms. ☐ Dr. ☐

Name (first) ☐☐☐☐☐☐☐☐☐☐☐☐ (M.I.) ☐ (last) ☐☐☐☐☐☐☐☐☐☐☐☐☐☐☐

Address ☐☐☐☐☐☐☐☐☐☐☐☐☐☐☐☐☐☐☐☐☐☐☐☐☐☐☐☐☐☐

City ☐☐☐☐☐☐☐☐☐☐☐☐☐☐ State ☐☐ Zip ☐☐☐☐☐ ☐☐☐☐

Phone ☐☐☐ ☐☐☐ ☐☐☐☐ Fax ☐☐☐ ☐☐☐ ☐☐☐☐

Company Name ☐☐☐☐☐☐☐☐☐☐☐☐☐☐☐☐☐☐☐☐☐☐☐☐☐☐

E-mail address ☐☐☐☐☐☐☐☐☐☐☐☐☐☐☐☐☐☐☐☐☐☐☐☐☐

1. Please check at least (3) influencing factors for purchasing this book.

- ☐ Front or back cover information on book
- ☐ Special approach to the content
- ☐ Completeness of content
- ☐ Author's reputation
- ☐ Publisher's reputation
- ☐ Book cover design or layout
- ☐ Index or table of contents of book
- ☐ Price of book
- ☐ Special effects, graphics, illustrations
- ☐ Other (Please specify): _____

2. How did you first learn about this book?

- ☐ Saw in Macmillan Computer Publishing catalog
- ☐ Recommended by store personnel
- ☐ Saw the book on bookshelf at store
- ☐ Recommended by a friend
- ☐ Received advertisement in the mail
- ☐ Saw an advertisement in: _____
- ☐ Read book review in: _____
- ☐ Other (Please specify): _____

3. How many computer books have you purchased in the last six months?

- ☐ This book only
- ☐ 2 books
- ☐ 3 to 5 books
- ☐ More than 5

4. Where did you purchase this book?

- ☐ Bookstore
- ☐ Computer Store
- ☐ Consumer Electronics Store
- ☐ Department Store
- ☐ Office Club
- ☐ Warehouse Club
- ☐ Mail Order
- ☐ Direct from Publisher
- ☐ Internet site
- ☐ Other (Please specify): _____

5. How long have you been using a computer?

- ☐ Less than 6 months
- ☐ 6 months to a year
- ☐ 1 to 3 years
- ☐ More than 3 years

6. What is your level of experience with personal computers and with the subject of this book?

	With PCs	With subject of book
New	☐	☐
Casual	☐	☐
Accomplished	☐	☐
Expert	☐	☐

Source Code ISBN: 0-7897-1134-6

7. Which of the following best describes your job title?

- Administrative Assistant ☐
- Coordinator ☐
- Manager/Supervisor ☐
- Director ☐
- Vice President ☐
- President/CEO/COO ☐
- Lawyer/Doctor/Medical Professional ☐
- Teacher/Educator/Trainer ☐
- Engineer/Technician ☐
- Consultant ☐
- Not employed/Student/Retired ☐
- Other (Please specify): _____ ☐

8. Which of the following best describes the area of the company your job title falls under?

- Accounting ☐
- Engineering ☐
- Manufacturing ☐
- Operations ☐
- Marketing ☐
- Sales ☐
- Other (Please specify): _____ ☐

9. What is your age?

- Under 20 ☐
- 21-29 ☐
- 30-39 ☐
- 40-49 ☐
- 50-59 ☐
- 60-over ☐

10. Are you:

- Male ☐
- Female ☐

11. Which computer publications do you read regularly? (Please list)

_____
_____
_____
_____
_____
_____
_____
_____
_____
_____

Comments: _____

Fold here and scotch-tape to mail.

BUSINESS REPLY MAIL
FIRST-CLASS MAIL PERMIT NO. 9918 INDIANAPOLIS IN

POSTAGE WILL BE PAID BY THE ADDRESSEE

ATTN MARKETING
MACMILLAN COMPUTER PUBLISHING
MACMILLAN PUBLISHING USA
201 W 103RD ST
INDIANAPOLIS IN 46290-9042

NO POSTAGE NECESSARY IF MAILED IN THE UNITED STATES